A History of Economic Policy in India

A History of Economic Policy in India provides an immersive, accessible yet rigorous understanding of the Indian economy through a political economy framework. It provides a birds-eye view of the politics, context, and ideas that shaped major economic policies in independent India and argues that they are the product of crisis, coalitions, and contingency – not necessarily choice.

Each chapter focuses on specific political regimes: colonial rule, Jawaharlal Nehru, Indira Gandhi, liberalization under coalition governments, the UPA government, and the NDA government. The book evaluates how well a government executed its policies based on the economic and political constraints it faced, rather than economic outcomes. The book's framework provides multiple perspectives and analyzes economic policies as an outcome of interactions between dynamics in the economy using theories to make sense of the economy, political ideology, historical conditions, and international context.

Rahul De teaches Indian economy and world economic history at Azim Premji University, Bengaluru. He is passionate about making undergraduate economics immersive and accessible. He has conducted workshops on economics teaching and written about it in the *Economic and Political Weekly* (2018). He is also interested in exploring topics not conventional to economics and has recently published on the economics of football (July 2023).

A History of Economic Policy in India

Crisis, Coalitions, and Contingency

Rahul De

Shaftesbury Road, Cambridge CB2 8EA, United Kingdom
One Liberty Plaza, 20th Floor, New York, NY 10006, USA
477 Williamstown Road, Port Melbourne, VIC 3207, Australia
314–321, 3rd Floor, Plot No. 3, Splendor Forum, Jasola District Centre, New Delhi – 110025, India
103 Penang Road, #05–06/07, Visioncrest Commercial, Singapore 238467

Cambridge University Press is part of Cambridge University Press & Assessment, a department of the University of Cambridge.

We share the University's mission to contribute to society through the pursuit of education, learning and research at the highest international levels of excellence.

www.cambridge.org
Information on this title: www.cambridge.org/9781009362672

© Rahul De 2023

This publication is in copyright. Subject to statutory exception and to the provisions of relevant collective licensing agreements, no reproduction of any part may take place without the written permission of Cambridge University Press & Assessment.

First published 2023

Printed in India by Avantika Printers Pvt. Ltd.

A catalogue record for this publication is available from the British Library

ISBN 978-1-009-36267-2 Hardback
ISBN 978-1-009-36268-9 Paperback

Cambridge University Press & Assessment has no responsibility for the persistence or accuracy of URLs for external or third-party internet websites referred to in this publication, and does not guarantee that any content on such websites is, or will remain, accurate or appropriate.

Contents

List of Figures and Tables	vii
Preface	ix
Acknowledgments	xi
List of Abbreviations	xiii

Introduction	1
1. Colonialism and the Indian Economy	12
2. The Drive to Industrialize under Nehru's Leadership: 1950–66	40
3. The Turn to Populism under Indira Gandhi: 1967–79	69
4. The Early Liberalization Years: 1980–2003	96
5. Maturity of Reforms in the UPA Years: 2004–13	123
6. Reforms under the NDA Government: 2014–19	151

Index	173

Figures and Tables

Figures

2.1	Trends in investment (percent) from 1950 to 1967	59
2.2	BOP from 1950 to 1966 (rupees, crores)	66
3.1	BOP from 1967 to 1980 (rupees, crores)	70
3.2	Trends in investment in proportion (percent) from 1967 to 1980	81
3.3	Trends in components of revenue expenditure from 1970 to 1992 (rupees, crores)	92
3.4	Trends in fiscal deficit as a proportion of GDP from 1970–71 to 2008–09	93
4.1	Trends in investment in proportion (percent) from 1980 to 2007	108
4.2	Trends in BOP from 1980 to 2003 (rupees, crores)	109
4.3	Trends in revenue expenditure from 1980 to 2011 (rupees, crores)	113

Tables

2.1	Period-wise growth rate: GDP and aggregate demand (percent)	58
2.2	Period-wise growth rate: sectoral (percent)	58
2.3	Trends in inequality: Gini coefficient based on monthly per capita expenditure	60

Preface

This book was born out of more than a decade of research on understanding the contours of, and teaching a course on, the Indian economy for the last six years – more pertinently, a response to multiple discussions about the contemporary economy with people from a wide range of occupations from social activists, construction workers, shopkeepers, taxi drivers, and journalists; chance encounters with people in the upper management of multinational corporations; and the comments sections of discussions on Indian economic policy on social media. My interactions bore out two general observations: first, people are interested in understanding how the economy affects their lives – irrespective of the kind of work they do – and second, there is a serious dearth of accessible resources on the Indian economy.

In this book, I present an accessible history of economic policies in India from colonial to contemporary India. This book is meant to serve as a representative sample of important academic literature on the Indian economy organized thematically. It aims to provide a socio-historical narrative to explain economic policies in contemporary India. This work will be of particular value to readers who do not have a background in economics and might not have the time or inclination to read multiple works to understand a particular period or policy in Indian history. It can also serve as a complementary resource to a teacher as it provides a coherent and accessible narrative connecting different periods and different data sources, public documents, and academic literature that can be brought to the classroom.

I have been part of designing the economics curriculum at Azim Premji University (APU), Bengaluru. I believe that undergraduate economics education in India, especially in teaching economic theory, is abstract and focused on modelling and quantitative analysis; students are not well exposed to different trajectories of analysis within economics and complementary concepts provided by other disciplines like history, politics, and sociology. Other economics educators who I have interacted with have felt the same.[*] At APU, the economics curriculum has attempted to embed the historical, political, social, and intellectual

---

[*] R. De and A. Thomas, "Rethinking Undergraduate Economics Education," *Economic and Political Weekly* 53, no. 3 (2018): 21–24.

within economic courses. The emphasis is on understanding theories within the context in which it was shaped. I start our Introduction to Economics class with the Industrial Revolution and explain how colonial intervention born out of the need for industrialization shaped the global capitalist economy. Further ahead in the course we study cases of market failures through examples of oil spillage, deforestation of rainforests, and a discussion on how capitalism has shaped global climate change. The need to contextualize economics within history and social structure was an important intervention for me as a teacher. The Indian economy course that I teach emphasizes contextualizing economic policies and events in India as being shaped by global dynamics. One point on which my views may differ from other commentators on the history of the Indian economy is the focus on embedding it within a global history of capitalism through colonialism, interactions with international agencies, through economic dynamics of the global economy, or indirectly through political and economic ideas from the Western, developed world – often brought in by Indian economists and policymakers trained in the United Kingdom and the United States of America.

There is no way to cover more than 200 years of history in one book without making tough choices. I have generalized both for time periods and have also had to sacrifice many regionally specific issues and themes in India. This is particularly true for the first chapter on economic policies in colonial India. The mandate of the chapter is to explain primarily how the economic problems faced by independent India were created by colonial economic policy and secondly how the choice of policies by Jawaharlal Nehru was influenced by events in the global economy in the 20th century. Since this book is directed towards readers who may not have been exposed to the academic literature on the Indian economy, this chapter covers a long period for the sake of narrative continuity. Readers can refer to the bibliography for detailed and scholarly works on policy in colonial India.

Even though this is a historical book, I have not explicitly engaged with the question of histography: how different accounts of the Indian economy serve different political agendas. To add another conceptual layer of how writing history itself is a form of politics would make this book too abstract for the reader.

I have written the book from a Marxian political economy framework, which I have explained in more detail in the Introduction, and this means that I have used Marxian concepts such as accumulation, class, and crisis to understand the trajectory of the Indian economy. I have embedded the narrative on the development of the Indian economy within the dynamics of global capitalism. However, politically I have been agnostic – as far as possible – as I believe that my political stance should not affect the analysis I am presenting to the reader, and I hope that readers from across the political spectrum will read this book.

Acknowledgments

Thanks to all my students batch of 2015–2020 who were the test audience for this manuscript. Your joys and pains in class and response to the course motivated me to write this book.

Thanks to my colleagues at Azim Premji University for having a shared sense of purpose about the importance of teaching and openness to engage with ideas from other disciplines.

Thanks to Arjun Jayadev for his encouragement and belief that I could finish this manuscript.

Thanks to the faculty of the economics group at APU for the formal and informal discussion about all things economics and providing insights into society through WhatsApp memes and Twitter beefs.

Thanks to Vaishnavi Pandalai, who assisted me with my research. Our weekly conversations and your enthusiasm regarding budgets and five-year plans were the fuel that drove my writing process.

Thanks to Alex Thomas for all our discussions on writing, teaching and not following the straight path in research.

Thanks to Vamsi Vakulabharanam, my PhD dissertation supervisor, with whom I took the first baby steps to understand the Indian economy using the frame of crisis and conceptualized the periodization for this book.

Thanks to Azim Premji University for providing research funding and a conducive environment for writing.

Thanks to the staff of the Teen Murthy Library who assisted me in accessing archival material.

Thanks to Saswata Guha for our collaborative analysis on macro-economic data in India and open-ended discussions on all things economics.

Thanks to Reetika Khera for providing new insights into the policymaking process under the United Progressive Alliance (UPA) government.

Thanks to all my teachers over the year for inspiring.

Thanks to Pratham, Jean Drèze, CORD India, and Vidaranya School for providing opportunities to gain meaningful insights about India.

Thanks to Rohit De for his guidance and mentoring regarding writing: Your feedback on my research proposal was invaluable. Your book was an inspiration for me.

Thanks to Anwesha Rana, the editor of this manuscript, for guiding me through the whole process of ideating to finishing the full manuscript.

Thanks to the staff of Cambridge University Press who assisted with producing the final draft of this book.

Thanks to Neeraja Sundaram: your interest in understanding political economy provided me with a window into the minds of how non-economists access economics.

Thanks to Ma and Baba for supporting me through every endeavor.

Thanks to Amma, Patti, and Charu for warmly welcoming us whenever we came over.

Abbreviations

AICC	All-India Congress Committee
APC	Agricultural Price Commission
APMC	Agricultural Produce Marketing Committee
ASER	Annual Status of Education Report
ASI	Annual Survey of Industry
BJP	Bharatiya Janata Party
BOE	Bank of England
BOP	balance of payment
CEGC	Central Employment Guarantee Council
CMP	Common Minimum Program
CPI	Communist Party of India
CWC	Congress Working Committee
DBT	direct beneficiary transfer
DMK	Dravida Munetra Kazhagam
EGOM	Empowered Group of Ministers
EIC	East India Company
FCI	Food Corporation of India
FDI	foreign direct investment
FERA	Foreign Exchange Regulation Act
FICCI	Federation of Indian Chamber of Commerce and Industry
FRA	Forest Rights Act
FRBM	Fiscal Responsibility and Budget Management
FYP	Five-Year Plan
GDP	gross domestic product
GFCE	government final consumption expenditure
GFD	gross fiscal deficit
GST	Goods and Service Tax
HYV	high-yielding variety
IAAP	Intensive Agricultural Area Program
IADP	Intensive Agricultural Development Program

ICDS	Integrated Child Development Scheme
IIP	Index of Industrial Production
IMF	International Monetary Fund
INC	Indian National Congress
LARR	Land Acquisition and Rehabilitation and Resettlement
MKSS	Mazdoor Kisan Shakti Sangathan
MRTP	Monopolistic and Restrictive Trade Practices
MSP	minimum support price
NAC	National Advisory Council
NAS	New Agricultural Strategy
NCEUS	National Commission for Enterprise in the Unorganised Sector
NCPRI	National Campaign for People's Right to Information
NDA	National Democratic Alliance
NFSA	National Food Security Act
NGO	non-governmental organization
NREGA	National Rural Employment Guarantee Act
NSSO	National Sample Survey Office
OBC	Other Backward Caste
PC	Planning Commission
PDS	public distribution system
PIL	public interest litigation
PL 480	Public Law 480
PM-JAY	Pradhan Mantri Jan Aarogya Yojana
PPP	public–private partnership
R&D	research and development
RBI	Reserve Bank of India
RTI	Right to Information
SC	Scheduled Caste
SEZ	Special Economic Zone
SEZA	Special Economic Zone Act
TDP	Telegu Desam Party
UIDAI	Unique Identification Authority of India
UK	United Kingdom
UPA	United Progressive Alliance
USA	United States of America
USSR	Union of Soviet Socialist Republics
WW1	World War 1
WW2	World War 2

Introduction

I was a child of reforms: I grew up in the 1990s and remember the constant delight of experiencing new things. My earliest memory of liberalization was the incursion of private cable television in Indian households in 1991 and getting access to international programming: sports, cartoons, and movies available at any time. I still have foggy memories of the 1980s when all of India would be sitting in front of the TV on Sunday mornings to watch *Ramayan* and *Mahabharat* – the previous generations were not entitled to a choice in entertainment. Choice and desire were a constant theme growing up. The personal computer arrived in households in the mid-1990s; I learned how to manipulate the keyboard and mouse to a higher degree of wizardry than any computer programmer could at that time. Then, in 1999, I visited the first multi-storey music store in Delhi: Planet M, where one could actually purchase original international albums in the same year they were released; no more illegal downloads from the internet or sneaky forays into the back alley of Pallika Bazaar – a haven of piracy located in the underbelly of central Delhi. The internet had seeped into Indian consciousness by now, and half of the country's city youth had discovered a new way of making friends and finding love hidden from the eyes of our parents. I visited my first mall in Delhi in 2002, something that I had heard about from friends who had made foreign trips. I still remember the thrill of just walking around in a shiny, air-conditioned building filled with the biggest brands that I could recognize – Nike, Adidas, McDonald's, Crossword, Music World, Barista, and pubs. Last but not least came affordable cell phones, and before we knew it we had forgotten how people met in the times before cell phones, we had forgotten the endless arguments with our parents about using the phone all the time, and we survived many hours of boring class trying to create a new record on Snake. New things and choices were unheard of a generation ago, especially for the large part of the upper class who were dependent on a fixed income. I was constantly reminded by elders that life was very different before, they had to wait for years to get any kind of consumer durables – phone lines, cars, scooters, fridge. Things were used until they broke down, and even then Scotch tape and home repairs could salvage devices for a couple of years more. The only choice for most consumer goods were either you could afford it or you could not; most people learned to make a moral value out of saving and curbing desire before liberalization in 1991 – or that is what I believed.

After school, I decided to pursue economics partly because it was the safest option for those of us who had decided to avoid the rat race of a professional degree: engineering, medical, architecture, or law school, but was also partly inspired to study something that had an impact on "everyday life." I had a paper in Indian economy in my third year of college at Delhi University; the course was quite comprehensive. However, on the first day of class we were told to focus on the exam and use previous year's test papers, assignments, and notes by senior students to prepare for the paper. The Indian economy was perceived as a boring subject not eliciting the interest of any students or the teacher, the readings were long and filled with jargon, and the lecture was filled with information and detail; most students left the class happy to have seen the back of it and hoping to never have to return to it again.

As I pursued a Master's in Economics, I learned that liberal reforms were not beneficial to most Indians and that the agricultural sector had stagnated since the 1990s, leading to widespread immiseration of peasants and farmer suicides on a scale that bordered on genocide. Class and regional inequality increased like never before, and I was part of a small privileged class who had immediately benefitted from liberal reforms. I was shocked to come to terms with the fact that all my influences – friends, families, teachers, newspapers, and television – had failed to register or communicate this. How had we insulated ourselves from such a stark reality, how had we built a bubble so thick that we believed the media but not the economic reality in our backyard? Visit any construction site, and I guarantee you that you will not doubt the claim that reforms did not benefit most Indians.

In order to make sense of liberal reforms, I pursued a PhD in Economics and went about researching: why were liberal reforms perceived as an economic success and how did it get political backing in a country where the majority did not benefit from them? As I researched economic policy, data, and the discourse on reforms, I learned that very little popular knowledge about policies is true, that policymaking is immensely complicated, and that the media has little interest or benefit in reporting about the economic reality of the nation, that most people have no access to information and little energy to go looking for it. But I also discovered that the youth, especially

Introduction

those who face the tangible effects of policy in their day-to-day lives, have a strong passion to understand and intervene in the world around them. This trajectory informed my endeavor to write an accessible history of the Indian economy, one that does not require specialized economic knowledge, one that does not bore students or anyone interested in knowing more, one that makes the economy relatable to all and inspires them to engage with policy in their household, in their neighborhood, in their schools and offices, in their villages, and on social media.

In this book, I present an accessible history of economic policies in India, from the colonial to contemporary periods, as I have found that there is a dearth of accessible and comprehensive histories of economic policies and the Indian economy. There are some gems on economic policy which are specific to a certain period; there are multiple books that analyze the contemporary Indian economy. However, there is an emphasis on writing about the liberalization period and generalizing about the period before. There also exist multiple accounts by policymakers about economic policy and the Indian economy. Lastly, there exists extensive academic work on specific policies, sectors, macroeconomic variables, and economic institutions. This project is not a substitute for the extensive literature on the Indian economy. It aims to provide an accessible introduction for non-economics readers and economic students on the history of economic policy in India and inspire them to read in more depth. I aim to reach those who on a whim want to learn more about economic policy, and I hope to make them feel more connected and curious about economic policy and the Indian economy.

It is an impossible task for one person or one work to summarize and provide a coherent narrative to understand a long period; therefore I have made decisions about what to include and what not to based on certain principles and mandates that I set out on in this project. It was important for me to have a narrative connecting different periods that the Indian economy went through, both to give a sense of continuity and to emphasize that history has a strong bearing on the contemporary. An important mandate for this project was to engage a generation that does not view reading in the same way as the youth did 20 years ago. I frequently lecture my students about the importance of reading history only for them to show me how much information can be learned through a well-made 10-minute video on YouTube. I do not believe this is an indictment of written histories but evidence that young people in general and informed readers in India are interested in different perspectives on economic policy. However, this has to be presented in a relatable and accessible way. Keeping this in mind I wanted this book to be readable like a novel from chapter to chapter, but I also wanted to break out from writing norms and habits I find common in writing on economic policy: writing from a position of academic seriousness and objectivity, cold and distant tone, focus on data speaking for itself, and using numbers and economic concepts to obfuscate and confuse rather than clarify, politically biased or provocative for the sake of eyeballs. If nothing else, this has driven away readers from engaging with the Indian economy and made it into a sphere of interest for professional economists.

I believe that this project is an important contribution to the contemporary intellectual space in India, especially as it is increasingly driven by social media which rewards simplification, generalization, and controversy and tends to drive people into echo chambers: we tend to follow those who we agree with. Two particular aspects of the nature of discussion on social media bother me – first, how important themes and questions are framed as either you are for it or against it and, second, how easy it is to find spaces to get approval for one's view, leading to what is referred to as confirmation bias. I hope this book will provide nuance, context, and perspectives but most importantly will inspire the curiosity of the reader to aim to be informed, balanced, and articulate in an environment that rewards being banal or controversial.

This book provides a history of economic policies and foregrounds policies oriented towards questions of growth and welfare: policies influencing gross domestic product (GDP), agricultural production, industrial production, and redistribution. I focus on these policies because these are the most fundamental issues that anyone should be informed about, these are policies that have a tangible impact on the daily lives of millions of people. Further, this provides a heuristic device to discuss other policies meant to complement major policies such as foreign trade policies, monetary policy, and fiscal policies. For example, to evaluate import substitution policies under Jawaharlal Nehru's government, one has to address how this contributed to industrial policy.

To provide a structure to the narrative in this project, I have broken the Indian economy into different periods: the choice of a period has been founded around political stability or the idea that we can glean a particular vision or philosophy of development within a stable political regime – a politically stable government can gain support for policies that fit in with their larger vision. Further, each of the periods is divided by an economic or political crisis. While standard economic theory frames a crisis as an economic problem that has to be solved by policy intervention, my theoretical framework assumes that a crisis is an organic culmination of instabilities within the economy. A crisis might present itself through a particular sector or economic process.

Introduction 5

However, it is indicative of broader structural imbalances within the balance of policies. Moreover, a crisis creates conditions for political and policy changes as these are volatile times, and voters and politicians are more amenable to sudden changes. This logic, of course, cannot be homogeneously applied across all periods, therefore I modify this logic for some periods. However, in all cases the periodization has been created to support the needs of the narrative, not some objective framework for periodization. The following is a summary of each period and the reasons behind it.

The Colonial Economy – 1776–1947

This chapter will summarize the nature of colonialism and how the colonial relationship between India and Britain changed from the 19th to the 20th century. One key insight in this chapter is how the two world wars and the Great Depression of 1929 shaped the world economy and consequently India. I will analyze how these changes shaped the freedom struggle in India. This chapter will conclude by describing the conditions faced by India on the eve of independence. This chapter will not be a comprehensive survey of colonialism in India but will focus on how certain colonial policies shaped the constraints faced by the Indian economy. The year 1947 is a period of political and economic crisis and provides conditions for changing policies.

The Drive to Industrialize under Nehru's Leadership – 1950–66

This chapter will discuss the main economic policies of the Nehruvian government: planning, mixed economy, heavy industry driving the growth process, and import substitution policies. Nehru was the prime minister throughout this period, and I discuss how policies were consistent with a larger development vision. I will evaluate the policy options that Nehru had and why he chose these specific policies. I will explain the impact of these policies on the Indian economy and the external conditions which influenced the implementation of these policies. This period ended with Nehru's death and the food crisis of 1965–66 which highlight the lack of policies to address the issues in the agricultural sector in India. The crisis and leadership vacuum created the conditions for a policy change.

The Turn to Populism under Indira Gandhi – 1967–79

This chapter will discuss the first tenure of Indira Gandhi's prime ministership and analyze the changes she made to Nehru's policies – which tapered towards socialist and populist policies. I will argue that these changes were a response to shifting power within the Indian National Congress (INC) and the government responding to the economic consequences of Nehruvian policy, which led to increasing political consciousness amongst the masses. I will study how Indira's policies affected the economy and led to social unsettlement and strikes, culminating in the Emergency period. This chapter will conclude with Indira losing power and India facing the Organization of the Petroleum Exporting Countries (OPEC) oil price crisis and industrial stagnation in 1979, leading to a crisis in the dynamics of a regime.

The Early Liberalization Years – 1980–2003

This chapter will discuss the period in which India transitioned from a mixed, inward-oriented, planning-based economy to a liberalized, external-oriented, market-based economy. In a shift from other academic literature, I will argue that liberalization began in the 1980s and was a fairly long period of transition. The beneficial effect of liberalization, especially in driving growth, exports, and investment, was experienced only after 2003. This chapter will be framed around the following questions: the conditions which led to the introduction of liberalization policies, why liberal reforms were politicized in 1991, and why liberal reforms did not have much of an impact on the manufacturing sector or the export sector in the 1990s. The year 2003 is not a crisis year in itself but marks the end of a period of economic and political uncertainty; the periods following this saw politically stable governments and reforms translating into higher growth.

Maturity of Reforms in the UPA Years – 2004–13

This chapter will focus on the two tenures of the United Progressive Alliance (UPA) government. I will analyze why the Indian economy was able to achieve high growth after more than two decades of liberal reforms, and how the UPA government used a different process to introduce "reforms with a human face" to make them more politically palatable. I will also discuss a change in philosophy within welfare policies referred to as the rights-based socially redistributive policies like the Mahatma Gandhi National Rural Employment Guarantee Act (MGNREGA), the Right to Education, and the Right to Information (RTI). This chapter will evaluate why the UPA government was able to achieve high growth – unlike the INC and the Bharatiya Janata Party (BJP) governments in the previous regime.

Introduction

Reforms under NDA – 2014–19

This chapter will focus on the first tenure of the National Democratic Alliance (NDA) government. I will analyze how the BJP gained an electoral majority for the first time in Indian history and examine major economic policies introduced by the NDA, such as demonetization, Goods and Services Tax, and Farm Bill. I will analyze how reforms under the NDA were different from those under the UPA. At the time of writing, the economy was under the tenure of the second NDA government and going through the COVID-19 lockdown crisis. I have decided not to include this period in this manuscript as it was difficult to comprehend the impact of lockdown on the Indian economy and how these would influence policies in the future.

Why is historically researched and politically neutral discourse on economic policy needed? Well, it is largely because there is no way to be completely informed or objective when understanding and evaluating economic policy; the more nuance one can get about a policy, the more balanced one's understanding of a policy becomes; and the more detail one has about the historical trajectory of a policy, the better one can answer the question of why this and why now. An important lesson that I try to imbibe in my students is that there is no objective evaluation of a policy because every policy has someone who benefits and someone who does not, and evaluation is colored by one's own biases. Therefore, one has to understand the logic and reasoning that shapes a policy instead of limiting oneself to evaluating the benefits and criticisms of the policy.

I ask my students to ask five basic questions about assessing a policy: (*a*) why was this policy introduced? (*b*) what was the problem that it was meant to fix or, broadly, how did historical context frame this particular problem and create this policy? (*c*) what were the politics which shaped this choice of policy or how did the logic of politics and institutions shape this policy? (*d*) what were the alternative policies available or what were the other theories available to solve this particular problem, and (*e*) how was this policy perceived or what do empirical data and reception tell us about this policy? In answering these questions, readers need to imagine themselves in those times: historical consciousness, the ability to imagine a decision from the perspective of those who are making it, is an important weapon in the historian's toolkit. In one of my first classes in the Indian economy course, I ask students to imagine that they are part of the Planning Commission under Nehru and reflect on what would be the primary problem that economic policy should address on the eve of independence. Initially, students struggle with this question and project the problems that still exist today onto that period – they say poverty and basic needs: water, sanitation, housing, clean drinking water, lack of infrastructure, corruption, and so on, are the major problem that needs to be addressed. At this point, I remind them to reflect on the nature of colonial economic policy and how it affected the structure of the Indian economy. This provides a starting point to think about the problems faced at the time of independence. One of the ways I prepare students to be historically conscious is to read documents from that period: popular documents such as Nehru's and Gandhi's speeches on economic issues and policy, budget documents, or other public documents like parliamentary debates, Congress Working Committee reports, and newspaper reports. Even accessing literature or cinema from that period apprises one of the issues that were considered important then, especially for the common man. These are some thinking exercises through which I hope to build historical consciousness amongst the reader through this book.

This book applies a political economy framework that borrows from both of its Marxist and liberal traditions. Political economy provides an innovative theoretical framework to study historical questions through the lens of multiple disciplines. Political economy as conceptualized by the first generation of European economists – Adam Smith, David Ricardo, Thomas Malthus, John Stuart Mill, and Karl Marx, amongst many others – was an object of study: it referred to the study of the emerging political–economic system which affected every aspect of the human experience. It was one of the earliest articulations of capitalism, but the original thinkers did not separate the economic, social, and political consequences of economic activity. Over the 20th century, the economy was analyzed as being independent of social and political dynamics. This empowered economists to analyze economic policy through an objective lens as they did not have to address moral questions regarding justice, equality, and environmental sustainability. Political economy in the 20th century transformed into one particular method of studying economic policy which foregrounds analysis of how politics affect economic outcomes. In the spirit of political economy inquiry, especially the form inherited from 19th-century economists, I presume that economic reality – economic policies and their tangible effect on people – is determined by political, social, economic, cultural, and intellectual factors; this means that there cannot be one causal explanation for any policy or economic outcome. For example, to understand why Nehru after independence adopted the planning-based heavy industry-oriented development model, one has to understand the challenges or problems Nehru was trying to address, the popular ideas at the

Introduction

time, the history of this institution or idea in colonial India, and how the social composition and political system in India shaped this change.

The political economy framework has been used by different commentators on the Indian economy differently; the following are some of the theoretical principles that I have followed. A political economy framework provides space for explaining a change in economic policy through multiple levels of abstraction and not one causal explanation, such as the ideas or theories shaping this policy, how political contestation has shaped the form of a policy, and how implementation challenges have affected the execution of the policy. For example, the Farm Bill Act introduced by the NDA in 2018 can be understood through ideas: the pros and cons of liberalizing the agriculture sector, the politics of the NDA government, and the process of implementing through political institutions in India. Second, the framework assumes that history has no design or goal, and therefore every moment, outcome, and policy is a culmination of multiple processes and also the beginning of the next set of processes. I do not assume that the present is a culmination of the events of the past nor do I evaluate whether a history of policies can be considered progressive or stagnant. For example, to analyze and evaluate liberalization in 1991, one has to study reforms introduced before 1991 and also how liberal reform policies have been modified or changed after 2003; reforms cannot be understood at just one point. Third, the political economy framework assumes that different classes have different economic and political interests, and consequently every policy has winners and losers. This leads to different perspectives and responses to policy. However, classes are not necessarily homogenous or conscious of their interest, which is why we find both coalitions between classes that do not share an interest or lack of consciousness amongst a class about their common interest. As a consequence, political parties play an important role in articulating class demand and contesting policy. Two examples stand out from my narrative: first, the lack of an organized national agricultural lobby at the time of independence led to the dilution of public investment in agriculture under Nehru. This changed over the 1970s and 1980s as agricultural powerful lobbies got political representation. In the 1990s and early 2000s, civil society organizations played a key role in articulating the demands of the landless and tribals and reshaping social rights policy under the UPA government. While data provides a window into understanding the impact of a policy, interesting insights into the policymaking process can be gleaned by paying attention to the discourse around it: the final form of a policy is influenced by its reception; a critical understanding of the government's and national media's presentation of a policy adds another layer of nuance, which is not captured through data, by demonstrating what determines the popularity of a policy. This is particularly true for populist policies, such as socialist policies introduced by Indira Gandhi or demonetization by the NDA government which had little impact on the economy. Economic theory and development discourse have generalized that the state is homogenous and has a conscious and coherent developmental philosophy. I do not assume through this political economy framework that the arms of the state are homogenous in identity or unified in interest. Instead, I describe how political infighting between central and state governments, within the central government and the opposition, between the bureaucratic arms of the state, and even within the ruling party shape policy outcomes. Second, periodization plays a foundational role in political economy analysis. While evaluating policy within a period, I analyze how the timing, sequence, and form of a policy is influenced by the development philosophy in a period. For example, how did a social rights policy such as the MNREGA fit within the UPA's brand of reforms?

I have consciously ignored or given lesser attention to some important caveats of economic policy analyses. Given the breadth of regional, social, and political diversity in India, it is impossible to analyze a policy from regional perspectives. Therefore, I focus my analysis on presenting the logic of a policy from the perspective of the central government; in some sense the central government is the central protagonist of this novel. There are some components of policymaking, which are central in most analyses of economic policy, such as the role of monetary policy and the Reserve Bank of India (RBI), how fiscal sustainability constraints decisions, the role of macroeconomic variables such as inflation, the balance of payment (BOP), interest rate, and so on, in shaping policy decisions. These have been peripherally mentioned and under-represented in the analysis in this manuscript. The primary reason for this is that explaining the role of these themes requires conceptual grammar which can alienate readers without formal training in economics – I believe that a reader can understand a policy without understanding some of the theoretical underpinnings of the policy. Lastly, identity in the form of caste, region, and gender has become an important part of social science analysis in India in the 21st century. I have focused more on class as a category for understanding the impact of policies on social groups; this is primarily because there exist good data and secondary literature analyzing class in India. Caste is an important axis through which economic inequalities are reproduced, and there is a dearth of databases and empirical studies to elucidate this mechanism – this is an important area for scholars to contribute to. I have tried to identify, wherever possible, the impact of policies on excluding marginalized castes as well as

Introduction

how the rise of vernacular regional parties has brought certain backward castes into the national policy discussion. However, there is an urgent need for a more detailed analysis of how economic policy shape and reproduce caste inequities.

The title of this book is motivated by the political economy approach to understanding history. The subtitle "A Story of Crisis, Coalitions, and Contingency" emphasizes that history is connected to the past and future, that human actors cannot plan and control the outcome of developmental plans, and that there is no design to history. As we study the history of the Indian economy, one finds ample evidence that decisions have been shaped by factors outside the control of the decision-makers. A corollary to this idea is that one cannot generalize that economic policies have unanimously been progressive or stagnant or improved or harmed people's lives. Instead, a rigorous evaluation of a policy should first ask why, why now, and for whom?

Before ending, I will provide one interesting question from each period covered in this book in the hope that it would motivate the reader to read more about the period. In Chapter 1, I analyze how the independence movement in India was shaped by colonial economic policies. In Chapter 2, I discuss why Nehru decided to have a planning-based mixed economy instead of a market-based private-sector-driven economy. In Chapter 3, I evaluate whether Indira Gandhi's policies can be considered populist or socialist. In Chapter 4, I argue that 1991 was not the year of liberalization in India. In Chapter 5, I address why the UPA was successful in introducing reforms that translated into high growth. In Chapter 6, I address how reforms under the NDA were different from the UPA.

1

Colonialism and the Indian Economy

In this chapter, I will describe and analyze the historical process through which colonialism shaped the structure of the Indian economy before independence, by understanding the nature of the global economy in the 19th and 20th centuries and how these dynamics shaped the colonial relationship between Britain and India. Further, I will describe the colonial policies that created and transformed the Indian economy, a critique of and resistance to these policies by Indian political actors, and how these dynamics shaped the economic policies of independent India. This chapter is global in outlook and will digress from India to explain how changes in the world economy affected the Indian economy. This will provide a context to understand the structural issues that the economy faced after independence and the trajectory of economic policies that were implemented. Throughout this chapter, I will frame the importance of contingent events, contestation between different interest groups, the crisis in shaping colonial economic policies, and the independence movement in India.

The Great Divergence

Look closely at a graph of GDP growth over the course of the millennia (Bowles 2013, fig. 1.1a) of countries in the world, and you will find that most countries or regions in the world had experienced similar low-level steady growth for 1,500 years. Then something happened in western Europe in the 16th century, when some countries such as Portugal, the Netherlands, and Spain started growing at a slightly faster speed. Then in the mid-18th century, Britain's growth rate took off and left all other countries behind. It took more than half a century for some of the early developing countries like the United States of America (USA), Germany, and France to catch up to Britain. It took more than two centuries for other developed countries in the world to catch up. India joined the race in the mid-20th century, and there's still a long way

Colonialism and the Indian Economy

to go before it catches up. The initial jump in growth experienced by Britain is referred to as the Great Divergence (Pomeranz 2021). This phenomenon is referred to by terms such as the Industrial Revolution, and the birth of capitalism is marked by major social and political transformations in the world – such as the French and the American revolutions, the institution of representative democracy in Britain and France, urbanization, and colonization of land, labor, and resources – on a hitherto unseen scale. The transformation that Britain went through over the late 18th and 19th centuries shaped the modern global economy and provides the foundation for understanding the modern Indian economy.

To appreciate the transformations brought by the Great Divergence, one has to understand the structure of the global economy before it. There is a misconception in the modern media that globalization is a modern phenomenon – that there were few interlinkages or interconnections between countries and regions in the world before the modern epoch. The global economy was thriving, even as far back as the end of the first millennium, with the movement of goods, people, and capital across all corners of the globe. Trade was largely self-contained within regions of production with the most profitable being the Indian Ocean, the Middle East, and China. Merchant classes in different regions created the infrastructure for international trade and profited the most from it; nations and governments had little involvement in the trade regime. Europe – especially western and southern Europe – was an important trading region that had little access to the Asian economy. Europe had a huge demand for goods produced in China and the Indian Ocean: textiles, garments, spices, silk, paper, porcelain, and tea. However, they did not produce anything demanded by this region.

It should be noted that the Indian economy, in its present form, did not exist in this period. The Indian Ocean was an important trade region containing a necklace of ports ranging from Lahore, Surat, Travancore, Bengal, and Malaysia. These ports were dominated by merchant classes. The Indian polity was divided into a few kingdoms, the most dominant of which was the Mughals coexisting alongside more than 500 princely states. The Mughal kingdoms had nothing in common with modern nation states; most areas were locally governed and shared revenue relationships with the Mughals in exchange for centralized security, infrastructure, and monetary systems. Goods produced in the Indian hinterland were transported to the ports, where they were bought in auction by traders who then sold them in different parts of the world – especially in ports in China and the Middle East. There were no unified laws, currencies, or standards of weights in India, and no centralized authority governing the functioning of ports or foreign trade.

The subcontinent dominated the production of textile and garments in the global economy and also provided cotton, pepper, grains, pulses, and vegetable oil. India produced a surplus quantity of cheap goods due to its fertile land, diversity in geographical conditions, and the availability of cheap labor. Regions within the subcontinent had few interlinkages with each other, and the surplus or profits accumulated by trade were rarely reinvested in production. The advantages of production in the Indian economy did not translate into economic growth or productivity gains. This is not unusual as there is no evidence of large-scale accumulation in any of the prosperous regions of the world before the 18th century.

The shift in growth trajectory experienced by Britain was not an outcome of design, policy, or planning, but a culmination of the right conditions, historical processes, and certain contingent developments. By the 20th century, all European and American economies had joined the race to significantly improve their GDP, and Britain had become an exemplar to study and follow. The Industrial Revolution in Britain was powered by producing cheap textiles and flooding the markets of other countries. Historically, China and India produced cheap textiles because labor was much cheaper than in the United Kingdom (UK). Britain managed to produce cheaper textiles in the 18th century due to access to cheap cotton in America and technological innovations. British textile mills created spinning jennies that used steam power to produce textiles at a faster pace. Coal was cheaper than labor in Britain, and the technological innovations were a consequence of circumstance rather than intent; high labor costs had forced British manufacturers to innovate new designs which led to the spinning jenny, an apparatus that increased the productivity of textile production by using the cheap source of coal found in Britain. Similarly, the discovery of the cotton gin in America sped up the process of turning cotton into yarn. The production of cheap cotton in America was pioneered by the British and Europeans, who had colonized the land and resources of America and used enslaved labor to produce cheap cotton. As the British increased its trade linkages and acquired colonies, it faced a growing demand for its cheap textiles which British producers could not match. This unprecedented increase in textile demand spurred increased investment in the textile industry in the form of scientific innovation and improvements in transport and communication. A class of rich British landlords infused capital and influenced colonial policies to create the conditions necessary for significantly increasing the

Colonialism and the Indian Economy

output of textile at a lower cost and steadily taking over the world market. This virtuous cycle of gaining new colonies, facing increased export demand, spurring investment in increasing the productivity of textile production, and increased profits became the backbone for sustained growth which is termed as the Great Divergence.

Why India Was Important to Britain

The East India Company (EIC), along with Portuguese, Dutch, and French Indian companies, entered the subcontinent in the 17th century and built a network of middlemen, agents, and contacts to trade regularly within the Indian economy. Since Britain did not produce anything of interest to India, they traded silver appropriated from Latin America. By the late 18th century, Britain had got a firm foothold in Bengal by gaining revenue collection duties. The British expanded their sphere of influence by collecting revenue on behalf of different rulers, and by the mid-19th century most of the provinces in India had become part of British administration. Under that, the Indian economy was oriented towards foreign trade through policies and became a British trading outpost to make trade linkages with other Asian economies. This sphere of influence allowed the British to directly acquire productive land in India and initiate commercial production of highly demanded agricultural goods: indigo, opium, cotton, and silk.

Before the entry of the British, Indian agriculture was carried out by peasants and small farmers for self-subsistence. Surplus agricultural produce was sold in the local market, and few regions catered to the needs of foreign trade. The importance of India as a trading outpost for the British is demonstrated by the increase in terms of trade between exports and imports from 84.3 in 1861–65 to 123.6 in 1911–15 (Roy 2020, 76). Terms of trade refers to the ratio of exports over imports – this ratio is more than 100 when exports exceed imports. This translated into an increase in exports of commodities from INR 7 crore to INR 18 crore from 1814 to 1844 (Rothermund 1993, 23) and an increase in import of commodities and precious metals at an even faster pace from INR 2.5 crore to more than INR 15 crore. The vast majority of these exports went to Great Britain and China. Entry into the Chinese economy was pivotal to Britain as they produced certain goods such as porcelain, paper, silk, and so on, which had a high demand across the world and provided a vast market for British goods. A triangular trade relationship was formed, where goods from India were exported to China to gain a trade surplus, which was leveraged to import goods to Britain through India. This led to a positive trade balance for India, and the extra income was transferred back to Britain as remittances.

How Did the EIC Create the Indian Economy?

The British colonial empire linked most of the world through its trade relations: the cotton plantations in North America, sugar production in the Caribbean, slave trade with Africa, precious metals in South America, production of capital goods and textile in Great Britain, opium and indigo production in India, and tea, porcelain, and paper production in China. As Great Britain linked up multiple parts of the world, a coordinated world market started appearing where price changes in one part of the world would affect production patterns in other parts of the world. This led to the movement of capital and labor around the world to access better interest rates, wages, and cheaper raw material, and resulted in geographical specialization of production – for example, opium was not locally consumed in India in a large quantity; however, the land was conducive for opium production, and there was a great demand from China for it. This had important consequences for the shaping of the Indian economy.

Across India, the rural economy had followed a similar pattern of agricultural production and trade for centuries based on customs, seasonal rain, and social networks. However, with access to a world market, Indian capitalist classes, merchants, traders, moneylenders, and landlords, eager to benefit from speculative trading, started changing agricultural production away from local demand products to commercial crops which have global demand. Indigo, opium, and cotton were the primary cash crops in the early 19th century, while jute, tea, and wheat became increasingly important over the late 19th century. The growing value of commercial agriculture propped up the price of land and led to the creation of a land market. As the value of land increased, in a land-scarce nation, capitalist classes started to appropriate common land and wasteland, displace tenants and peasants, and increase the pace of deforestation to bring new areas into agricultural production.

In a capital-scarce economy like India, capitalist classes tended to look for guaranteed short-term returns; this was provided by investment in land and precious metal. While investment in the land led to speculative gains from the rising prices of commercial crops in the world market, there was little incentive to invest in improving the factors of production or quality of the land. The favored mode of production was to give cash advances to peasants or

Colonialism and the Indian Economy

tenants working on the land and to procure their produce at a fixed price; the peasant took on the risk of a bad monsoon or low produce. From the peasant's perspective, the moneylender provided a link to the world market as there was no substantial local market for these commodities in India. Moreover, the lure of cash advances was difficult to resist for the peasant who had little savings and needed cash to fund the harvest season festivals and family celebrations. The peasants would frequently get indebted to the moneylender due to a bad harvest. The moneylender would use this indebtedness to maintain a steady supply of commercial crops at cheap prices, which could be turned around into a nifty profit based on the world market. The lack of availability of financial capital, due to the low penetration of banks in India, led to an unwillingness to invest the profits in improving the productivity of land or investing in industrial production. This process of commercialization changed the structure of the agricultural sector into becoming labor-intensive, peasant-based production on small landholdings controlled by merchant classes. The degradation of land by intensive commercial farming, appropriation of common land, hoarding, and rent-seeking behavior by merchant classes coupled with the lack of tenancy rights and social security created the conditions for impoverishment and immiseration of agricultural producers – a malaise that the country is still dealing with.

Colonial policies such as discriminatory tariff policies benefitted the EIC by providing preferential access to Indian commodities and over time transforming the Indian economy into an essential part of their colonial empire. The increased embeddedness of the Indian economy in foreign trade contributed to creating a national economy: unifying production patterns across India, creating interlinkages across different regions, and generating a class of Indian capitalists who benefitted from the commercialization of the economy. Such a change was necessary for India to embark on the road to becoming a capitalist economy.

The Indian economy, before the colonial incursion, did not function as a national economy. Instead, there was a dual economy: well-governed regions connected to a port – for example, Surat, Bengal, Travancore, and proximate princely states – were deeply embedded in the global economy, while most of the densely populated hinterlands were local, self-sufficient economies. There was no national market connecting different parts of the country, and a lack of infrastructure, common laws, and administrative apparatus discouraged anyone from trying.

After the 1857 uprising, the British crown took parliamentary control of India from the EIC and centralized power in the hands of the governor-general of India. Before this transfer of administrative responsibilities, EIC officers had worked autonomously in different regions to further their financial interests. There was very little coordination between officers and the home office in London due to the difficulty of travel and communication. The centralization of power and control by the British crown was assisted by the advent of the telegraph and faster travel due to the opening of the Suez Canal. Economic gain was not the sole motive of the British government; instead, they started treating India as an administrative extension, building the governance apparatus and infrastructure required to administer it: dividing regions into administrative units like districts and *tehsils*, organizing the administrative bureaucracy in hierarchies, and homogenizing governance apparatus and chains of power in all regions. An important institution introduced by the British was their legal system in India, which included contract laws, property rights, uniform weights, and processes of resolving economic disputes. In the past, these had been addressed at a local level and contributed to uncertainty regarding trade and production across different regions in India. Homogenous law created national markets: production de-linked from local demands and movement of goods, capital, and labor across the economy driven by price differences. Equally importantly, the army got unified under the civilian governor-general with the commander-in-chief as the second in command. The civilian control of the military led to a more organized and rational dispersion of the troops towards issues and conflicts of national importance. In the past, the army was divided among different commanders in different presidencies, creating conflicts and making coordination impossible amongst the different troops without a proper chain of command. The British also made silver currencies produced by the mint as the universal currency, allowing easier transactions across regions. Furthermore, the British physically linked different parts of the country with the construction of the railways. The British government's interest in constructing railways in India was to expedite the movement of goods, labor, and troops. However, the success of building the railways was contingent on attracting British capital. The government guaranteed a 5 percent rate of return on any British capital invested in Indian railways paid for by public revenue. The railways along with the telegraph created the conditions for the functioning of a national economy and production for a national and international market.

How Colonial Policies Shaped Indian Industries

One common critique of colonialism is that the British de-industrialized India. While there is a certain truth to this claim, it is equally unsubstantial to claim

Colonialism and the Indian Economy

that India would have become an industrialized economy without colonialism. This chapter will not resolve either of these claims, but instead will address the question of how industries were shaped by colonial mediation and policies and how this contributed to the development of industries after independence.

India had a substantial handicraft industry – a precursor to the manufacturing sector – which was supplying a quarter of the world's production of goods in 1750 (Tomlinson 2013, 101). The Indian handicraft industry in the 18th century was at par with other manufacturing sectors in other economies. However, the conditions required for it to expand such as an expanding market, access to capital, physical and social infrastructure, and conducive policies were not available. The handicraft manufacturing industry existed in two forms in India: the first was based in rural areas and served local demand, while the other was located in towns and served larger markets. Local handicraft industries were caste-based and were not a full-time occupation: handicraft makers subsisted on their income by working in the agricultural sector. These craftsmen produced simple consumer goods, such as cloth and basic implements for agriculture like plows and pots for storing. The other form of handicraft production was full-time and organized around guilds, with different specializations in different areas which served the needs of the military, luxury consumption, and export. The handicraft sector was highly decentralized: there were almost no backward or vertical linkages, and they were dependent on a trading class or local patronage for demand. The technology used was simple, and there were no formal institutions to raise capital. The Indian handicraft sector was not able to innovate or create new products to compete with British-made goods; this was not due just to a lack of technical know-how or access to technology but also due to colonial tariff policies – which will be discussed later in this chapter. Indian handicrafts stagnated over the 19th century due to the loss of power of princely states and changing preferences towards imported British-made consumer goods.

In the 18th century, cotton textile was India's main manufacturing export – this remained true until the time of independence. India was the largest supplier of calico – coarse cloth – from the ports of Gujrat and fine muslin from the ports of Bengal. These were largely exported by the EIC, and these regions developed into the main industrial areas in independent India. By the year 1800, Lancashire cotton and yarn had flooded the Indian market, and even with access to a large reserve of cheap labor, Indian textiles could not compete with their British counterparts. It must be noted that British textiles were not of the same quality as Indian, and the technological innovations used in the Industrial Revolution could be imported by Indian manufacturers.

Still, British textiles outcompeted Indian handlooms due to multiple factors, including cost, control of information, and the ability to access markets across the country. At a similar time, jute industries started emerging in Calcutta.

Infant factory production emerged in India by the late 19th century. The first steam-powered textile mill in India was built in Mumbai in 1856. The capital was raised through multiple Indian investors, and machinery was imported from Britain. Bombay became the first major industrial center for textiles and was followed closely by Ahmedabad. Textile industries originated in western India due to the existence of capital-owning classes, well-developed roads and ports, and a lack of intervention by local rulers. These industrial centers possessed a close integration of trading, money lending, and industrial know-how within the city's family community – Marwaris, Parsis, Jains, and so on, who formed an incipient industrial capital class in India.

Indian heavy industries were structurally different than handicraft industries. Unlike the handicraft industries which got out-competed by British imports, Indian factories would benefit from the structure of the economy and colonial policies. Before 1914, most of India's cloth imports came from Lancashire; these producers lobbied the British government to decrease tariffs in India so they could compete with Indian production. The decision of the British crown to reduce import tariffs to 5 percent and then abolish them completely by 1882 would go on to become one of the most criticized policies by Indian nationalists. When import tariffs had to be increased due to revenue requirements of the economy, Lancashire textile lobbied for excise duties on Indian manufacturing to make them less competitive.

The tariff policies were symptomatic of the changing nature of intervention by Britain in the world economy. Contrary to popular narratives, the early phase of industrialization in Britain, the USA, and France was based on protectionist trade policies and monopoly trading. Home industries in Britain were protected from foreign competition by high tariff barriers, while a market for British commodities was founded on getting monopoly rights of trading with different countries. By the mid-19th century, European countries had stopped importing manufacturing goods from Britain and protected their own domestic industries. There was a tariff war between different countries such as Germany, Belgium, France, and the USA. Britain, however, could produce goods more economically than other countries due to their access to cheap labor, cheap capital, state investment in physical infrastructure, and falling cost of transport and communication. Britain started advocating and practicing free trade policies precisely because its industries could compete with their counterparts in the global economy. At a time when protection would have helped Indian industries grow, the colonial government imposed low tariff barriers and placed excise duties on Indian industries. This constrained the readiness of Indian capital to invest in projects with a long gestation period – a malady that would haunt them after independence. This tariff policy shaped both the structure of the economy as well as the independence movement in India.

The Roots of Colonial Resistance

The colonial government had globalized the Indian economy and embedded it within its colonial empire. The British had created an administrative apparatus, infrastructure to improve connectivity (for example, railways, roads, and so on), a homogenous legal system, and policies to make the economy profitable for British manufacturing and trading interests. While reliable and comprehensive data about the Indian economy is unavailable, economic historians have provided rough estimates of data to understand the trajectory of the Indian economy in this period. The importance of Britain in shaping the Indian economy, especially after coming under the British crown, is demonstrated by the economy achieving a growth rate of 1.76 percent in 1865 and 1 percent by the turn of the century (Roy 2020, 5). While these growth rates may seem low in comparison to the growth rate achieved in the 21st century, at that time it was on par with European economies. The population rate was still low in India, hovering around the 0.5 percent mark, owing to a significant death rate and lack of modern healthcare and low literacy. As a consequence, the per capita national income was growing at a rate of 1 percent – that is, every year a person's income was increasing by 1 percent. Given the extent of economic inequality, this meant that significant profits were being earned by certain people, such as trader and merchant classes, British expatriates, administrators and company servants, and professionals dependent on colonials – agents, lawyers, doctors, teachers, and middlemen.

This was the first period of growth on a national scale experienced in the country and contributed to the growing consciousness amongst the elite about the loss of economic opportunity to the people. In the past, economic activity had been determined largely by regional considerations, caste links, local customs, and cultural habits. However, with increased economic opportunities available on a national scale, there was growing political consciousness about the detrimental effects of colonial rule on the economy and the need for political action to engage with the colonial government about national policies.

This crystallized into the economic critique of the colonial government and shaped the economic policies of independent India.

The Critique of Home Charges

The INC was created in 1885 by a group of British-educated Indian lawyers who initially wanted to negotiate about policies but morphed into an organization that would successfully mobilize the masses of the country and thrust itself into the forefront of the independence movement. The INC's ability to mobilize the growing national consciousness about discriminatory colonial policies was crucial in their ability to shape the Indian economy after independence and gain popular consent for doing so. In the early 20th century, the colonial critique was framed around home charges. Home charges were a transfer of funds from revenue collected in the Indian economy as a payment for British capital used to fund the railways, irrigation, and infrastructural work, purchases of equipment for Indian stores, charges for services of British troops on Indian soil, and payment of wages and salaries of administrative staff working in India and the home office in Britain. These home charges were substantial and funded by the trade surplus of the economy. In essence, the home charges were a transfer of Indian revenue to support British capital, create demand for British industries, and provide employment to British troops and administrative staff. Trade had been the generator of economic growth for Britain. The increasing dependence on foreign trade for the Indian economy contributed to the drain of trade surplus by the British in the form of government and private remittances. The drain was significant enough that India's export surplus was reduced to a deficit that had to be funded by loans from Britain.

The first generation of Indian nationalists, including Dadabhai Naroji, R. C. Dutt, and Rajaramohan Roy, argued that this drain was a theft of resources from India by Britain. This criticism, which in hindsight seemed obvious, was not of interest to the Indian economic elite, especially those who had benefitted from British colonial rule: forward castes who were given land revenue collecting rights and transformed it into ownership over the land; professional and educated classes who got employment directly or indirectly with the British government; merchant classes and traders who benefitted from contracts to supply the British government as well as gained access to new markets; and blue-collar workers who got jobs in factories made possible by British rule. Paradoxically, for a substantial part of India's population, which included poor peasants, backward castes, and tribals, economic life under

Colonialism and the Indian Economy

British rule was no different from the subjugation they faced under Indian feudal lords. What was significant about the drain critique of colonialism was the argument that something that was 'ours' is being stolen by an outsider. This implied the existence of an economy that generated returns which should be used as an engine to improve the standard of living of the population of the country. This implied that the economy was a shared resource – devoid of regional, caste, and ethnic rivalries – meant to serve all Indian citizens. The efficacy of this argument came from the presence and intervention of the British across the national territory, and the threat of a common enemy implied all Indians as stakeholders in the economy.

World War 1
World War 1 and Its Impact on Indian Industries
Political events in the late 19th century and the beginning of the 20th century are some of the most important for understanding the development of capitalism on a global scale. Western European countries, Russia, the USA, and Japan industrialized and competed across the globe for access to cheap resources, land, labor, and markets to sell machinery and mass consumer commodities. This period is the closest the world has come to experiencing a free international trade regime, as countries reduced their tariff boundaries, while tariff boundaries in colonies and newly emerging economies were kept very low. Capital from these countries flowed around the world, searching for profitable outlets for investment. The Indian economy found itself firmly embedded within the needs and ambitions of the British Empire; then in 1914 the assassination of Franz Ferdinand sparked World War 1 (WW1) and consequently reshaped the global economy and with it the trajectory of the Indian economy.

The initial impact of WW1 was the collapse of the international trade regime, with countries unable or unwilling to provide passage for goods, capital, and services, while triggering a reshaping of the global power structure: Britain lost its dominance in the world economy, while the USA emerged as the main economic power. The international economy, before WW1, had been stabilized by the gold monetary standard. This allowed traders to convert currencies of different countries at a stable exchange rate. The gold standard was an anomalous monetary system as no country or financial institution controlled its supply; instead, a country's exchange rate was determined by its gold reserves. In theory, the discovery of new gold, hoarding, and speculative activity or contingent events could lead to a change in the value of gold, affecting the global economy. However, the Bank of England (BOE) maintained the stability of the gold reserve. They were able to do so because of their large positive BOP, funded by interest earned on capital exports and remittances from its colonies – especially India. The role of the BOE in maintaining the gold standard was crucial to making London the financial center of the world and establishing its political clout in maintaining the international economic order. The economic damage that WW1 unleashed – instability of global trade, breakdown of trade relations, economic losses due to war, war repatriation paid by Germany for war damages, and the breakdown of cooperative behavior amongst the colonial powers – eroded the efficacy of the gold standard. While Britain struggled to maintain its BOP surplus, other countries like France and the USA started hoarding gold in anticipation of a pending crisis, which would contribute to the end of the gold standard during the Great Depression of 1929.

The war unevenly affected the global economy. Britain, France, and Germany had faced the bulk of economic damage, including deaths, destruction of infrastructure, stagnation of production, and loss of capital to war efforts. Russia and the USA had come out of the war with limited damage and were well placed to become significant powers in the global economy. The forces of capitalism – business, trade, banking, and finance – had suffered due to a breakdown in trade relations between European countries, money, and resources needed to repair countries, loss of productive capacities due to unused machinery, decrease in productive labor, and fall in demand due to impoverishment in the economy.

The war was immediately beneficial to the infant manufacturing sector in India, especially given the rise in the price of all commodities and the closure of maritime trade routes with Europe. The industrial sector got a boost in this period due to government contracts and protection from imports. This contributed to an increase in employment in industrial centers. However, the increase did not compensate for the fall in employment in the small-scale sector. The greatest benefit was received by the steel industry, especially the newly created Tata Steel plant, which got a contract to be a government supplier for railway tracks and construction steel. The cotton textile industry also faced a surge in demand. Textile imports declined from 2.1 billion yards in 1906–08 to a wartime average of 1.6 billion yards in 1916–18 (Rothermund 1996, 67). Indian textile mills stepped up their production from 0.6 billion yards to 1.3 billion yards, and the number of mill hands increased by 12 percent in this same period. The mining industry also benefitted as coal imports dwindled from 500,00 tons to an insignificant amount by the time of the war, while coal exports increased to a million tons by 1916. Similarly, the jute export

Colonialism and the Indian Economy

industry experienced increased demand due to the need for sandbags for the wartime effort.

While WW1 started reshaping the global economy and brought a surge in growth in the manufacturing industry in India, it did not translate into the path to industrialization, partially because the global economy went into cycles of recession over the next few decades but also because Indian agriculture was not equipped to develop. Between 1900 and 1914, the economy grew at a rate of 1.95 percent (the highest in colonial India) and per capita income grew by 1 percent. From 1914 to 1917, the economy grew by 1.14 percent, but per capita income grew by only 0.06 percent due to a surge in population growth and structural and regional inequality (Roy 2020, 5).

WW1 contributed to the divergent development of small-scale and heavy industry in India. Domestic industries benefitted from the changes in the global economy over the 20th century. However, there was a curious transformation occurring within. Its contribution to the national income increased from 11 percent to 17 percent, while its workforce share decreased from 13.6 percent to 9.6 percent from 1900 to 1947 (Roy 2020, 71). Small-scale and handloom industries suffered in this period due to shrinking export markets, smaller surplus available for producers as they faced higher agricultural prices (Rothermund 1993, 79), and a shortage of capital in an uncertain market. This impacted employment as workers and producers who lost their jobs in the small-scale sector had to return to the already overworked agricultural sector.

Colonial Policies Encouraging Domestic Industries

Incipient heavy industries needed protection from foreign competition to develop; crucially, investors had to be assured a rate of return to make the long-term investments required for projects with long gestation periods, such as the guaranteed rate of return on British capital invested in railways. The Tatas had been an exception investing in steel at a time when there was no guaranteed market, and they were fortuitous for the change in demand created by WW1.

In the 19th century, the colonial government would have no incentive to develop the domestic industry. However, with the changes in the global economy in the 20th century and increased dependence on the Indian manufacturing sector, the colonial government was becoming aware of the strategic necessity to have policies to encourage industrial development and appointed an industrial commission to consider future options. The *Report of the Indian Industrial Commission 1916–18* urged the government to play an active role in the industrial development of the country. The policy did not have much political impact, and its recommendations – improvement in technical education and encouraging private agencies to provide industrial finance – were toothless. The policy itself was diluted by 1919. However, its importance owes to the fact that this was one of the first instances of discussion of an industrial policy that would benefit Indian industries. This was an important foundation for policy discussion on the importance of import substitution and the complementary role of the state and large domestic capital.

The increasing expenditure faced by the British government in WW1 required an urgent increase in revenue collection in India. As a consequence, the general rate of import tariff was continuously increased and hit a high of 25 percent by the mid-1920s. The government of India, building on the recommendations of the industrial commission, initiated a policy of "discriminating protection" in the early 1920s, based on the recommendation of the *Report of the Indian Fiscal Commission* (1922). The commission had recommended protection to domestic industries for a limited period if they were able to demonstrate the ability to compete with imports. A tariff board was set up which provided protections to 11 industries between 1923 and 1939. Protection was provided to heavy industries requiring modern production systems, such as iron and steel, chemicals, textiles, and consumer industries, such as paper, tea, salt, matches, and so on. Contracts from the government, protection from foreign imports, and state support for the development of domestic industries in the aftermath of WW1 provided the foundation of the industrial policy which would be adopted in independent India.

The period from WW1 to independence is also the period that brought into focus the economic and social issues that would plague independent India – but let us not get ahead in our story. The agricultural sector barely grew in the 20th century (Roy 2020, 71), and its contribution to the economy dwindled. All new land had been exhausted, and there were no investments to improve productivity. The best land was allocated to commercial crops, which were monopolized by a small section of the population. The dependency of the majority of the population on the agricultural sector, without any social security nets, created a recipe for immiseration and tragedy.

The Great Depression of 1929
The Great Depression of 1929 and How It Impacted the Satyagraha Movement
Some events reshape global dynamics overnight; how nations react to these changes determines the winners and losers. The Great Depression of 1929

Colonialism and the Indian Economy

was one such event, borne of American creditors' overzealousness to profit and heightened by structural issues with financial regulation in America. It spread like a contagion across the world and touched every economy embedded in the global trade regime. India lacked a safety net to face the Depression, but this spark set the flames to the independence movement.

In the 1920s, the world economy had been recovering from the damage wrought by WW1. The USA had played an active role in negotiating peace in Europe and providing credit to war-ravaged countries. This led to the phenomenal growth of the USA economy, and it became the financial leader of the world. Along with the growth of Russia, the global economy had started experiencing an upturn in prices over the 1920s. In the middle of 1929, USA stock markets crashed. The crash had a domino effect across stock markets all over Europe. The primary reason for the crash was an overproduction of wheat and unregulated banking and financial markets in America. The Depression led to a deep deflation or fall in prices and unemployment. Moreover, there was an overproduction of goods and no demand for it. With profit rates falling, there were no funds available for credit. The American economy went into depression – a steady fall in GDP that affected the entire global economy.

The Depression affected the European economies significantly, especially Britain, which had not yet recovered from the ailments of the war. The response of Western economies to the Depression created more problems than it solved. Classical economic models posited that the functioning of markets would resolve an economic crisis – prices of goods would adjust to create demand for industries that were depressed. As stocks of goods were cleared a virtuous cycle would be created: income received by firms would provide a new round of investment, and a new round of production would generate more employment which would translate into increased demand for goods. Over a few business cycles the economy would start growing again. Governments did not intervene much in times of the Depression, and banks generally followed deflationary policies – policies that curb the supply of money in the hope that interest rates would increase in the future and the amount of savings and loanable funds available to banks would increase. However, the Depression of 1929 showed no signs of recovery, unemployment soared, there was no demand for goods and services, stock and financial markets were spiraling downwards, and banks which had sunk their capital in the financial market were unable to recover from the losses, and filing for bankruptcy. People had lost their trust in the financial system and were hoarding money, and there were no funds available to capitalists to start a new cycle of production – there was no outlet for the economy to return to a growth trajectory.

The American government responded by adopting a protectionist trade policy – the Smooth Hawley Act of 1930. They increased tariffs and devalued the currency, making imports more expensive. A protectionist trade policy immunized the American economy from price fluctuations in the world economy and made imports more expensive, ensuring that American money is not drained and foreign competition cannot enter the market. Further, they started hoarding gold and left the gold standard since the international monetary system was unstable. The BOE had historically acted as the lender of last resort for the gold standard and bailed out banks and economies to maintain stability in exchange rates. However, following the American adoption of protective measures, countries got embroiled in tariff wars and international trade receded to WW1 level. This adversely affected countries which were highly dependent on foreign trade, especially Britain as it lost its importance in the global economy. The Depression came at an important historical juncture as Britain had started losing the economic dominance required to maintain its colonies, and had a secondary impact on countries of the periphery since their government did not provide policies to protect the nation.

The Impact of the Great Depression on the Indian Economy

India did not have a central bank, and the exchange rate was controlled by the secretary of state in London. Colonial discrimination policies meant that import tariffs were low, and the Indian economy had no cushion to face the uncertainties of the world market. Moreover, the colonial dependence on home charges and the need to increase revenue collection drained the scarce resources available in the economy. The Depression had a massive impact on the foreign trade-oriented Indian agriculture sector which simultaneously experienced a fall in world agricultural goods prices and access to credit. Each level in the hierarchy of agricultural trade passed on the economic challenges to the next level. Dietmar (1996, 94–98) has analyzed this web of credit connecting financial institutions in England to Indian peasants. British banks provided loans to traders who participated in forward trading: agreeing on the price of the commodity in advance and minimizing the risk of volatile prices, these traders paid advances to wholesalers and merchants in India to procure agricultural goods. These funds were passed down to moneylenders, landlords, and traders at the local level, who provided advance capital to peasants for their crops.

This chain was important for two reasons: first, there was no formal institutional credit available in India; second, peasants were dependent on credit to start the agricultural cycle, and the chain of credit passed on the risk

Colonialism and the Indian Economy

of failure of the monsoons onto the peasants. With falling agricultural prices, a rising rate of interest on credit and rising land revenue – due to the increased need for revenue by the British government – peasants in India were unable to generate livelihood and pay their debts. The British laws in India favored creditors, and they could force peasants to pay up. This led to a massive loss of land and the sale of distress gold by peasants, who fell into poverty traps as they sold their assets, and had no social insurance or public benefits to support them. Fiscal stimulus in the guise of government spending or inflationary policies would have helped the Indian economy face the consequences of the Depression. However, the British government responded by exporting the distress gold at below market prices to Britain to buttress a positive BOP to cope with the Depression. This loss of the gold reserve further deflated the money supply and contributed to the low availability of credit.

The nationwide immiseration of the peasants and the contraction of the export-dependent agricultural sector affected the Indian masses; this turned out to be a boon for the fledgling efforts of the INC to create a mass movement. The INC had been spearheading the freedom struggle since the turn of the century. However, their impact was largely centered around urban areas in north India. The INC leadership was British-educated, and their interventions to colonial rule had been couched as political and legal critiques. Mahatma Gandhi's incursion into the INC had made them more visible to the masses. However, the INC had failed to unite different strands of Indian society in the independence movement. Gandhi launched the Satyagraha movement in January 1930, with an 11-point program. At first glance, the demands made seem unconnected, but on closer inspection many of these deal directly with the economic impact of colonialism. Two points stand out about these demands: first, they successfully brought together the economic interests of different classes and framed it as a critique of colonialism; second, they targeted economic policies that had exacerbated the impact of the Depression.

Countries all over the world had devalued their currency; this made imports more expensive and exports cheaper, creating export demand while preventing the nation's income to be drained by imports. This provided an incentive for the production of import substitutes by domestic industries to fill the demand gap, protected the agricultural sector from cheap imports, and stabilized prices from being affected by the volatility of the world market. However, the Indian government did not control the exchange rate. The currency was controlled by the secretary of state in London, and it was in Britain's interest to maintain a high sterling–rupee exchange rate – to ensure that there was not a sudden flight of demand from the rupee, but also because customs duties and tariff earned on Indian imports provided one-third of the total revenue generated by the Indian government. The British government needed revenue to balance its budget and maintain its superiority in the global economy. The second demand made by the Satyagraha movement was to change the ratio between the rupee and the sterling or devalue the currency.

The other important sources of revenue for Britain were land revenue and salt taxes, which accounted for another third of revenue (Rothermund 1993, 103). The British could have increased income tax. However, they did not want to affect the urban upper classes and British employees as this was a vocal political base. The government maintained a high rate of land revenue, at a time when agricultural prices plunged, credit was scarce, and peasants were being forced by the court to pay back moneylenders. The third demand in the Satyagraha movement was to reduce the rate of land revenue. Salt taxes affected all citizens. However, they disproportionately hurt the poor as salt is an inelastic good: the demand for it does not reduce even when its price rises. As the salt tax was increased, a larger part of the shrinking budget of the poor went into paying tax. The fourth demand was the abolition of the salt tax, and Gandhi's Dandi Salt March resonated with the masses and gave immense visibility to the independence struggle.

From the early 19th century, the British ensured preferential treatment for themselves, over both Indian and foreign competitors, by controlling the import tariff rate. This ensured that there was low or no tariff on British imports to India. By the 20th century, Britain was one of many countries having strong trade relations with India. Japan had become the biggest textile exporter in the world, benefitting from low salaries and state support. It had dethroned Britain and its colonies as the main supplier of textiles in the global economy. By 1930, Japan was a major exporter of cotton textiles to India and a major importer of raw cotton. Japan had devalued the yen after the onset of the Depression, and even with high tariffs, they were outcompeting Indian mill traders. The Indian Tariff Board of 1932 (Rothermund 1993, 105) had strongly recommended a high tariff boundary. However, preferential treatment to British traders prevented the administrators from doing so. The Depression highlighted one of the contradictions of colonial and dependent economies – the need to protect the Indian economy from foreign competition versus the need to make policies to benefit the colonizing country. The Indian textile magnates grumbled about these policies, and by 1934 a pact was made between Indian and British textile for a lower tariff rate. At the same time, quota agreements were made with Japan which allowed them to export a certain amount of cotton textiles in exchange for importing a certain amount of raw cotton.

Point seven of Gandhi's demand was to impose customs duties on foreign cloth; this directly benefitted the textile-producing industry but also symbolically resisted the domination of Britain built on textile production.

The Satyagraha movement's demand for changing the exchange rate, tariff rate, and tax rates collectivized the economic interest of multiple groups – peasants, the common man, textile- and cotton-producing industries, producers, and merchants involved in foreign trade – and framed these demands as a critique of colonialism. Gandhi's demands were not very successful, and a parley was placed called the Gandhi–Irwin Pact, which negotiated suspension of the Satyagraha movement in exchange for the opportunity for Gandhi to directly address the British parliament. But this did not translate into any policy changes. By 1931, as the Indian economy faced the aftermath of the Depression, public sentiments crystallized around Gandhi and translated into the INC's victory in the first election in 1935. The Great Depression of 1929 had created the conditions for a national independence movement at a time when Britain was at its weakest.

The Changing Structure of the Indian Economy in the Early Twentieth Century

India experienced between 2 percent and 3 percent GDP growth at constant prices (Tomlinson 2013, 5) in the 1920s, benefitting from the euphoria and the buoyancy in the world market following WW1. This is the highest recorded growth in GDP in any decade in pre-independent India. In the 1930s, the growth rate plunged to between 0.5 percent and 1 percent and negative growth in per capita income. As population was growing, per capita income fell. This was a consequence of the shrinking of the global economy after the Depression but also symptomatic of the changing structure of the Indian economy. Colonialism had embedded India firmly within the British Empire's market for goods, commodities, labor, and capital. In 1860, 43 percent of India's exports went to Britain, while 84 percent of their imports came from Britain (Tomlinson 2013, 54). Another 35 percent of India's exports went to China; India was part of a triangular trade relationship, where India had an export surplus with China and provided Britain entry into trade with China. The Indian economy in the 19th century was oriented towards exports of primary goods: British administrative mechanisms, investment in infrastructure, and policies were oriented towards maintaining this trade regime.

As the British Empire waned after WW1, and other developed countries dominated the global economy, trade relations with Britain also diminished.

By the 1930s, only 23 percent of exports went to Britain, while imports had decreased by more than half to 37 percent. Trade relations with China had also become negligible. Japan and America had become the second most important trade partner with around 10 percent of imports and exports each, while continental Europe had contributed 10–15 percent of trade. This diversification in trade had changed the composition of commodities traded: raw cotton and foodstuff were the most important exports, while jute, manufactured jute products, tea, and oilseeds were the other important commodities. Opium and indigo exports had completed stopped. The majority of the population was dependent on agriculture. However, the agricultural sector was stagnating with low productivity, disguised unemployment, negligible investment in infrastructure, and diminishing availability of arable land. India's dependence on foreign trade had been decreasing steadily, and there were no avenues available through which the agricultural sector could have grown.

Indian industries and infrastructure, cotton textiles, jute manufacturing, tea plantations, oilseed production, iron and steel, sugar, and paper had grown in this period. However, most industries made little contribution to the GDP and employment. Improvement in agricultural productivity, supply of cheap and surplus labor migrating from agriculture, and export of manufactured products had been the key to growth and development for the early industrializing countries. Colonial policies such as preferential tariff structure and import substitution policies had buttressed the process of industrialization. The Indian economy had developed in complementarity to the needs of the British economy; once the colonial empire started waning, it highlighted the structural deficiencies in the Indian economy. Certain classes such as urban professionals, colonial administrative staff, workers in factories and secondary sectors, and rural elites like landlords, moneylenders, merchants, traders, and wholesalers benefitted from the structure of the colonial economy. The vast majority of the population were small-scale or landless peasants, who were stuck in deep debt, with little or no assets, and no prospect of improvement or upward mobility. The government did not pursue any policies to redistribute income, provide basic needs or any kind of social insurance, or provide measures to dampen economic shock caused by the Depression through policies such as devaluation, protective tariffs, deflation of currency, fiscal stimulus, and so on.

The Rise of the INC as the Face of the Independence Movement

Immiseration and chronic poverty in the agricultural sector broke through barriers of language, region, religion, and caste in the Indian population.

Colonialism and the Indian Economy

It was at this opportune moment that the the the INC under Gandhi's direction launched its Satyagraha movement. Gandhi had already garnered support from Indian capitalist classes, by framing different economic issues as a common problem, he had managed to unify different economic interest groups across the country. The Satyagraha movement cobbled together different economic issues and framed them as a common problem: the discrimination of colonial rule. The addition of a vast army of peasants became the mass base that the INC needed to become a national party and provided the backbone to have giant rallies and marches as a public demonstration of the strength of the INC.

The Government of India Act of 1935 was symptomatic of the increasing realization amongst British administrators that India was too expensive to administer. The act itself was seen as a small step towards building a democratic apparatus in India. It divided the country into provinces that were allowed to elect their representatives and provided a legislative structure to mediate the administrative relationship between the federal and provincial governments. The British wanted to protect their interest in India and had secretly hoped that the INC would not gain a complete majority in the elections. They had designed electoral representation to have different parties gain the votes of different social groups: princes would form autonomous power groups, and peasants would vote for the National Agricultural Party composed of landlords. The hope was that the landlord would get allegiances from the peasants, who would be thankful for the improvements brought by the British government. However, the timing of the Depression and Gandhi's mass mobilization techniques meant that the agricultural sector which included landlords, moneylenders, traders, and factory workers blamed the British for the state of the economy after the Depression and voted for the INC.

The INC government emerged in power in eight provinces following the general elections of 1937. The formation of the government had a nominal impact on the polity and economy, and the ministers resigned in 1939, protesting India's involvement in World War 2 (WW2). Of note, however, was the formation of a planning commission in 1939 by the INC. This committee was headed by Nehru and involved ministers from all the victorious provinces. They had also invited independent experts and some delegates from the princely states. The report was largely qualitative and listed the priorities of industrial investment to develop the country. The report had little immediate consequence. However, it would foreshadow the direction of the INC government after independence.

India's Role in World War 2 and How It Contributed to Independence

The British economy had been unable to recover from the impact of the Depression and their loss of financial importance in the global economy with the demise of the gold standard. The British had been unable to finance the administration of its colonies, including India, and the British parliament was in a serious discussion regarding providing independence to its colonies – albeit maintaining their political and economic interests. Meanwhile, the German economy had made a swift economic recovery and, under the guidance of Adolf Hitler, started rebuilding its armaments. The Depression had changed the political circumstances in Europe, and with renewed hostilities across the continent and colonies, inevitably the world arrived at the brink of another war in 1939.

Britain, still reeling from the effects of the Depression, was highly dependent on its colonies, especially India, for funds, army personnel, and production. The British government staked a much higher claim to production in India than in the previous war. The British bought goods from India on credit and forced the country to save. While the purchase of goods was funded by printing more currency, these were kept in the accounts of the Reserve Bank in the BOE. India turned from a debtor into a creditor for Great Britain; this assisted India's demand for independence. However, it also suited the British politically. The British claimed a lion's share of India's jute production for sandbags, cotton textiles, soldiers' uniforms, and steel. The price at which the government procured this was fixed by the government itself. Indian industries had to produce at full capacity to meet the requirements of the war; there was no capital available in the economy for them to invest in increasing production.

After the depression of prices in the 1930s, agricultural prices started rising in anticipation of shortages at the time of war. The viceroy of India, however, did not take any precautions during this price rise – one can assume that he believed it would benefit the Indian agrarian sector. In May 1942, India lost Burma to Japan – a major rice-growing region. Cognizant of the effects this would have on supplies, the government fixed the price of rice. This policy backfired as instead of creating an affordable stock of rice, it led to hoarding by traders to maximize profit. The price of rice and wheat went up from INR 3 and INR 4 a *maund* (37.5 kilograms) in 1939, respectively, to INR 14 and INR 10 in 1942 (Rothermund 1993, 121). The government's feeble attempts to purchase grain from surplus provinces and sell it at cheap prices in deficit provinces were largely ineffectual in controlling prices; the colonial government had historically preferred free movement of market forces and did not have the experience or infrastructure required to ration food grains. Provincial governments took matters into their hands, and the governor of Madras banned the export of rice from the province and took state control of the rice trade. This move was successful in halting the price rise in Madras.

Due to political circumstances, the Bengal government was unable or unwilling to undertake similar measures. In 1943, Bengal was hit by a famine of unprecedented magnitude. Traders in Bengal had hoarded grains and sold them at profits outside the state. Agricultural peasants and industrial laborers who had no direct access to rice suffered the greatest. Since jute and rice are grown in the same field, one would expect an increase in rice production when prices rose. However, the prices of jute stayed stagnant in this period, while the price of rice exploded. This is evidence of the fact that the shortage of food grains was not a production crisis but a distribution crisis; this famine was a consequence of policies, not a natural disaster. Unofficially, it is estimated that two–three million people died, directly or indirectly, due to the famine. The famine was exacerbated as a result of a lack of government policies and infrastructure to deal with famines.

The famine forced the government to implement rationing measures. By 1945, more than 400 towns and cities were subjected to rationing. Wartime rationing led to the creation of institutional mechanisms and a new bureaucratic apparatus that would provide the foundation of the planning regime in India. The Bengal famine and the general fall in wages and standard of living culminated in a series of peasant and worker strikes all over India and represented a leftist challenge to the INC-led freedom movement, and would have major ramifications for India after independence. As the British began formal procedures to depart from India, and the INC government began uniting a country divided by religious differences, regional conflicts, and a crisis of sovereignty, class war was brewing in the economy which would significantly affect the direction of the economy.

While the INC had mobilized multiple class interests through their Satyagraha movement, this was largely due to their public visibility and ability to engage the colonial government. Sooner or later, the INC would have to confront the contradictory classes which were part of their vote base, which included the rural and urban elite and peasant masses. Until the 1939 planning committee report, the INC had not articulated its economic vision for India after independence; their dialogue with the British was a mixture of demands of different classes which would include boycotting of foreign goods, protection of domestic industries, abolition of the *zamindari* system, and state ownership of key industries. The INC had been garnering strong support from Indian infant industries and urban elites because there was a mutual acknowledgment of the contradictory position of the British government in India – balancing the requirements of the home country while meeting the needs of the Indian economy, which translated into a commitment to provide a market for British goods in India, maintain the home charges, and paying interest on the sterling debt.

On the other side of the fence, as peasant rebellion increased, the fledgling Indian left started becoming more visible politically – to the extent that moderate socialists in the INC became alarmed by the radical demands of the left. One event of particular note was the All India Kisan Sabha held in 1936 – strategically at the same time as the conference of the socialist wing of the INC. The main aim of the Kisan Sabha was to secure freedom for peasants – comprising more than 50 percent of the population – from economic exploitation through the abolition of the *zamindari* system and Soviet-inspired land reforms. In urban areas, worker unions had become capable of organizing strikes and *bandh*s which could shut down industries and cities. The largest trade union in India, the All India Trade Union Congress, had INC members but worked autonomously. In 1942, most INC leaders had been arrested after the launching of the Quit India movement, violent worker and peasant strikes had been occurring all over the country, and there was a real fear amongst the business community that the independence movement would turn into a socialist revolution. The success of the Russian Revolution and the fledgling revolutionary anti-colonial movements in South America and parts of Asia had made this a real possibility. The INC had representatives which were trusted by the business community, most importantly Vallabhai Patel, who raised funds for the INC on the promise of preserving the interest of domestic capital, and Gandhi, who favored peaceful protest and did not openly support the labor movement even though he was an avowed critic of industrialization.

In 1944, major industrialists in India, representing the different business communities, including Shri Ram, Tata, Birla, and Kasturbhai Lalbhai, presented the Bombay Plan to the government. This plan would become a footnote in history. But the contents of the plan and the politics that shaped it are important to understand the contestation of economic policies before independence. The Bombay Plan was a document that provided a model to achieve rapid economic development in India while improving the economic conditions of the masses. It planned to double the national income in 15 years

Colonialism and the Indian Economy 37

and projected investments required in different industries to achieve this end. The plan endorsed a mixed economy with state control of key industries and the need for coordinated strategies by public and private enterprises. It was an indication of industrial support for state control of industry and a planned economy in an attempt to influence the economic policies of independent India in favor of domestic capital. It is also important to note the items that were not listed in the plan, such as a strategy for agricultural development or structural changes to address the issue of poverty. The consequence of the plan will become clearer in the next chapter on the policies of the Nehru government.

State of the Indian Economy on the Eve of Independence

India gained independence on August 15, 1947. However, the euphoria of independence was short-lived. Communal violence had threatened the fabric of the nation. The partition of British India displaced millions of people, creating the largest migration in modern history. The uncertainty of sovereignty due to the unwillingness of various princely states to enter the republic and the threat of border incursions from China had made the state of the nation very uncertain. Moreover, the structural conditions of the Indian economy itself were a problem that could not have been sorted overnight. The economy had grown at a slightly better rate in the 1940s. However, it experienced a negative rate of growth in per capita income (Tomlinson 2013, 5). The vast majority of the population was dependent on agriculture, which had been stagnating due to low public and private investment and increasing population pressure and was left to cope with the vagaries of the monsoon and volatility of prices in the world market.

Poverty and inequality were both increasing with no major redistributive or poverty-alleviating public policy. The colonial government had initiated a public distribution system, but its functioning was not effective. The British had commercialized the Indian agricultural sector and embedded it in the world market, but with the closure of the global economy in the war, there was no prospect for this to be an engine of growth; on the contrary, linking with a volatile global economy would have severe adverse effects for peasants. The British had completely restructured Indian industries and created a dual structure: small-scale manufacturing units and handloom producers had been outcompeted by the flood of cheap British manufacturing goods while being constrained by a lack of rural demand. Large industries in India developed alongside British capital. Textile, jute, iron, and steel had become established domestic industries, while other fledgling industries, like sugar, cement, paper, and wool, were growing at an impressive pace. However, Indian industries were not equipped to drive the growth trajectory as none of these industries, barring jute, had any export potential. To make matters more complicated, the jute-growing region in Bangladesh had been lost due to partition. Indian industries were low on investments and did not contribute to creating employment. Moreover, India was still highly dependent on Britain for machinery. Independent India inherited this paradoxical industrial structure.

Britain had a parasitic relationship with India in terms of remittances and debt accrued over WW2. The flow of remittances back to Britain went up significantly as British citizens and businesses started withdrawing from India due to the threat of nationalization and socialism. The British remained the most important trading partner with India, but the USA was very close, with an almost equivalent percentage of imports coming from there and Japan. It was crucial for India to maintain autonomy, to break away from its dependency on Britain, but also to avoid a dependent relationship with other imperial powers. The colonial government had also played a minimal interventionist role in the sphere of production or capital formation: their economic role had been to collect revenue and maintain discriminating taxation and tariff policies. Revenue was collected through customs and indirect taxes (Tomlinson 2013, 150). The majority was spent on tax collection, debt servicing, defense, wages, and salary (Tomlinson 2013, 151). India inherited a deficit BOP, unbalanced industrial structure, underdeveloped capital markets, high poverty, and regional imbalance from the colonial economy. However, it is also worth noting that crisis, contingency, and contestation played a key role in the unfolding of the colonial economy. The crisis faced by Indian peasants in the aftermath of the Great Depression created the conditions for the mass national independence struggle. The two world wars were contingent events that helped shape Indian heavy industry: WW1 created conditions for government policies that assisted infant heavy industries, while WW2 sharpened the class divide in Indian industries and paved the way for a coalition between the INC and large industry. Lastly, class contestation played a pivotal role in the 1930s and 1940s and would go on to shape the policy direction of Nehruvian India.

On the eve of independence, the Indian government faced the challenge of changing the structure of the economy which had little prospect of growth; further geographical and social diversity in different regions in India meant homogenized policies would be toothless to deal with regional issues. Moreover, they had to bring political consensus to a nation that had a significant rural semi-feudal population that was highly dependent on privileges granted by the British administration. The emergent and incipient domestic capitalist

Colonialism and the Indian Economy 39

class and privileged factory workers were small in number, but they were vocal, politically engaged, and organized. India was highly dependent on the British government, which, even after granting independence, wanted to preserve their economic interests in the country. It was in the face of these deeply divergent and sometimes contradictory interests that India had to shape an economic policy, which aspired to bring it out of economic servitude and make it one of the most powerful economies in the world. The rest of the book narrates this story. But it is important to be conscious of the condition that two centuries of colonialism has created in India and the patterns, relations, and mentalities that it had shaped, which had to be overcome or destroyed to transform into a modern growth-oriented economy.

References

Bowles, S. (ed.). 2013. *Core Economics*. 3rd ed. New York: Worth Publishers.

Pomeranz, K. 2021. *The Great Divergence: China, Europe, and the Making of the Modern World Economy*. Princeton, NJ: Princeton University Press.

Rothermund, D. 1993. *An Economic History of India*. 2nd ed. New York: Taylor & Francis.

Roy, T. 2020. *The Economic History of India, 1857–2010*. 4th ed. New Delhi: Oxford University Press.

Tomlinson, B. R. 2013. *The Economy of Modern India: From 1860 to the Twenty-First Century*. 2nd ed. New York: Cambridge University Press.

The Drive to Industrialize under Nehru's Leadership
1950–66

At the stroke of the midnight hour on August 15, 1947, the world slept while India awoke to life and freedom. The Indian economy, however, would not be free of its structural deficiencies and uneven developments from colonial rule – even after achieving political sovereignty. The primary task facing Nehru and his advisors on the eve of independence was clear: India needed to grow at a fast pace and achieve industrial development to catch up with the rest of the world while breaking away from its economic dependency on Britain and other superpowers. The tricky task facing the government was how they intended to achieve these goals while facing constraints of capital resources and accommodating the diversity of economic interest groups that existed in the country. In this chapter, I will explain the economic development goals of the Indian economy after independence and the choice of policies to achieve them. This explanation will include studying the historical context of these policies, the internal and global contestations around these policies, and the role of contingent events in shaping them. While the institutions of colonialism and its critique paved the direction of the development trajectory, historical contingency and the impossibility of balancing contradictory and antagonistic interest groups and global politics eventually shaped the application and impact of these policies. It is important to be mindful of these circumstances to appreciate how Nehruvian policies have both shaped the institutions and trajectory of India's future economic growth but also passed on the deficiencies and imbalances that existed within the economy. It is not the mandate of this book to evaluate whether the policies were right or wrong; instead, I hope to show the multiple and contradictory forces that shaped the policy choice and simulate the reasoning behind these choices.

Inheriting the Colonial Economy

The new government had adopted an economy shaped by almost two centuries of colonial rule. The agricultural sector was highly unequal in terms of land ownership and access to capital. The majority of the population was dependent on the vagaries of the monsoon and markets and caught in webs of debt. The added pressure of an increasing population with limited land meant that the majority of peasants were poverty-stricken, with no opportunity to increase the productivity of the land. The landlord class thriving within ancient feudal hierarchies had little incentive to improve production. While a large part of the agricultural economy was self-subsistent or small surpluses generated were sold in the local market, commercial forms of agriculture oriented towards exports – plantations and globally demanded agricultural produce coexisted. The economy, however, was not equipped to produce enough food stock for the whole economy, and there were frequent shortages in some regions while others had excess. The industrial sector had a clear dual structure: developing factory production in manufacturing goods and light consumer goods which, while small in scale, had entrepreneurs capable of scaling up, and a large but stagnating small-scale and handicraft industry with little scope for growth. The economy was also characterized by an underdeveloped financial market and dependency on other countries – England, the USA, and Japan – for producer goods. Probably the biggest challenge the economy faced was uneven regional development with some well-developed regions, especially near the coast and metropolitans, and underdeveloped and unconnected hinterlands and border regions.

The nation had adopted certain socio-economic contexts and colonial institutions which would assist in the mammoth task of shaping the economy. Most importantly, there was no dominant regional or ethnic group that could grab military control of the nation; many newly independent countries had an oligarchical class that embedded the economy within the colonial relationship of the past, such as the Latin American countries, wrecking any opportunity for independent economic development. The INC government was committed to democracy and the development of the nation. Moreover, the colonial bureaucracy had created a literate section of the population who were experienced in managing the different arms of the bureaucracy – courts, police, army, civil services, revenue collections, and so on. The independent economy had geographical advantages such as highly diverse terrain and climate, producing diverse kinds of agriculture, well endowed in natural resources and minerals, and well-located and developed ports at multiple points on the coastline. The economy had surplus quantity of cheap labor and the potential to develop large domestic markets, as well as a small but rising class of skilled labor and managers. These endowments created opportunities for the government which were missing in many other newly independent countries.

Models of Economic Development

The primary objective of the Nehru government was to grow at a fast pace and catch up with other developed countries in the world. This was necessary to transform the highly unequal and poverty-stricken economy and to escape from dependence on other global powers. Rapid growth and development are tricky problems as there is no universal solution for an economy to follow; instead, every policy has its pros and cons. The earliest developing countries such as the UK, the USA, France, Germany, and other Western nations achieved growth through industrialization, or when the majority of the GDP and employment in an economy is generated by the industrial sector. An economy does not organically transition from agriculture being the dominant contributor to the GDP to industries being the overriding coordinator; different countries have industrialized through different policies. The earliest developing countries had achieved industrial development through colonial extraction and protectionist economic policies. The colonial government had guaranteed markets for their products, access to cheap land, labor, and resources, and protection through tariff policies from other competitive economies. As industries developed, they transitioned from the export of primary products and light manufacturing goods to heavy industrial goods. This fast-growing export sector pushed the economies on an upward development trajectory through its linkages with other industries and sectors. There was no dearth of accessible colonies in the 19th century, and these economies developed over more than half a century and consolidated their domination of the global economy. As the available colonies got mopped up in the 20th century, the developed nations were pushed into a war which severely damaged the global economy. However, the end of WW2 brought a renewed cooperation amongst developed countries under the global leadership of the USA and the Union of Soviet Socialist Republics (USSR); moreover, the level of development allowed them to survive the difficulties of the war and depression.

A second route to development was the Japanese case of export-oriented development. Japan had a strong central government and bureaucracy which subsidized and disciplined the textile industry to compete in the world market. Coordination and disciplining by the government, cheap labor, and demand from the populous Asian economies provided the conditions for Japan to develop through exports. The increased demand for exports created linkages with other parts of the economy and created a growth trajectory. This mode of development required a strong government that could subsidize and intervene with efficiency in the economy, coordinating the needs of the export industry

The Drive to Industrialize under Nehru's Leadership

with other sectors. This route is preferred by small economies that do not have sufficient domestic demand to kickstart the development process.

A third model of development was followed by Russia. The Bolshevik government came to power in 1917 and socialized the economy: public control of means of production. The first step was to collectivize land through public or collective ownership of productive land and funnel public resources to the agricultural sector to develop it at a fast pace. The surplus generated by the agricultural sector was invested in the nationalized industrial sector. Unlike Japan where private and public sectors existed together, the Russian economy was highly coordinated through a complete control of industries by the Bolshevik party. Since there was no private ownership of land and enterprise, it was possible to coordinate the production of different sectors according to a predetermined plan. The dictatorial government used coercive methods to ensure that interest groups followed plans. Russia achieved industrial development in two decades – a rate faster than that experienced by any other country.

Industrial development was achieved differently in diverse economies, but a common thread was access to capital – usually, surplus generated from agriculture, colonization of land, and access to the international market to provide demand for industrial goods. Russia could partially skip this step as it had a huge domestic market and political and social stability. The early developers – especially those constrained by landmass such as Britain – were highly dependent on colonies. These economies had well-developed agricultural sectors and supportive governments which protected industries with trade policies and conducted wars and expansions to meet the interest of industries. In the case of Japan and Russia, the state played a much more interventionist role – actively coordinating the industries to achieve steady growth and industrial development.

India's Unique Development Path under Nehru's Direction

While political independence gained a break from colonial discriminatory policies, economic independence through self-sustained growth was necessary to break out of the network of the colonial economy. The historical trajectories of industrial development and the critiques of colonialism provided the context for Nehruvian policies. It was not possible for the INC under Nehru to have a policy direction that would address the issues raised by different economic interest groups: industry, labor, landlords, professional classes, peasants, and so on. Moreover, it was not possible to replicate the development trajectories of other economies, partially because the nation adopted a democratic framework – none of the other developed economies had universal democracy and could disregard issues of inequality and injustice – and partially because the socio-economic diversity in India was unique.

Nehru's decision to follow the industrialization-focused development model was based on suggestions of academicians and policymakers. The method adopted to reach this goal distinguishes India from the path of any other developing economy. Nehru's policies were defined as the middle way and were implemented through a planning process. He chose to focus on the industrial sector over the agricultural sector and domestic capital over foreign capital. The rest of the chapter will discuss the specificities of this policy and the reasoning behind them, how the economy performed under these policies, and the challenges and constraints that the government faced.

The INC adopted a mixed-economy, industrialization-led development model which was based on their critique of colonialism but also borrowed colonial economic policies and institutions. The INC had made many piecemeal critiques of colonialism, the most potent of which was that the British had limited the developmental possibilities of the Indian economy by draining resources in the form of sterling home charges, de-industrializing the handicraft industry by flooding the Indian market with British goods, and transforming the agricultural sector towards commercialized export-led growth – ignoring the needs of the local market and embedding peasants in a chain of debts. The legislative and bureaucratic institutions introduced by the colonial government would be an important part of India's planning apparatus. Moreover, colonial policies supporting Indian industries in the early 20th century such as fiscal support, government contracts, and planned development would form the foundation of Nehruvian industrial policy.

Mixed Economy: The Middle Path

Nehru and the Planning Commission (PC) charted out the fastest and most efficient path to industrialization, knowing well that it would take a long gestation period of unprofitable investments while having to balance multiple political and ethnic interest groups in an economy undergoing intense social transformations. Policymakers around the world had to choose which path to follow to industrial development – the one represented by the USA, driven by export markets, private enterprise, and minimal government intervention, or by Russia, fueled by careful planning, public ownership of means of production, and state control of the economy. But Nehru and the PC did not consider

The Drive to Industrialize under Nehru's Leadership 45

there to be any choice at all, as he wisely noted in his speech (Publications Division 2017, 46),

> There are in the world various policies, ideologies, and theories. I suppose there is some truth in each of them. However, my personal feeling is that while it is very important to have a theory as a logical way of thought, it is not reasonable to apply it ... you have to take the facts of the situation and adapt either yourself or your theory accordingly.

For Nehru, the social context was key to the path of development to follow; he reasons in the quoted speech that the socio-economic conditions, nature of capitalism, and colonial history were different in 19th-century USA and 20th-century Russia from independent India.

Nehru's solution was characteristic of his solution to many decisions, the Buddhist-sounding middle path. When asked to choose between the USA's free enterprise-based capitalism or the USSR's state-controlled capitalism, Nehru retorted:

> That is a very hard choice indeed and I do not see why I should be forced to make it. It is inevitable that those countries, which do not want either of the two extremes must find a middle way ... or a mixed economy, if you like to call it that, is inevitable. (Publications Division 2017, 45)

The middle way was conceptualized as taking the best of both systems and finding a complementary role of public and private enterprise in achieving the mutual goal of industrial development. The middle way fit in neatly with India's foreign policy of non-alignment, of abstaining from supporting either superpower in a rapidly polarizing world – the USA or Russia – while hoping to get support from both; but more on that later. The middle way was not a specific policy direction but a philosophy providing room to maneuver in a politically sticky situation. More than just balancing the American or Soviet ideologies, it was predicated on balancing different interest groups and ideologies. Primarily, it avoided confrontation with the socialist, Gandhian, or rightist critiques of industrialization and tried to accommodate all these interest groups. While the mixed economy provided the structure for industrialization, the key institution to achieving it was planning.

Planning

In contemporary times, planning is seen as the opposite mechanism to market-directed development. However, in most forms of planned economies, both mechanisms coexist. Planning is an approach used by a government to industrialize the economy in a short period. European and the American economy took more than half a century to industrialize. However, for economies developing in the 20th century, this was not an option, as they were falling behind other economies. Planning was a method through which a developing economy could coordinate the accumulation of capital, invest it in a coordinated manner in specific industries, and make policies to speed up the growth in the industrial sector. Planning uses an input–output model to derive the relationship between different industries; it uses a matrix to depict how much output from an industry contributes as input for another industry. For example, if an economy wants to grow the iron and steel industry by 7 percent per year, then the input–output matrix can be used to estimate how much electricity, ore, minerals, and chemicals are required to achieve the production target. Planners can allocate capital to each industry according to this plan. A plan requires that the government can control capital resources in the economy, incentivize production for different industries, and create complementary policies and infrastructure to assist these industries. While the plan is a technical document, the planning mechanism needs institutions that can coordinate and execute the plan.

Planning had been an important institution in capitalist economies in the mid-20th century. European wartime economies – Germany, France, Britain, and so on – used a form of planning as material, labor, and capital had to be allocated towards industries that contributed to the war and, concurrently, created government apparatus to ration necessities which were short in supply in times of war. Western, developed countries applied the planning mechanism to restore the economy from the damage done during the war – notably, the Monet plan in France and Germany using a form of planning under the Third Reich to restore the economy from the damage done by payment of wartime repatriations under the Treaty of Versailles. Soviet Russia was the first country to successfully use a plan by implementing policies appropriating excess capital from the agricultural sector and channeling it into heavy industries. Other successful planning regimes for India to emulate were Japan and South Korea: both followed mixed economy models and used a planning apparatus to drive growth in the textile industry. India itself was no stranger to planning as the colonial government applied a form of planning during the Bengal famine. These historical examples demonstrate that planning is a versatile tool that is used to coordinate production and investment to push an economy back to a growth trajectory, especially when there is an imbalance or crisis

The Drive to Industrialize under Nehru's Leadership

in the economy, and scarce capital resources need to be invested in particular industries to get the economy back on the development course.

Planning in India was founded on three key institutional mechanisms that were necessary for its success. The first was the adoption of a mixed economy which allowed both private and public enterprises to coexist. However, the government determined which sectors were available for private enterprise. The mixed economy model allowed the government to determine the pace and direction of industrialization. The second institution essential to planning was the PC, a committee that created the technical plans for the economy. The plan determined how the government would raise its revenues and how the revenue would be allocated. Moreover, it also determined how the government would fund any excess expenditure over revenue. The plans provided a road map for the government and a basis for private enterprises to plan their production cycles. The plans were not legislatively enforceable, but they formed the foundation of the annual budgets. The PC included Nehru as the chairman, a nominated deputy who was a cabinet member, and heads of important ministries such as finance, agriculture, home, defense, and experts from the field of economics, industry, banking, science, and so on. The committee was different from other government bureaucracies as they were largely nominated by the government and did not have a set tenure – this was meant to immunize the PC from the politics of election cycles. Moreover, they did not directly come under the jurisdiction of the executive and the judiciary. It was an advisory body that would assist the finance ministry in making the budget, recommend targets to ministries, and provide advice on economic policy. The PC was not empowered with any administrative mechanism to ensure compliance from ministries, but Nehru as the chairmen could coerce ministries to follow the plan. The third institution of planning, closely connected to the PC, was the Five-Year Plan (FYP) to demarcate the budget of the government over the next five years; in India, the FYPs took on a different connotation as they coincided with the political tenure of a government.

Let us take a hypothetical example to understand how plans were conceptualized and implemented through these three institutions. Suppose the government decides that the textile industry in India will drive industrialization by 5 percent annually. According to calculations made based on the input–output matrix, the plan will estimate how much industries providing inputs to textile industries need to grow. For example, the production of power may have to be increased by 10 percent, and railway lines will have to be built to connect the textile production area to the market, which means iron and steel and railway equipment production will have to be expanded, and procurement of cheap raw cotton from Japan may have to be increased. The plans will provide production targets for each of these different industries and allocate inputs and raw materials accordingly. These technical requirements will have been calculated in the plan. The PC will ask individual ministry heads to coordinate with the different enterprises in the industry to achieve the target. A tremendous amount of forward planning and bureaucratic coordination is required for plans to be maintained over the years.

One of the challenges of the planning process was to get industries to follow the plans. Different institutional mechanisms had been used in different economies to achieve this. Russia nationalized all industries and could intervene through government orders. South Korea and Japan allowed private enterprise to coexist and could not coerce industries. However, they followed a strong carrot-and-stick practice where cheaper credit, protection from foreign and domestic competition, and coordination with raw material providers were given as an incentive to follow plans; the state could punish the enterprises for not meeting targets by imposing high taxes or nationalizing an industry. The government was able to use such disciplinary measures because they were an authoritarian government, and its political tenure was not affected by backlash to policies. Planning in India did not have access to any institutions to discipline industries and was dependent on cooperation from the ministries to achieve plan targets. The repercussion of this will be discussed later in the chapter.

Political Responses to Nehruvian Mixed Economy Industrialization Development Model

Large industrialists in India supported the mixed economy and protective policies – partially because they could not compete with the global economy and also because they needed central government support to build an infrastructural base for the growth of the manufacturing sector. They indicated their support through the presentation of the Bombay Plan. In some ways, rapid industrial development was palatable for capitalists and industrialists in India primarily because of widespread fear of the influence of multinational corporations in the economy – as was the case in other newly independent countries of South Africa and those in Latin America and East Africa.

Small firms working in regional markets in the manufacturing sector did not have much of an impact on the national debate. Probably the strongest voice came from the Swatantra Party – an independent political party that

The Drive to Industrialize under Nehru's Leadership

represented the interests of former princes and regionally powerful landlords – who argued against strong central control rather than any specific form of economic liberalism. A few decades on, they would merge with other rightist parties to form the BJP.

The leftist and socialist parties formed a formidable challenge to Nehruvian industrialization policies, especially government support of private heavy industries. Their major premise was that the subjugation and immiseration of peasants were not due to only colonial policies but the structure of the rural economy and society in India which reproduced unequal relationships. For them, independence was meaningless if peasants were subjugated in the hands of Indian feudal elites. The Indian peasantry had been organized around Kisan Sabhas by the radical left in the aftermath of the Great Depression around the plank of radical land reforms and collectivization. Another tract of the leftist movement was organized around trade unions in cities and industrial towns, demanding improvements in their wages, conditions of work, and job security. While minuscule in size in comparison to the Indian peasantry, this group had a powerful vote bank in cities and industrial towns. Lastly, we cannot undermine the impact of Gandhi's moralistic critique of not only colonial rule, but also his philosophical critique of industrialization, urbanization, and modernization as it had an important influence on the masses.

In the earlier chapter, I analyzed Gandhi's demands in his Satyagraha movement: this is not a good representation of Gandhi's economic philosophy. While Gandhi's method of politics and critique of colonialism were borne of his philosophies, the specific demands made were connected to the context and the impact it would have on colonial rule. Gandhi's larger economic vision was embedded in morality and Indian tradition and resonated with Indians from many walks of life. It is worth exploring this in more detail – even though Gandhi never wrote a specific work on his economic philosophy – because it challenges both the standard economic vision of growth through industrialization and the tenets of modern economics. Nehru had to negotiate Gandhi's vision, and it shaped many of the agrarian and distributive policies in India. It is hard to summarize Gandhi's vision as it was embedded in individual and community life and there was no coherent macro idea to explain how his philosophy applies to the whole nation or how it negotiates with some of the larger economic issues of financial independence, backwardness, and poverty.

Gandhian economic philosophy was a challenge to modern industrial life, claiming that industrial society was embedded in material wants, desire fulfillment, and increasingly complicated means of production. In one of his early lectures on his philosophy (Economic Society of the Muir Central

College, Allahabad, December 22, 1916), aptly titled "Does Economic Progress Clash with Real Progress?", Gandhi defines progress as moral progress which is in opposition to material progress. Gandhi defines material progress as contributing to the alienation of man to fulfill his duty in society and achieve growth through attaining its highest form. This includes renunciation of material desires, working in cooperation with fellow workers, and working ceaselessly for the upliftment of the weak and poor. Gandhi's reasoning for perceiving industrialization as being detrimental to moral progress was clear: the early developing countries had achieved industrialization by appropriating land, labor, and resources from around the world, and India would have to do the same just to compete with the rest of the world, and chances were that they would still struggle to close the economic gap.

Gandhian philosophy is distinct from Marxism in his belief that private property and enterprise could coexist with the socialist way of life. When asked about whether private enterprise and competition are better than planned economy by the state (1959, 11), he responded:

> I believe in private enterprise and also in planned production. If you have only State production men will become moral and intellectual paupers. They will forget their responsibilities. I would therefore allow the capitalist and the Zamindar to keep their factory and their land, but I would make themselves trustees of their property.

Gandhi's notion of economic change or transformation was suffused with his idea of non-violence. He believed in equality and collectivized ownership but would condone any violent means to achieve this end. He was skeptical of too much power with the state as it would use violence and coercion to achieve its ends. Instead, he espoused the idea of trusteeship – that is, landowners and capitalists should use their capital for the upliftment and betterment of their workers rather than amassing wealth for their gain. Fundamentally, Gandhi's economic vision was based around a community free from material poverty and subservience in a hierarchy.

This quote smoothly dovetails into Gandhi's larger vision of idealizing village life: of a community with strong generational connection, of maintaining the social hierarchies in rural India while working together and fulfilling responsibilities of providing the basics for all and renouncing any excess. While Gandhi's overall philosophy is fragmented, its application found widespread appeal, especially in bringing ideas of equality, collective participation, and skill-based and traditional production techniques. Social movements took inspiration from Gandhian methods of politics but also his philosophy.

The Indian government had a hard time distilling his ideas, and eventually, they coagulated around his idea of trusteeship and the constructive program which wanted to ensure equitable distribution of political and economic power. This program included providing basic amenities such as sanitation, education, knowledge of health, removal of social barriers such as untouchability, and encouragement of village and small-scale industries. I will revisit Gandhi's influence on Nehruvian policy later in this chapter.

I have outlined the foundations of Nehruvian policy; the next section will discuss the specific industrial, agricultural, and external policies that were implemented to achieve the aims proposed by the mixed economy-planned industrialization model.

Industrial Policy

India's industrialization policy had been shaped by the 1938 PC report (Nehru 1988), the Bombay Plan, and the Industrial Policy Resolution of 1948. However, a heavy industrialization strategy became the primary path to development with the introduction of the second FYP and the Industrial Policy Resolution of 1956. The first FYP was used to bring balanced development in agriculture and establish the institutions of planning; with the fundamentals of the economy in place and after Nehru had monopolized control over the party, the economy embarked on the path of accelerated industrial development.

In order to follow the heavy industrialization path, public investment in infrastructure – power, transport, roads, ports, and public enterprise – had to be increased at a substantial rate. In a capital-scarce nation, this would mean that resources would have to be taken from the agricultural sector. High agricultural output and low prices were necessary for creating agricultural surplus which could be invested in the industrial sector, but the agricultural sector was not equipped to meet this need. If India faced a food grain shortage due to monsoon failure, then it would have to spend scarce foreign currency on importing food grain. The plan to follow the path of heavy industrialization was a leap of faith, with multiple conditions required for its success. The conviction of Nehru and planners made India stick to the plan even in the face of adversity.

The second FYP was drawn by an eminent statistician and Nehru's trusted advisor, P. C. Mahalanobis, and was based on the idea that industrialization creates growth through its forward and backward linkages: heavy industry creates a demand for basic industrial goods and raw materials and decreases the costs of producing final or consumer goods. A good case study of the economies of scale generated by heavy industries can be found in 19th-century America where railway lines were expanded to trade or procure raw materials with new regions, and demand was created for multiple industrial products which ranged from railway lines, machinery, power, metals, minerals, and so on. The increased demand for industries provided the impetus for entrepreneurs to invest and expand the production of these goods. Moreover, as railways increased their coverage, the cost of transportation went down for all goods, providing an incentive to further increase production and tap the expanded market. Railways were a crucial cog in the industrialization of the American economy in the 19th century.

The industrial policy of 1948, later updated in 1956, divided up all industries into three buckets. In 17 basic and key industries, including iron and steel industries, heavy machinery required for other key industries, mining and processing of minerals, aircraft, railways, ships, and so on, the public sector would have a monopoly or an exclusive right to new investment. A private enterprise which historically existed in this industry was allowed to continue, but no new firms were allowed to enter these industries. In another 12 industries, needing high investment but not as technology-intensive, including fertilizers, machine tools, and ferroalloys, both private and public investment would be encouraged, although the state was committed to investing in these industries. Schedule C contained all other industries which were open to private capital. Some cottage industries were restricted to small-scale industries, to protect them from competition from large enterprises. These measures were welcomed by private capital as they were assured good infrastructure and long-term support for the industry. The industrial policy was buttressed by restrictive foreign trade policy and the planning mechanisms which coordinated investment and production between different key industries.

Foreign firms were perceived as a source of foreign exchange and technology. While foreign exchange limits discouraged foreign firms to enter India, the government encouraged collaboration with Indian firms. Collaborations between Indian and foreign firms increased from around 50 a year in the 1950s to 300 a year from 1958 to 1968. Foreign capital controlled 40 percent of assets in the organized large-scale private sector by the 1960s. The collaborations were mainly in manufactured luxury consumer goods industries such as radios, refrigerators, luxury clothes, and processed food.

The second FYP increased the budget outlay in industries and minerals from 12 percent of the total expenditure to 27 percent (Tomlinson 1996, 176). The increased resource allocation was taken from the agricultural sector whose outlay decreased from 27 percent to 19 percent. These changes were maintained in the third FYP, where 25 percent was allocated to industry and 18 percent to agriculture. More importantly, the total budget outlay was almost doubled from the first to the second FYP, increasing from INR 19,600 million to INR 46,720 million. This was further increased to INR 85,700 million in the third FYP (Tomlinson 1996, 178). The planners were well aware that these increased outlays could not be simply funded by an increase in taxes – especially since the majority of the country were subsistence farmers on the brink of poverty. Private capital lobbied strongly to not increase taxes, and an overvalued exchange rate and quota tariff regime reduced the opportunity to raise revenue through customs duties. The majority of resources were raised by increasing fiscal deficit – funding the excess of government expenditure over revenue via loans – through domestic borrowing. Another important component was contributed by foreign aid provided by the Aid India Consortium, created in 1958, by Canada, West Germany, the USA, Britain, and the World Bank. The increased dependence on deficit financing and aid from Western, developed, democratic countries placed constraints on the industrialization path which India would have to face up to in the future.

Agricultural Sector

The agricultural sector in India was an enigma wrapped in a contradiction. It employed almost three quarters of the population of India and was key to achieving successful growth, as well as overcoming the widespread poverty that afflicted the nation. Historically, capitalist development in the agricultural sector has fueled industrialization in the early developing countries. British landlords during the 18th century, through the parliament, shaped policies that contributed to the growth and commercialization of the agricultural sector. The Inclosure Act of 1773 allowed landlords to evict tenants, appropriate common property lands, and create a commercially viable land market. The surplus generated from the agricultural sector fueled the heavy initial cost of industrialization (Wood 2013). Russia approached the problem from a completely different perspective, acknowledging that surplus capital and labor from the agricultural sector was a prerequisite for industrialization. The Russian government collectivized land, maximized production in the agricultural sector, and invested the surplus into the industrial sector. Britain and Russia represent the two extremes of development; neither option was available to India as it followed a parliamentary democratic system. However, the decision to focus scarce resources on industrialization constrained the agricultural sector to a degree that policy could not resolve. The fate of the Indian agricultural sector was strongly connected to its social structure and colonial policies.

In a land-scarce nation like India, the fertile regions had developed a social structure that allowed the sustenance of a large part of the population – although it should be noted that for a vast population of scheduled and lower castes in India, the share of land was disproportionate and unequal. Individual landowners did not own enough land to invest in improved technology and increase the productivity of land; instead, landlords depended on cheap labor and social customs to siphon off any surplus generated from the lands. The colonial government had reshaped the social relations in agriculture by changing the tenure system, allowing certain dominant castes in each region to monopolize common land. Moreover, they set up infrastructure, legal apparatus, and trading networks to commercialize the agricultural sector and embed it within their global empire. Farmers' decisions on what and how much to produce were shaped by global markets, not local demand or social customs. Consequently, changes in the global market shaped the fortunes and hardships faced by Indian farmers. The collateral damage was the displacement of tenants, appropriation of forests and common lands from tribals, and the creation of a class of highly indebted small farmers.

There existed no swift solution to centuries of immiseration and lack of development in the agricultural sector while negotiating multiple layers of social structure resistant to change. The agricultural sector provided insurmountable obstacles to the government's vision for rapid industrialization. In hindsight, we can say with clarity that the government under Nehru was unable to solve the malaise of the agricultural sector or achieve self-sufficiency in food production. However, it is of interest to contemporary readers to understand the context and constraints that shaped agricultural policies. The INC was cognizant of the social structure which reproduced poverty, and immiseration in the agricultural sector was scaffolded by *zamindar*s and moneylenders. There was a strong interest in the abolition of *zamindari* well before independence. However, the government did not have the resources to develop the agricultural sector. Instead, they had to choose whether to target self-sufficiency in food production or address inequality and poverty issues through redistributive policies.

Agricultural Policy
One path to self-sufficiency was through – what would be later termed the Green Revolution – the Intensive Agricultural Development Program (IADP),

The Drive to Industrialize under Nehru's Leadership

which provided a technocratic solution to increasing food production, by providing incentives to increase private investment such as subsidization of modern agricultural inputs like fertilizers and pesticide and provide public investment in infrastructure to the regions which yield maximum output. This would improve agricultural production and exacerbate regional and class inequity in an already unequal sector. The alternative approach was to introduce land reforms in the agricultural sector to alter the pattern of land distribution. Unlike in socialist and dictatorial political structures, the INC was constrained in taking land directly from landlords and redistributing it to tenants and landless labor: Feudal heads and landlords played an important role within the INC in mobilizing votes in rural areas, and the party could not threaten this delicate balance; there was unease amongst the party heads that radical reforms would provide the impetus for violence at the grassroots level. Though there was clear logic to the first set of policies, the INC decided to follow a piecemeal version of the second set of policies – specifically to assuage the leftist and Gandhian interest groups within the party.

The INC abolished *zamindari* and placed a ceiling on land ownership, in the hopes that landlords will voluntarily relinquish land which can be redistributed to their tenants or small landholders. The second part of the strategy was to invest equitably in the agricultural sector, instead of focusing on high productivity areas, through community projects. The community project, inspired by Gandhian philosophy, was a multi-pronged mechanism for the government to resolve the specific problems associated with the agricultural sector. A community project would focus on a development block comprising a hundred villages and have a team of specialized project staff diagnose the issues faced in an area and recommend practical solutions, the government would allocate funds for these solutions, and the project staff would oversee the implementation of the solutions such as common water sources, drainage, farm management, health and education, use of fertilizer, and so on. The program was supported by American technical and financial assistance funneled through the Ford Foundation. The community program was a middle-way approach to functioning in the agricultural sector, and it was hoped that the community projects would provide a non-political approach to tackling the social issues facing rural areas and would translate into community ownership of the agricultural sector and cooperative behavior while avoiding the destabilizing effects of class conflict.

The first FYP prioritized the agricultural sector and started the community program in 55 blocks. It allocated (Tomlinson 1996, 176) 17.5 percent of the budget outlay on agricultural and community development and an additional

56   A History of Economic Policy in India

27.2 percent to irrigation and power. In comparison, only 8.4 percent was allocated to industry. The first FYP hoped to cover a quarter of the villages in rural India and planned to allocate the resources equitably across all regions.

External Policy

International trade policy which includes policies determining exchange rate and balance of payment played a crucial role in supporting industrial and agricultural policy. India had been deeply embedded in the global economy under colonial rule; this dependency had decreased over time as the Depression and wars had led to a contraction of the world economy. British investors were keen to maintain their stakes in the Indian economy and were nervous about the prospect of nationalization by the new government. Domestic private enterprise expected protection from foreign competition from the government after independence. The Nehru government advocated a planning-based industrialization model and protected infant industries from global competition. Protection of the infant industry is based on the idea that heavy industries initially cannot compete with foreign competitors, and they require a long gestation period before they can break even and produce at an efficient rate. Every economy that industrialized in the 19th and early 20th centuries used a form of infant industry protection. Britain protected markets in their colonies through discriminatory tax policies to ensure guaranteed markets for British textile mills. The American Revolution of the late 18th century led to the protection of American industries from British competition. Other major European developed economies such as France, Germany, and Belgium issued a protective tariff barrier in the late 19th century to prevent British companies from flooding their markets.

There was another variable that influenced India's trade policy: its dependency on the global economy for heavy machinery, oil, and food grains. The last was particularly disconcerting as the inability to invest in the agricultural sector made the economy vulnerable to food prices in the world market. India adopted an overvalued exchange rate to protect Indian industries: the rupee was artificially maintained to be able to purchase a higher amount of dollars. Let us take a hypothetical example to understand how an overvalued exchange rate would function: assume the market rate was INR 10 to a dollar. Then an overvalued exchange rate will make a dollar equivalent to INR 7. This means that imports would be cheaper for the economy as fewer rupees need to be spent to purchase a dollar's worth of goods. This would benefit the economy as imported machinery, petrol, and food grains would be cheaper. However, exports would become more expensive and industries dependent on exports would be affected. Moreover, there was a danger of cheaper imported goods flooding the market and out-competing infant import industries such as textiles, paper, cement, sugar, basic consumer goods, and so on. The Indian government maintained a complicated system of trade quotas and erected high tariff rates for imported products to check the deleterious effects of free trade in imports. Crucial imports such as petrol or heavy machinery had a higher quota available. However, permission to import these goods was given to only a few industries to ensure that they were protected from both global and domestic competition. Other goods, especially in the luxury and consumer categories, had a higher tariff to discourage people from purchasing them, especially when cheaper Indian alternatives were available.

Nehruvian trade policy completely changed the direction of foreign trade from colonial India: exports plummeted in India with the overvalued exchange rate, especially commercial agricultural products such as raw cotton, sugar, rice, and so on. Even with import quotas and high tariffs, imports increased at an exponential rate – particularly due to the economy's demand for food grains. India faced an adverse current account balance and needed to generate a surplus on its capital account to finance external payments. Current account refers to the balance of trade or the balance between export and import of goods and services. The capital account consists of foreign investment, foreign borrowing, and external assistance or aid. Even with encouragement towards foreign capital, India attracted minimum new investment, and the foreign corporations slowly disinvested or left the economy – adding to the drain of current accounts. Given the rigid rules and industrial policy, foreign capital had no long-term guarantee, and the threat of nationalization was high in the Global South in general. India's ability to get commercial borrowing was limited, and even though it took loans, they were insubstantial to fund the current account deficit. India had to depend on substantial foreign assistance, especially from the USA, to fund its current account deficit. Foreign assistance is a tricky element as it comes tied in with multiple conditionalities such as having to purchase only goods from that country providing aid or certain bilateral agreements or expectation of cooperation in the global economy. However, without gaining self-sufficiency in food grain production, India had little choice but to depend on foreign aid. One particular foreign aid policy would play a crucial role in the economy, referred to as PL 480 aid; under this act, India imported wheat from America at highly subsidized prices to meet the food grain needs of the growing economy.

How Did Nehruvian Policies Affect the Indian Economy?

The public-sector-led heavy industrialization policy was successful in propelling India onto a growth trajectory. The Indian economy grew at 3.66 percent (Table 2.1), which was more than twice the growth rate achieved in the early 20th century under colonial rule. The growth was driven largely by the industrial sector which grew at a faster pace than the GDP at 6.1 percent (Table 2.2). Growth in the industrial sector was driven by public investment and government expenditure. Investment grew by 6.8 percent a year – an unprecedented growth rate not matched by any government until the 1990s. The government share of investment increased from 28 percent to 50 percent (Figure 2.1) over this period, indicating the increasing role of public investment in the economy. Government expenditure grew at 6.81 percent,

Table 2.1 Period-wise growth rate: GDP and aggregate demand (percent)

Period (base year 2004–05)	Private final consumption expenditure	Government final consumption expenditure	Gross fixed capital formation	Exports of goods and services	Imports of goods and services	GDP at market prices
1950–66	3.12	6.81	6.8	0	2.56	3.66
1967–80	3.08	5.23	3.86	8.6	3.69	3.62
1980–2003	4.7	5.7	6.6	9.2	10	5.62
2004–14	7.4	7.31	10.53	13.81	14.77	7.52
Period (Base Year 2011–12)	Private final consumption expenditure	Government final consumption expenditure	Gross fixed capital formation	Exports of goods and services	Imports of goods and services	GDP at market prices
2014–19	7.24	7.86	7	3.6	5	4.8

Source: Calculations by author using National Accounts data from RBI's *Handbook of Statistics on Indian Economy*, table 4.

Table 2.2 Period-wise growth rate: sectoral (percent)

Period (base year 2004–05)	Agriculture	Industry	Services (including construction)
1950–66	1.8	6.1	4.85
1967–80	2.6	4.58	4.1
1980–2003	3.5	5.95	6.81
2004–13	3.3	7.2	9.4

Source: Calculations by the author using National Accounts data from RBI's *Handbook of Statistics on the Indian Economy*, table 3.

The Drive to Industrialize under Nehru's Leadership

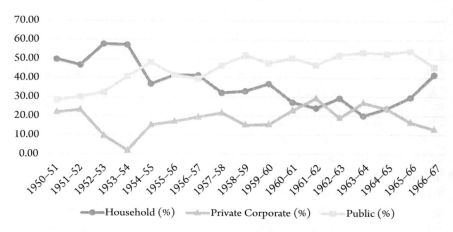

Figure 2.1 Trends in investment (percent) from 1950 to 1967

Source: Calculations by the author using National Accounts data from RBI's *Handbook of Statistics on the Indian Economy*, table 13.

a growth rate unmatched until 2003. The heavy industry-oriented growth in the economy was driven by public investment and expenditure which produced structural imbalances in other parts of the economy.

The majority of investment was in the capital goods industry and infrastructures like electricity, mining, coal, and transportation, which grew by 20 percent in this period. Four industries – namely food products, textiles, wood and furniture, and basic metals – accounted for more than two-thirds of industrial production. One of the unique features of industries in this period was the high-capacity utilization and total factor productivity (McCartney 2009, 286). The reason for this higher productivity was that a substantial diversification in the structure of production was achieved. The nature of growth was balanced amongst industries due to effective planning, avoiding major supply blockages.

Agricultural output grew at around 1.87 percent (Table 2.2) from 1949–50 to 1964–65. During the first period, rise in land-use intensity contributed approximately 45 percent to crop output, a major part of which was attributable to cropping pattern shifts across regions and over time (Rao and Storm 2000). There were few gains in productivity in food grain production, partly due to a lack of public investment and partly due to the semi-feudal structure of agricultural production which provided few incentives to private investment.

Exports registered negligible growth (Table 2.1), indicating the structural change from the colonial economy dependent on foreign trade. Imports grew at a significant rate of 2.56 percent (Table 2.1), largely spread over the import of machinery, oil, and food grains. An overvalued exchange rate and import substitution had contributed to a complete break from the foreign trade dependency of the colonial economy. This imbalance in foreign trade led to an unprecedented dependence on foreign aid to fill the foreign exchange gap. The Indian government was unable to increase savings and generate an internal solution to raise resources.

Due to the dearth of data, it is difficult to determine trends within income distribution in this period. The increasing allocation of resources to investment led to greater urban–rural inequality and a concurrent slowdown in consumption. Based on calculations made from data provided by Suryanarayana (2012) that are available for the period 1961–62, the extent of inequality measured by Gini coefficient – it provides a number from 0 to 1 to represent the extent of inequality in a region, a higher number representing higher level of inequality – decreased both in rural areas from 0.31 in 1961–62 to 0.29 in 1967–68 and in urban areas from 0.357 in 1961–62 to 0.332 in 1967–68 (Table 2.3). These years were marked by a near absence of any real welfare policy, except in health and education. State policy was geared towards economic development, and distributive matters were folded into the domain of economic planning (Chibber 2012, 173). Urban inequality declined due to public sector job creation in the urban industrial sector. Rural inequality declined even in the absence of major land redistribution and is difficult to explain through the impact of economic policies.

Table 2.3 Trends in inequality: Gini coefficient based on monthly per capita expenditure

Year	Urban	Rural
1961–62	0.357	0.313
1967–68	0.332	0.291
1968–69	0.329	0.305
1977–78	0.346	0.336
1983–84	0.34	0.31
1993–94	0.344	0.286
2004–05	0.376	0.305
2009–10	0.393	0.3

Source: Compiled by the author with figures for 1961–62, 1967–68, 1968–69, and 1977–78 from Suryanarayana (2012, 79) and figures for 1983–84, 1993–94, 2004–05, and 2009–10 from Vakulabharanam (2012).

The Political Economy of Nehruvian Policy: Who Benefits?

The largest benefits of this regime were reaped by domestic capital and urban skilled workers. Chibber (2006) has traced the history of the coalition between domestic large capital and the state to the Bombay Plan (cited in Baru and Desai 2018, 233). Nehru was careful to keep public sector expansion within bounds that were acceptable to Indian business houses. Almost every major body set up to design policy and new state institutions, in the aftermath of independence, was dominated by business leaders (Chibber 2012, 175). Moreover, the INC curbed the power of organized industrial labor through the Industrial Dispute Act of 1947, which curtailed the union's ability to go on strikes and gave the state government more bargaining power. Further, the Nehru government protected domestic capital from competition by instituting an import-substituting external regime. Urban skilled workers benefited from the significant increase in public sector jobs.

Nehru had planned extensive land reforms. However, efforts to introduce land redistribution were blocked by large landlords who controlled state legislatures. While there was some success in the acquisition of surplus land, the progress of land to tiller reform was not promising. Landed power remained largely intact in many parts of the country. Through the limited redistribution of land, a new stratum of rich landed peasants was created. Low growth in the agricultural sector and lack of land reforms left a large ocean of agrarian laborers clutching on to marginal holdings. The lack of redistributive measures by the government forced many of these rural dwellers to become underemployed landless proletariat or migrant workers (Chibber 2012, 176). I will revisit this dynamic in the fourth chapter when we discuss how migrant landless labor forms the backbone of the informal sector.

Shortcomings of Nehruvian Policy
The Failure of Land Redistribution

While the government had been successful in generating growth through industrialization, a raft of structural imbalances and clashing interests would affect the efficacy of these policies. Political stability and consistency of economic direction are crucial in ensuring that the gains of industrialization translated into the future growth and development trajectory of the nation. However, the development process was hampered by issues – some structural and inevitable, and some unforeseeable or an outcome of the varied forces shaping the economy.

One of the primary structural challenges to implementing Nehruvian policies was negotiating the complicated demands brought on by federalism. The Constitution has instituted a clear set of guidelines about the zones of powers of the central and state governments and the institutional processes through which they could coordinate their functioning. However, there was not any mechanism available to the central government to force a state government to implement its economic policy. Having the same parties at the center and state assisted in coordinating actions, but in a nation as diverse as India, there were frequent differences with no formal institutional mechanisms to redress.

One of the key contradictions which got inscribed in the economic policies of India was the difference in authority in different sectors. While industrial policy and its implementation were in the hands of the central government, governance of the vast rural sector was under the control of the state legislation. This included control over key areas such as agricultural credit, land revenue, taxation on agricultural income, and land reforms. The Nehru government had focused its resources, especially from the second FYP, on the industrial sector. This caused a fall in the investment in agriculture. However, the success of the industrial strategy required high food production to keep food prices down and generate surpluses for the industrial sector. The Nehru government did not have a clear principle for growing the agricultural sector and had wavered between building on its community development program and land redistribution policies. The INC and the Lok Sabha had endorsed the plan for ceilings on land ownership and the formation of cooperative farms. The extra land appropriated through the Agricultural Land Ceiling Act, 1972–75, would be distributed to cooperatives, where small and medium landowners would combine their land to benefit from capital-intensive agricultural technology such as irrigation, mechanized harvesting, use of chemical fertilizers, and so on. Moreover, planners in the second FYP increased the targets of agricultural production to the states, as rising agricultural prices were threatening to affect the industrial plans. Further, the government wanted states to procure surplus stocks and provide price ceilings to ensure equitable availability of food grains.

However, state governments remained recalcitrant towards such policies because redistribution of land required political force, which a newly elected state government was wary of. Moreover, members of state parties were invariably large landlords who were opposed to such policies. They feared that agricultural reforms would eventually translate into a socialist revolution and collectivization of all land. States were unwilling to procure food grains and sell them at a lower price or have price ceilings or place taxes on agriculture.

As agriculture and rural development were the main areas of intervention for the state governments, barring leftist parties, no one was willing to upset the local status quo. By 1957, the food ministry also rejected the recommendations of the PC, sparking an ideological difference that would lead to a complete change in agricultural policies by the mid-1960s.

The Zamindari Abolition Act and the Land Ceiling Act collectively ended up being more harmful than beneficial for tenants. There were multiple loopholes in the rules and regulations. Moreover, the INC failed to establish support from state leaders or establish a cadre of local party workers to set up institutions at the village level to apply these policies. The Land Ceiling Act allowed land for personal cultivation – defined as land cultivated under the person's supervision and farmers were swift to register as much of their land as possible under the names of other family members. The states did not invest in the sizable bureaucratic staff required to update land records, and corruption was rife at the local level. Tenants and sub-tenants were dispossessed of their land or lost their customary rights and had to pay higher rents to be allowed to continue working on the land.

Land reforms were a complete failure in India; in hindsight, it is hard to believe that land redistribution was imagined in a democratic set-up with the agricultural elite controlling public office. Some regions – especially those with leftist governments – had some success in redistributing land. However, even in these areas, these were used to enrich certain communities at the cost of others. The government did not have the resources to allocate to poverty alleviation or public works programs, and state governments were selective in the changes they made to rural areas, leading to the lack of any safety net or policy for the most impoverished and marginalized. Nehruvian policies built a perception, which continues to this day, that the INC is not a farmer-friendly party.

The Problem with the Planning Mechanism

The planning process had been beneficial to private enterprises as the public sector provided underpriced inputs such as power, steel, transportation, and so on. However, public sector enterprises would at times become an obstacle to growth as they were unable to consistently meet the targets set by the planners – symptomatic of the differences between a plan on paper and reality. Public sector enterprises faced different problems from not functioning in a competitive environment: labor issues, difficulties from being situated in economically backward regions, inefficient management, intervention by government bureaucrats, supply shortages, and infrastructural issues. There was no pressure on public sectors to generate profits but just meet targets, and no disciplinary measures to rectify low or bad quality production, barring transferring management. Further, the planning apparatus was manipulated by private enterprises, using political clout and relations with bureaucrats and ministers, to block new competition from entering these industries. This resulted in frequent underutilization of production capacity or an inability to maximize returns. For example, Indian steel production rose from 1.5 million tons in 1951 to 6.2 million tons in 1970. However, this success did not translate into the profitability of steel industries, as demonstrated by Hindustan Steel which made a loss of INR 1.4 billion on investment of INR 11 billion by 1970 (Tomlinson 1996, 184).

The licensing process was complicated and gave inordinate power to bureaucrats who lacked industrial experience. Large private enterprises had both the staff and extra funds required to thrive in such a system; and they would frequently pre-empt bids for licenses to ensure that other companies did not get it, even if they did not invest in these sectors – for example, in the process of procuring import license planners used an in-principle argument to determine whether an industry or company is required to import some material. Imports were not allowed in goods that in principle Indian industries could manufacture. Some companies managed to get licenses for certain imports that they did not need, ensuring other companies that could have benefited from it did not have access to it. In some cases, the government did not have the requisite knowledge of current industrial technology or a clear set of rationales to make such decisions. Certain imports could have made some industries more efficient, but they did not get a license because the government believed that they could be manufactured at home; this was particularly true in the nascent electronics and automation revolution, which quickly bypassed Indian industries before the government could establish their future importance.

Chibber (2012), one of the prominent commentators on Nehruvian policies, notes that the issues with Indian industries were not a result of competence or corrupt intentions but one of lacking the institutional framework to ensure that plans could be established. Nehru, as the head of the PC, could ensure that all ministries and cabinet members accepted the plans in principle. However, implementation of plans required close coordination, which required incentives and disciplinary mechanisms. For example, if the plan required increasing the production of railway carriages in one year, then production targets of steel, machinery, carriages, and power industries must also be increased.

The Drive to Industrialize under Nehru's Leadership

However, if one of these industries did not meet the requirements, then it would affect the targets. The PC had no mechanism to ensure that each ministry and public enterprise met its requirement. This is in stark opposition to the South Korean planning mechanism where an array of incentives and punishments were used to make industries fulfill requirements. The Korean government, after a military coup that placed president Park Chung-hee as the dictatorial leader of the economy in 1962, wanted to push the production of textiles to bolster the economy towards industrialization. The new regime demanded private corporate textile producers increase output even at a loss; in exchange they devalued the currency and provided subsidies such as cheap procurement of raw material, land, access to cheap infrastructure, and so on. They also threatened nationalization as well as the appropriation of surplus to ensure that private enterprises followed their plans. The Indian government did not have recourse to such power, and frequently ministers, bureaucrats, management, and labor unions would resist or take a conflictual stance towards the government. Given the lack of resources, the government was unable to create a better incentive structure to encourage enterprises to follow plans; the Korean government, which was equally short of resources like India, could appropriate resources from other sectors, as they could not be politically challenged.

The 1965 Food Crisis and the End of the Nehruvian Policy Regime

As the economy entered Nehru's third tenure as prime minister in the 1960s, multiple challenges to Nehru's dominance within the party started to emerge. Of particular note was the rise of the rightist parts of the party under Morarji Desai and Kumaraswami Kamraj, but also a steady suppression of the leftist and socialist cadres in the INC from important roles in the organization. As India's dependence on foreign aid increased, there was pressure from the USA and the aid consortiums in India to introduce liberal reforms and allow more foreign direct investment in the economy. While India was fairly independent in the international power structure to be directly coerced by the USA, it was vulnerable to their demands, as they were highly dependent on the USA for building food stocks and precious foreign currency.

Two expensive wars against China in 1962 and Pakistan in 1965 pushed the already difficult demands on public expenditure to the limits. However, it was the lack of monsoon and severe droughts between 1965 and 1967 that pushed the Nehruvian regime into a state of crisis. Agricultural production fell by more than 10 percent, which led to a significant fall in private consumption.

The government was forced to import food grains in 1966 to compensate for the shortage. The current account deficit almost doubled from 1964–66. The sudden spurt in imports led to a severe balance of payment crisis and an urgent need for foreign exchange.

Apart from the external imbalance alluded to earlier, the imbalances of the Nehruvian regime were felt most strongly in the agricultural sector. Agriculture was the largest employer and the largest sectoral contributor to national income before independence. However, the focus on industries in independent India meant that public investment in agriculture was not adequate. The agricultural sector grew by only 1.8 percent (Table 2.2) in this period. This sector was highly unstable and dependent on the vagaries of the monsoon. There were early warnings that agriculture was structurally unstable, with negative growth in 1955 and 1957. However, the government deflected this issue by importing cheap food grains, through the PL 480 agreement with the USA: Public Law 480, known as 'Food for Peace', was a funding avenue through which American food was given as overseas aid to India. By failing to invest in agriculture, Nehru missed an important opportunity to significantly alleviate poverty. The Nehru–Mahalanobis plan had envisaged large-scale

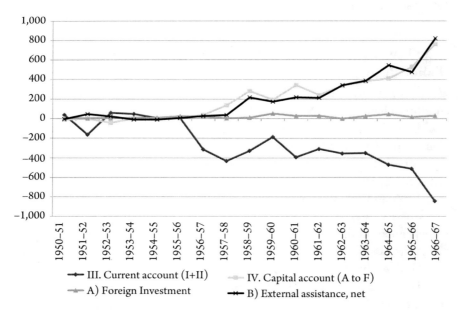

Figure 2.2 BOP from 1950 to 1966 (rupees, crores)

Source: Calculated by the author using data from National Income Accounts from RBI's *Handbook of Statistics on the Indian Economy*.

The Drive to Industrialize under Nehru's Leadership 67

land reforms in agriculture to compensate for the lack of public investment, but this turned out to be politically infeasible. The structural imbalances of the Nehruvian regime would culminate in the agricultural and balance of payment crisis of 1965 and 1966 (Figure 2.2).

Moreover, after Nehru died in 1964, there was a vacuum of power in the INC and infighting amongst different sections. These factors highlighted the structural instabilities in the Nehruvian regime: failure to develop the agricultural sector and build self-sufficiency in food stocks, lack of redistributive policies, failure to implement land reforms and tackle the state of poverty in the economy, inability of the planning regime to discipline the economy to the needs of industrialization, dependence on aid and foreign countries to execute the plans, culminating in the crisis of 1965–67. While the crisis affected the external and agricultural sectors, these were symptomatic of imbalances in the Nehruvian policy regime, and the lack of political organization and economic resources required for the planning-based industrialization model. In the end, the Nehruvian regime kick-started growth in the Indian economy and placed it on the path of industrialization but left significant imbalances that would force major changes in economic policy in the next regime.

This chapter discusses the context and rationale of following a planning-based industrialization-led growth path. Liberal economists, who advocate the superiority of markets over planning, have criticized Nehruvian policies on multiple grounds, but have failed to account for the historical, economic, and political constraints that shaped these decisions. Most importantly, they fail to appreciate the importance of the middle-way philosophy in balancing or compromising with multiple antagonistic interest groups globally and within the nation. This is an important lesson, especially for contemporary economic policies which lack a coherent philosophical underpinning and become exercises in empirical justification. Nehruvian policies gambled on planning-led industrialization and contested legitimate critiques from leftists, Gandhians, and liberals. Eventually, contingent events such as bad monsoons, expensive wars, and the death of Nehru would exacerbate the shortcomings of the Nehruvian policy regime, and political changes in the INC would ring the death knell of Nehruvian policies.

References

Baru, S., and M. Desai. 2018. *The Bombay Plan: Blueprint for Economic Resurgence.* New Delhi: Rupa Publications.

Chibber, Vivek. 2006. *Locked in Place: State-Building and Late Industrialization in India.* Annotated ed. New Jersey: Princeton University Press.

———. 2012. "Organised Interests, Development Strategies and Social Policies." In *Growth, Inequality and Social Development in India: Is Inclusive Growth Possible?*, edited by R. Nagaraj, 168–93. New York: Palgrave Macmillan.

McCartney, M. 2009. *Political Economy, Growth and Liberalisation in India, 1991–2008*. 1st ed. London: Routledge.

Nehru, Jawaharlal. 1938. *Report of the National Planning Committee 1938*. Indian Culture Division. http://indianculture.gov.in/report-national-planning-committee-1938. Accessed September 14, 2022.

Publications Division. 2017. *Jawaharlal Nehru Selected Speeches: Volume 2, 1949–1953*. New Delhi: Publications Division, Ministry of Information & Broadcasting.

Rao, M. J., and S. Storm. 2000. "Distribution and Growth in Indian Agriculture." In *The Indian Economy: Major Debates Since Independence*, edited by T. J. Byres, 193–248. New York: Oxford University Press.

Suryanarayana, M. H. 2012. "Economic Development and Inequalities." In *Growth, Inequality and Social Development in India: Is Inclusive Growth Possible?*, edited by R. Nagaraj, 63–90. New York: Palgrave Macmillan.

Tomlinson, B. R. 1996. *The Economy of Modern India, 1860–1970*. New York: Cambridge University Press.

Vakulabharanam, V. 2012. "Class and Inequality in India over Three Decades." Presentation at a conference commemorating 40 years of the School of Social Sciences, Jawaharlal Nehru University (JNU), New Delhi.

Wood, E. M. 2013. *The Origin of Capitalism: A Longer View*. 1st ed. New Delhi: Aakar Books.

3

The Turn to Populism under Indira Gandhi
1967–79

The Nehruvian Regime and the Crisis of 1965–66

The Nehruvian policy regime was focused on industrial development and self-reliance. The state channelized its resources towards the development of key infrastructural and heavy industries through the public sector. It institutionalized the planning mechanism to ensure coordination with private industries, protection from foreign competition, and subsidization of imports. The focus on developing a self-reliant heavy industry-intensive form of capitalism came at the cost of reduced public investment in the agricultural sector. Further, the lack of redistributive policies under the Nehruvian government translated into increasing rural inequality, as the gains in the sector were made by the landowning classes. The alarming aspect of Nehruvian policies – especially one aiming for self-reliance – was its heavy dependence on foreign aid. External assistance increased from INR 6 crore in 1955–56 to INR 822 crore in 1966–67, which translated into 90 percent of the BOP deficit being funded by foreign aid (Figure 3.1).

The crisis of 1965–66 was a consequence of the development trajectory followed under Nehru and was indicative of the instabilities within the choice of policies. The crisis was itself triggered by a spectacular fall in agricultural production and private consumption due to two extensive droughts in 1965–66. India, having lost an expensive war with China and amidst another crucial one with Pakistan, did not have the resources to import food without serious consequences to budgetary surplus. It was at this crucial juncture that the USA government started negotiating conditions tied to its PL 480 aid program. In the meantime, India had no other choice but to import food grains to compensate for the losses caused by the drought; lower supply led to higher agricultural prices and, consequently, unleashed crippling inflation upon the lower-income classes in the country. These imports severely damaged India's BOP position and undermined the state's effort to maintain an overvalued currency to protect imports. At this crucial juncture, Nehru passed away,

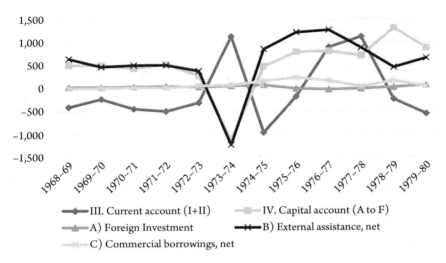

Figure 3.1 BOP from 1967 to 1980 (rupees, crores)

Source: Prepared by the author using data from RBI's *Handbook of Statistics on the Indian Economy*.

creating a leadership void in the INC and providing the opportunity for multiple vested-interest groups to struggle for control. The crisis had not only destroyed the dynamics of the Nehruvian policies but also created the conditions for political change. In the next section, I will argue that the policy changes in the Indira Gandhi regime were an outcome of conditions created by the crisis of 1965–66. In times of crisis, it is easier to mobilize political support for change, especially from interest groups affected by it.

Dilution of Nehruvian Policy and the Turn to Liberal Reforms
Internal Struggles in the INC and the Weakening of the PC

Nehru had played a crucial role in ensuring the involvement of the PC in the policymaking process. He headed PC meetings and ensured that members were well-positioned in different ministries. These steps were taken to ensure that the recommendations of the commission were implemented by the ministry, and while the PC did not have the disciplinary powers to punish ministries that did not comply with its recommendations, as long as Nehru was the prime minister, he maintained its stature in policymaking circles. With Nehru's death, rightist vested-interest groups who believed in market reforms and a more prominent role of private enterprise, headed by Morarji Desai and Kumaraswami Kamraj started vying for leadership. After a lot of lobbying and infighting, the INC chose a neutral candidate as their new prime minister, Lal Bahadur Shastri.

The Turn to Populism under Indira Gandhi

Shastri had stature within the party, due to his active role in the independence movement, but had little experience in economic policymaking and had not shown any indication of support for Nehru's policy ideology.

With Shastri at the helm, the INC slowly started demolishing the PC, which had been one of the key institutions for regulating and sustaining the heavy industry-oriented model of capitalism followed in the Nehruvian regime. Within the first few months of Shastri's leadership, the balance of power between the PC and the ministries was transformed. He divested the members of the PC of their long-standing privilege of indefinite tenure and placed them on fixed-term contracts – in essence connecting their tenure to their performance in the commission (Frankel 2006, 251). Moreover, Shastri stopped attending commission meetings and started appointing liberal reform-minded bureaucrats to key positions in the ministry – for example, L. K. Jha, a strong advocate of liberalization, as head of the prime minister's secretariat, C. Subramaniam to the agricultural ministry, and Desai as the finance minister. The dilution of the powers of the PC continued after Shastri's death and culminated in a complete overhaul in March 1967, with the appointment of D. R. Gadgil as its head. Gadgil was a staunch critic of the powers of the PC and turned the commission into an expert advisory body. He dismantled the PC's de facto controls over the allocation of investment; instead, resources were to be assigned based on a specific formula, also referred to as the Gadgil Formula. Moreover, PC members were not allowed in ministry meetings anymore. In essence, while the PC could still make recommendations, it no longer had the power or clout within the secretariat to influence policies. This is in stark contrast to the South Korean planning mechanism, mentioned in the last chapter, where the government used a carrot–stick approach to get private enterprises to cooperate. The demolition of the PC can be considered the first step towards the breaking of the Nehruvian regime and planted the seeds of the future liberalization of the economy.

Devaluation and the Dilution of Import Substitution Policies

Following the drought and high inflation of 1965–66, the government was forced to import food grains to ensure sufficient stock. At this crucial juncture, the American state under Lyndon Johnson held back aid when it was required the most, during the agricultural crisis, even though the Ford Foundation and the World Bank (*The Hindu* 1967b) recommended that India should continue getting aid. The decision to withdraw aid was probably based on geopolitical considerations and an outcome of increasing Cold War hostilities.

India had headed the non-alignment movement and had not supported either the USSR or the USA in the global economy shaped by the Cold War. They had been receiving significant aid from both superpowers with the intent of making allies. The USA used the opportunity brought by the 1965 crisis to pressurize India to accept market-based reforms and have stronger economic relations with American firms.

India was extremely dependent on aid to finance its import bill and had to take action soon to curb the back-breaking inflation that was wreaking havoc on the economy and polarizing opinion against the central government. It was in light of these factors that India decided to devalue its currency by 36 percent in March 1966 and implement other measures of liberalization like the delicensing of industries (*The Hindu* 1966c) and crucially the removal of import licenses in critical industries like fertilizers and agricultural machinery (*The Hindu* 1966g). While it is well established that these liberalization measures were brought in under the duress of American pressure (*The Hindu* 1966d), the political pressure faced by the state (*The Hindu* 1966a, 1966b) forced the Indian government to argue that devaluation would benefit the Indian economy (*The Hindu* 1966e, 1966g). It was pretty clear that in the short run, devaluation would hurt the economy as imports would become more expensive and the BOP would continue to deteriorate due to the inelastic demand for crucial imports like food grains, agricultural inputs, and petroleum. While demand for most goods decreases at a faster rate as their price rises, inelastic goods such as essentials do not see much drop in demand even after a price rise as they are necessary for survival.

Devaluation and the introduction of a few liberal measures failed to convince the American leadership that the Indian economy was conducive to market reforms, and the promised American aid came much too late and was a lot less than promised. The USA was not satisfied with devaluation and was lobbying for more liberal reforms in India. It was willing to increase investment in India, on the condition that its companies would get a stake in agricultural industries, especially fertilizers. However, American-owned fertilizer companies would import crucial inputs and raw materials. This would further dilute India's BOP status and provide a channel of diverting resources from India to abroad. The economic upheavals brought by the crisis and the consequent devaluation probably influenced the government to embark on a radically different agricultural policy from that of the Nehruvian regime and, as a consequence, diverted the direction and nature of capitalist development in the Indian economy.

Green Revolution: Liberalization in the Agricultural Sector

The crisis created conditions and a political appetite for liberal reforms in the form of devaluation of the currency and curbing the powers of the PC. However, it was in agricultural policy where the biggest shift from Nehruvian policy was achieved; this would be one of the first liberalization policies in India. In the Nehruvian regime, agricultural growth was de-prioritized, and the majority of public resources were allocated towards heavy industries. There were two different ideas regarding agricultural policies that were discussed in policymaking circles. The first was growth generated through public investment in infrastructure like irrigation, roads, power, and agricultural research. The second alternative, which had strong support from Nehru, was growth generated through changes in social structure via land redistribution and the creation of cooperatives. Nehru, in his tenure, flirted with socialist changes in the agricultural sector, such as land reforms, redistribution of land, and collectivization of land. However, the INC never had the political currency to undertake these policies: a large part of their vote base came via the patron–client networks of large landlords.

The crisis of 1965–66 exposed the frailties of the agricultural sector and its dependency on USA aid, and it became easier to build a certain consensus amongst the polity about the need for self-reliance in the primary sector. Due to historical social structures and the impact of colonial policies, agriculture in India was largely self-subsistence driven. Eighty percent of households (Tomlinson 1996, 194) had less than 3 acres of land, one of four of households had less than 1 acre, and only 3 percent of households owned more than 10 acres. Commercial agricultural production had been oriented towards global trade. However, this had been de-linked since independence. This provided a paradoxical structure to generate growth in the Indian economy as the inequality of land ownership was a severe constraint to achieving fast growth.

New Agricultural Strategy

In the face of an economic crisis, the INC suspended the FYP and adopted single rolling budgets; this allowed them to make fast decisions in the face of changing circumstances, such as the New Agricultural Strategy (NAS), which was officially announced in the fourth FYP in 1969. Under the NAS, the planners decided to focus on the 20–25 percent of land in India which had an assured supply of water and complementary public infrastructure to potentially grow fast. Second, they decided to adopt scientific and technological solutions to increase land productivity. This was a key requirement because in a densely populated country like India, the most productive lands had already been cultivated, and there was very little potential to increase output by expanding land usage. In October 1965, the new agricultural strategy was implemented as the Intensive Agricultural Area Program (IAAP) in 114 districts based on the pilot program, the IADP, implemented by the Ford Foundation in 14 districts in 1961. These were some of the most agriculturally productive districts in the country and included fertile districts like East Godavari (Andhra Pradesh), Tanjavore (Tamil Nadu), Ludhiana (Punjab), Burdwan (West Bengal), and Palghat (Kerala). The decision to follow the IAAP was strengthened by technological breakthroughs in Mexico and Taiwan in 1965 where they developed new varieties of paddy and wheat seeds, which provided a significantly higher yield – almost double the productivity of Indian seeds and could survive in Indian conditions. However, these variants had a higher vulnerability to plant disease and were more susceptible to weather and natural disasters, and required close monitoring and technological support. As a consequence, farmers adopting high-yielding variety (HYV) seeds in cultivation would have to invest in pumps or tube wells to ensure a regular supply of water, fertilizer to augment the seeds, pesticides to protect the plants, and mechanical modes of cultivation to minimize the time of cultivation.

HYV technology was meant to be scale-neutral. However, given the fixed costs of mechanization, it would only be profitable in fields of a certain scale – at least 10 acres. Farmers would require capital to sink in investment which would generate returns over some time. Given that the majority of Indian farmers had little to no savings, it would be unrealistic to expect farmers to adopt the new technologies. The government provided subsidized credit to farmers to adopt these new technologies and disseminated technical knowledge through government bureaucrats and public university professors. In short, the NAS took the most efficient path to increase agricultural production, which was to provide loans, subsidize inputs, and share technical know-how to farmers in highly productive, well-irrigated lands. An industrial equivalent of this would be to give cheap loans and subsidized inputs to the largest private industries. In some ways, liberalized agricultural policy was the opposite of Nehruvian industrial policy which was driven by public enterprise.

The Formation of the Food Commission of India

The second important change in agricultural policy as a response to the 1965 crisis was made possible by the appointment of market-oriented C. Subramaniam as the head of the agricultural ministry. Subramaniam took up a two-pronged policy of increasing the productivity of agriculture through subsidies and improving distribution through price incentives. In July 1964, Subramaniam announced the decision to establish a Food Grain Trading Corporation (also referred to as the Food Corporation of India, or FCI) with branches throughout the country and the parallel announcement of the Agricultural Price Commission (APC), which would compete with private traders in purchases in the open market to build up food stocks.

The FCI played a crucial role in changing the nature of the already existing public distribution system (PDS), and it is worth summarizing its historical role to understand this shift. The PDS was introduced in 1939 with the introduction of food rationing by the British government. Over the next decade, the PDS evolved into becoming a large-scale food rationing program meant to increase food security at both the national and household levels. The Indian government would procure food grains – mainly rice and wheat – from farmers, store buffer stocks, and provide them to consumers at a fair price through ration shops. In principle, all of India was meant to be covered, but there was a heavy urban bias in the 1950s as most shops were located in urban areas. Further, the PDS did not drain much of government resources as a large part of supplies came from subsidized American PL 480 aid. The year 1957 marked a turning point in food pricing policy when the economy faced a food shortage due to monsoon failures. Since agricultural prices in India had largely been determined by market forces, the Food Grain Inquiry Committee of 1957 felt that distribution to poorer sections at subsidized prices should be an additional goal for the PDS. The PDS got transformed from a food security policy into a social welfare policy in 1957 – that is, instead of subsidizing the cost of consumers, the policy directly targeted the poor and marginalized. From 1957 to 1965, both the amount of food grain distributed and the number of fair price shops expanded rapidly, and the PDS distributed 10 percent of all food grains produced in India.

The FCI and the APC introduced by Subramaniam were meant to influence the market price: by procuring food grains at a price above the market price to incentivize producers to increase production and adopt new technology, in effect raising the equilibrium market price. This was meant to be a complimentary policy to the new agricultural strategy. The shift to procurement at market rates rather than through direct government intervention, such as price controls or compulsory procurement of stocks, is indicative of a shift to market reforms. This was necessary because hoarding by agricultural traders in times of drought led to excessive price rises which exacerbate the effects of the crisis, especially on the wage-earning classes.

However, over time the PDS became an increasingly populist tool to gain political mileage from capitalist farmers, and the procurement prices became a point of negotiation.

Why Was It Referred to as the Green Revolution?

This progressive liberalization culminated in a host of policy measures, later dubbed by the media as the Green Revolution. The *Fourth Five-Year Plan* (1966, 26) stated:

> The broad objective of the fourth plan is the transformation of agricultural production from a traditional way of life to industry increasingly based on considerations of investment and return ... high priority will be given to the physical inputs needed by agriculture such as fertilizers, pesticides, agricultural implements, etc.... The new strategy which has been devised to raise agricultural output in intensive cultivation in areas where irrigation is assured. Improved seeds of food grains will be used.... Inputs like fertilizer, better seeds, pesticides, technical advice and know-how which are essential for raising agricultural production will be made available to the farmer.

The new agricultural policy was an immediate success, and India produced its highest wheat output of 16.6 million tons in 1967 (Frankel 2006, 7), a third more than its previous peak, and continued growing even in the face of sporadic droughts in 1968–69. Wheat showed an impressive increase in output growth rate from 3.99 percent under Nehruvian policies to 5.21 percent in this regime. This allowed India to achieve food self-sufficiency by 1971 and was dubbed in the media as the Green Revolution. Rice output took a longer time to grow, and output peaked in 1970 at 40.4 million tons (Rao and Storm 2000, 204). However, the improved growth in rice output achieved early in the regime could not be sustained, and the growth rate of rice fell from 3.49 percent to 2.16 percent by 1980. The growth rate for other major food grains such as *jowar*, *bajra*, maize, pulses, as well as non-food grains also fell in this period (Rao and Storm 2000, 204).

The Impact of the NAS on the Indian Economy

The impact of the NAS on food grain production was mixed, and it is worth taking a closer look at its impact on investment and land use to understand how this policy reshaped Indian agriculture. Public investment in rural infrastructure has historically been the leading driver of growth in the agricultural sector. Public investment in irrigation, research, and rural electrification had

The Turn to Populism under Indira Gandhi

augmented land productivity across the rural class spectrum and increased the floor of agricultural production. Public investment in transport, storage, and communication has been crucial in connecting rural hinterlands to national markets, improving the response to a change in prices. However, the Indian government was constrained in the 1960s due to fiscal challenges and heavy investment in the public sector. Therefore, private investment was encouraged through the NAS. As a consequence, by the 1970s private investment in agriculture was almost two-thirds of the total investment in agriculture (Rao and Storm 2000, 210).

The largest amount of private investment was in electrical and diesel pumps whose numbers increased from 1 and 2.7 per 1,000 hectares of gross cropped area in the 1950s to 52 and 50 in the 1970s. Chemical fertilizer use increased from negligible to 13.7 kilograms per hectare in the 1970s. Ten percent of agricultural areas adopted HYV seeds by the 1970s. The net irrigated areas increased from 20 percent in the 1950s to 30 percent in the 1970s with the majority of growth contributed by the introduction of tube wells (Rao and Storm 2000, 204).

The increased private investment in land-augmenting technology indicates that the NAS was successful in incentivizing commercial production. However, this increased investment did not translate into benefits for the region: the use of pumps and tube wells decreased water levels for other farmers, forcing them to procure private pumps, the use of fertilizers affected the local soil conditions, and HYV seeds attracted various pests which affected production in the whole region.

Mohan Rao argues that the reason for the NAS not translating into growth in the primary sector was that Indian agriculture was not structurally equipped to benefit from market reforms. Market reforms create incentives for farmers to invest in land-augmenting technology and gain higher returns in the market, which would be reinvested to expand production. This would have a domino effect on input markets, and allocation of resources would be based on the profitability of a product – labor migrating to profitable agricultural regions pushing down the wage rates, more capital moving to agriculture pushing down the interest rate, and more profitable farmers purchasing more productive land, increasing land prices. Policymakers envisaged that the surplus and profit made by commercial farmers would be reinvested in improving productivity.

Econometric studies in India have found that the supply response of aggregated crop output to prices is low in India. Typically, a 10 percent rise in prices will lead to an increase in total output in the long run of 2–5 percent

(Rao and Storm 2000, 197). The NAS, like any liberal market reform, was predicated on the assumption that the supply response of producers would be high. However, the agricultural sector was socially constrained from growing through market incentives: land, labor, and capital markets in rural India were not free and mobile but determined by social norms and rigidities. Bhardwaj (1974) and Bardhan and Rudra (1986) (cited in Rao and Storm 2000) demonstrated through their fieldwork that labor and capital are largely circulated within the village and rarely circulate between villages. Primarily, land and credit are used as means to monopolize and control the poorer peasants in a village already circumscribed between unequal caste and ethnic social relations. For example, a landlord or merchant will give loans to local farmers and peasants to keep them tied to the social hierarchy even if they are unable to pay the exorbitant higher interest rates, rather than loan the capital to other villages or regions where they can get higher assured returns. Similarly, labor tends to take lower-paid jobs or even remain underemployed in their village rather than higher-paid jobs in other regions because of the higher perceived cost of looking for a job in another area – labor has to negotiate different social customs and barriers when traveling to a new region. Further, land is considered an important marker of status in rural India, and landlords are unwilling to sell it to higher bidders unless they are absent or have shifted to urban areas. Therefore, even if a farmer wants to expand production due to market incentives, there are multiple social barriers and insufficient knowledge to respond to market incentives. Nehru was correct to believe that structural changes and the redistribution of land similar to those in Soviet Russia or China were key to creating dynamism in the agricultural sector. However, the government under him did not have the political muscle to enforce such structural changes.

Criticism of the NAS

The measures introduced under the Green Revolution led to self-reliance in food stocks by the 1970s. The primary sector grew at 2.6 percent in this regime as opposed to 1.8 percent (Table 2.2) in the Nehruvian regime. However, it comes as no surprise that increased production came mostly from the prosperous regions of Punjab, Haryana, Bengal, and Tamil Nadu, and led to a steady increase in intra-rural spatial inequalities. The gains from the new agricultural technology were reaped by fertile and well-developed regions and by farmers owning more than 10 acres, which included less than 5 percent of all land ownership. Due to underdeveloped labor and credit markets, these

The Turn to Populism under Indira Gandhi

benefits did not translate into higher wages or more employment opportunities. Further, the food crisis and concomitant imports of food grains contributed to inflation, and the marginalized faced increasing prices throughout this whole period. There were no substantial redistributive policies, and the PDS was not efficient in delivering to rural regions across India. This period experienced an increase in rural consumption inequality from 0.291 percent in 1967–68 to 0.335 percent in 1977–78 (Table 2.3), as the gains from the technologies were reaped by only a few.

The policymakers were well aware of the fact that they had essentially encouraged market-driven capitalist production in the primary sector, and these measures would further skew the already uneven distribution of gains in the primary sector. The government tried to assuage discontent by listing some land reform policies in the fourth FYP (Frankel 2006, 28) and emphasizing the fact that these measures were scale-neutral and could be undertaken by farms of any size. This claim has been debunked by Frankel (2015) who has demonstrated that even if we take the case of the biggest beneficiaries of the Green Revolution, the farmers located in Ludhiana district in Punjab, we get ample evidence against the claim of scale-neutrality of Green Revolution technologies. The gains made by large farmers (above 25 acres) in this district far outdid the gains made by medium farmers (10–20 acres). While cheap credit was available to both classes of farmers in Punjab, returns on investment were lower for medium farmers because these technologies were not scale-neutral. For example, tube wells and tractors provided maximum returns to investment in holdings of 25–30 acres. However, medium farmers in Ludhiana continued to take loans to mechanize production, leading many of them to become indebted to banks following one bad year of crop production (Frankel 2015, 12–31). Ludhiana is a good example because it is one of the few areas in India where there are substantial medium-sized farms; in most other areas like the Gangetic plains, the average landholdings are about 1–2 acres. This increase in regional and inter-class inequalities would culminate in the spread of discontent amongst rural masses and contribute to political destabilization within the state.

The First Moment of Liberalization

The response to the food crisis of 1965–66 and changing political context transformed economic policies from being public enterprise- and industry-centric to the agricultural sector and market reforms. The first moment of liberal reforms was the devaluation of the rupee enforced by American aid conditions.

Devaluation brought the Indian rupee closer to its market value and eased the artificial trade barriers and protection for Indian industries created by an overvalued exchange rate. The second moment of liberalization was the erosion and steady dismantling of the importance of the PC and its influence on policymaking. The third moment of liberalization was the NAS through which the government provided subsidies to incentive adaptation of new technology by producers, and the creation of the FCI provided price incentives for agricultural producers to expand production.

This shift in policy direction was a culmination of the structural shortcomings of Nehruvian policy: lack of growth in the agricultural sector, lack of redistributive policies, dependence on Nehru to make the institutions of planning function, and dependence on American aid. This transformation was heralded by the rightist elements in the INC who were supportive of liberal reforms and wanted a greater role for private enterprises in the economy. In the late 1960s, it would appear that the economy was moving from the Nehruvian development model to a more market-oriented economic model. However, certain political events would scupper the advance of reforms.

Destabilization of Government and the INC Split

The fall in USA aid (Figure 3.1) in this period and the concomitant diversion of government income to food imports led to a fall in public investment (Figure 3.2) and contributed to industrial slowdown, contributing to lower wages and working days for industrial labor. The food shortage crisis, lower growth rates, inflation, lower wages, lack of redistributive policies, and agricultural inequality had led to growing unrest amongst the masses. This was expressed through an increasing number of agitations, strikes, and cases of labor militancy (May 3, 1969) during this period.

Growing political unrest in the country was matched by increasing infighting within the INC with the Syndicate headed by the right-oriented Desai looking to control the organization and change its policy orientation. The party placed a young Indira Gandhi as its prime ministerial candidate in the 1967 elections and won a majority in the Lok Sabha elections. However, its total seat tally was significantly lower than in the previous parliament, and it lost power in many state elections. The seats lost by the INC had been quite evenly distributed amongst leftist (Communist Party of India [CPI], Communist Party of India–Marxist [CPI–M]), rightist (Jan Sangh, Swatantra Party), and regional (Dravida Munnetra Kazhagam [DMK], Akali Dal) parties. This was a clear indication (March 22, 1967) that the support for

The Turn to Populism under Indira Gandhi

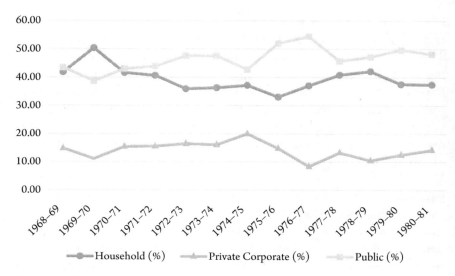

Figure 3.2 Trends in investment in proportion (percent) from 1967 to 1980

Source: Prepared by the author using data from RBI's *Handbook of Statistics on the Indian Economy*.

the INC was diluting. While Indira was the prime minister, there was a clear tussle for power within the INC, with the older heads trying to influence her to change the direction of the economy.

Infighting within the INC

The losses faced in the 1967 election led to reflection within the INC, and eventually the Congress Working Committee (CWC) came up with a – radically different but socialist at its core – 10-point program to rebuild the party's core philosophy. Socialist policies vary significantly from country to country but at its core is the idea that the means of production of a nation – land, infrastructure, machines, and heavy industry and essential inputs such as fuel, minerals, metals, and so on – are controlled by the state. The government controls the means of production to produce socially necessary goods and services rather than those that are most profitable in the market.

These recommendations included the nationalization of banks and insurances, export encouragement, the ban of princely private purses, curbs on business monopolies, and land reforms. The 10-point program was a reflection of the influence of leftist elements in the INC, and the growing fear that the economic hardships wrought by the 1965 crisis and the lack of redistributive policies would lead to revolutionary and radical politics. The 10-point program was ratified by Indira, who sensed that she could maintain her hold on the party by mobilizing support from the younger leftist influences in the party. These trends, however, alarmed the rightist old guard – Kamraj, Desai, and the Syndicate, especially since former princes and large businesses were an important source of funds and support for the party. Moreover, the Syndicate had successfully started diluting Nehruvian policies over the last three years, only to find Indira pushing the INC back towards socialistic[1] policies. The debates and struggles within the INC eventually got concentrated on the issue of nationalizing banks.

Bank nationalization implies that private banks are taken over by the government. This allows the government to invest the bank's finances into areas of public interest, which could include funneling them towards key and strategic industries or giving subsidized loans to the poor and marginalized. Bank nationalization, however, would be perceived as a threat to private enterprise, especially in a capital-scarce economy like India. In principle, the nationalization of banks was seen as necessary as the country had a shortage of investible resources, and most of the institutional credit was directed towards larger business houses. With softer loans provided as part of the Green Revolution package, there was an increasing consciousness of the need for investment resources to be more equitably distributed. However, there were great differences in opinion on how it should be implemented. The leftist vision for the nationalization of banks (*The Hindu* 1967c) entailed a complete takeover of large banks – those with an asset base of more than INR 200 crore – by the state and the distribution of capital according to government mandates. This would radically change the structure of capitalism in the country, with the state monopolizing the financial stage of production and deciding how to allocate funds instead of funds being allocated to those who can guarantee the highest returns. As a consequence, it would funnel funds to the less profitable small-scale industries and the primary sector and would force large private enterprises to raise their funds or/and reinvest profits. This would curb their ability to enter new or incipient industries and expand. The socialist implications of such policies were unmistakable.

The Syndicate was not against the nationalization of banks but wanted to implement it in a diluted form, referred to as 'socialist control of banks' (*The Hindu* 1967a). This essentially meant diversifying the board of directors in banks to include members from different professions such as economics, rural management, accounting, and so on. This would provide checks on

---

[1]   Socialist policies are defined here as policies which socialize the means of production.

The Turn to Populism under Indira Gandhi 83

banks from diverting most of their resources to a few profitable large private enterprises. While in hindsight the policies might not seem different, at that time they represented two vastly different visions for the economy (*The Hindu* 1969c). The first, which was closer to Nehru's policy regime, envisaged state control of capitalism, while the second (*The Hindu* 1969d) envisaged dilution of power amongst private stakeholders of capitalism as the state itself receded from being directly involved in the economy.

INC Split in 1969

The infighting in the INC was representative of the divergent class base of the party. Large private companies, formal sector employees and professional classes, former princes, and the rich landlord class were represented by the Syndicate. Small-scale businessmen, peasant farmers, and marginalized (caste, religion) classes were represented by the leftist elements. There had been a certain consensus amongst the masses about the INC's rule in the first regime owing to Nehru's influence and the positive perceived role of the party in the independence struggle. However, without Nehru and the old stalwarts of the INC, such as Gandhi and Vallabhbhai Patel, there was no person capable of bringing a compromise.

Amidst all the infighting, Indira Gandhi took matters into her own hands, and in the Faridabad session of the All-India Congress conference in April 1969, without warning, she sent a note titled "Note on Economic Policy" (INC 1969) to the CWC as an alternative to Subramaniam's liberalization-centric proposals. Her planned changes (Frankel 2006, 248) included proposals to appoint a monopolies commission, ban the entry of big businesses into the consumer goods industry, reorient credit policies to favor new enterprises, and place a ceiling on unproductive expenditure by private corporations. Earlier in the day, party president Siddavanahalli Nijalingappa had sharply criticized public enterprises and the growing burden they were placing on the public coffers. In her speech, Indira came to the defense of public enterprises, claiming "that heavy industries had to be set up in the public sector not only because private entrepreneurs were not interested in projects of long gestation periods but also because such large undertaking should not be entrusted to individuals" (*The Hindu* 1969b). The importance of public sector enterprise was at the heart of Nehru's development vision, and it became an object to articulate the differences in the party.

After the conference, the INC put up a united front to the media to avoid seeming unstable in public (*The Hindu* 1969e). This consensus lasted for

84 A History of Economic Policy in India

a short time until the death of the consensus presidential candidate, Zakir Husain, in May 1969. The Syndicate started pushing for its candidate as the next president, with the hope that they could topple Indira from the prime minister's seat. Indira countered unexpectedly by dismissing Desai as the finance minister on July 16. She placed herself as the finance minister and immediately announced her intentions by declaring the nationalization of the 14 largest banks in India on July 22, 1969, by a presidential ordinance. She justified her move in a broadcast on radio (All India Radio 1969), stating that "control over the commanding heights of the economy is necessary, particularly in a poor country where it is extremely difficult to mobilize adequate resources for development and to reduce the inequalities between different groups and regions." She further indicated that the classes she was creating policies for were "the millions of small farmers, artisans, and other self-employed persons. A bank can be a source of credit which is the very basis for any effort to improve their meager economic lot." She also strengthened her position in the government by the victory of her loyal party worker V. V. Giri in the presidential election.[2] The Syndicate had no real response to this grab of power by Indira and acceded to a split in the hope that Indira would not be able to keep power without their support.

The Populist Turn under Indira Gandhi

Indira continued to blaze a socialist trail of policies and followed bank nationalization with a bill to abolish princely privileges and private purses and placed restrictions on the unfettered expansion of monopolistic enterprises. This was followed by a bold move to bring about land reforms by amending the Land Acquisition Bill to provide stronger powers to the state to acquire land from private parties. These policies introduced by Indira were an attack on the primary beneficiaries of Nehruvian policies: large industrialists, agricultural landowners, and princes. These powerful interest groups successfully challenged the Land Acquisition Bill in the Supreme Court and got it overturned. Indira was unable to fight the legal challenges and took a radical move to amend the Constitution such that it could remove judicial intervention from the legislature (Lakhanpal 1970). However, she could not get legislative support for these changes.

It might seem counterproductive to attack classes that supported the INC traditionally, but this could be perceived as a political strategy by Indira to

---

[2] Largely with support from leftist opposition parties.

The Turn to Populism under Indira Gandhi

reframe her public image. Indira sacrificed the traditional supporters of the INC to capture the imagination of the masses by attacking industries and princes (*The Hindu* 1970a, 1970b). Having initiated a set of radical socialist policies, Indira had no other option but to continue with her policies (*The Hindu* 1970c). In a move that was part-desperate and part-inspirational, she decided to call for a new round of elections in the hope of capturing the legislature to push through her policy changes. This came as a surprise to the Syndicate and opposition parties which did not anticipate that Indira's Congress could win the election without their support.

Indira, sensing that she needed to carve out a new vote base, took advantage of the sympathy she had garnered for her socialist policies from the masses, and initiated the Garibi Hatao slogan as part of her 1971 election campaign. This campaign included piecemeal redistributive policies such as rural land redistribution, liquidation of rural debt, urban land ceiling laws, reallocation of credit, continued attacks on the vested-interest groups in the country, and a whirlwind campaign tour of the country. It is difficult to discern a coherent philosophy behind the list of redistributive policies under this campaign, but the fact that Indira could introduce such a major redirection of INC policies cemented her credentials as a pro-poor politician. Much to the Syndicate's surprise, Indira won the general election of 1972 with an absolute majority. With control of the legislature, she went about implementing the policies she had promised and a whole gamut of piecemeal changes (INC 1972) which belied any particular economic vision. We will refer to the policies under Indira's tenure as populist as there was neither any planning nor premeditation involved in these policy measures.

Populism is an instrument of mobilization or sustaining electoral support from a certain group. It refers to the set of policies that distribute goods and services directly to different social constituencies to get political support. One indication of policies being populist is when certain policies directly harm or benefit certain subclasses without necessarily impacting the general economy. For example, the Monopolistic and Restrictive Trade Practices (MRTP) Act, 1969, and the Foreign Exchange Regulation Act (FERA), 1973, curbed the capability of large private corporations. However, there were no policies or large-scale investment in public enterprise to compensate for the fall in production by private enterprises. Populist leaders tend to create a division in the voting base by identifying a major crisis or problem in the nation and pitching themselves as the saviors who can lead the nation away from this problem. In Indira's case, she pitched the political struggle within the INC as the economic elite capturing national economic policy and her policies as maintaining the socialist credentials of Nehruvian policy while also being pro-poor. A populist leader frequently uses popular symbols or slogans to mobilize groups, like the INC (Indira)'s Garibi Hatao campaign and use of symbols of motherhood to frame Indira. Historically, populist policies have been introduced in times of social unrest in diverse political contexts, which range from fascist movements in Germany and Italy, socialist movements in Latin America, and anti-colonial movements in Asia. What is common to these movements is a focus on short-term electoral gain over long-term development and use of public mass media such as newspapers, radios, social media, and rallies to reach the masses.

The core ideology of the Indira government, which came to power in 1972, was to remove poverty and inequality and achieve self-reliance (approach to fifth FYP). These goals were oriented towards redistribution of income rather than growth of the economy. However, most of Indira's policies seemed reactive rather than following any specific plan. Fresh from an election victory, the economic policy adopted at the Gandhinagar session of the All-India Congress Committee (AICC) in October 1972 stressed the following policies: reducing unemployment and adopting measures for job creation, meeting minimum basic needs, building housing sites for landless labor, land ceilings, and reforms. Moreover, the government nationalized general insurance companies and coal mines and introduced a whole gamut of resolutions to restrict monopolies and control the composition of the board of directors of companies.

By 1974, there was increasing restlessness amongst the polity, as there had been hardly any progress concerning poverty alleviation while crippling price rises were causing havoc to fixed-income classes. Desperate to regain public opinion, Indira, in a few months, adopted a slew of policy reforms and continued its attack on two of the biggest beneficiaries of Nehruvian policies.

The Attack on Heavy Industry

There was a secular decline in public investments in this period, and it is well established that public enterprises were used below capacity. This led to a fall in demand for industrial goods, especially for many large private industries, which were dependent on public enterprises, and the railways for the demand for their goods. Further, industrial licensing was required for investment above INR 25 lakh increased to INR 2 crore after 1974. Some estimates (Jha 1980, 83) conjecture that it took 400 days for an application to pass through various departments. This was not conducive for large-scale

The Turn to Populism under Indira Gandhi

investment dependent on timing. The state made it progressively easier for small-scale industries, by exempting them from licensing in 128 industries and providing easier terms of credit from 1970 onwards. Over the years (Jha 1980, 87), the government imposed stringent and often unrealistic price controls on vital commodities like steel, cement, aluminum, copper, zinc, coal, ships, fertilizers, bulk drugs, chemicals, and ferroalloys. By contrast, consumer industries such as refrigerators, air conditioners, pop-up toasters, blenders, radios, record players, soaps and detergents, cosmetics, cigarettes, alcohol, and hotels were subject to no price controls. This restricted the flexibility of large businesses that were involved in heavy industries. However, hardly any of the 128 industries which the government had reserved for small scale industries (SSI) suffered from this handicap. Thus, in industry after industry, while the final product was subject to price controls, the components that were produced by small-scale ancillary units were not. For example, automobile manufacturers faced price controls, while tire or interior manufacturers did not. These discriminatory policies curbed heavy industrial development and increased the profitability of small-scale industries by removing various regulatory controls.

Curb on the Bargaining Powers of Organized Labor
The continuous inflation and its deleterious effects on fixed incomes had led to militant strikes and agitations to increase wages in keeping with price rises. Indira Gandhi, especially during the Emergency, initiated a variety of regulations, under the garb of controlling inflation, to render unions useless. The state banned strikes and *gherao*s (the primary instrument of wage bargaining) and froze emoluments (dearness allowance, gratuity, and so on) other than regular wage increments. Complementarily, the home ministry under Yashwantrao Chavan expanded the powers of the Central Reserve Force and the army to being called in by state governments to protect property from labor agitations.

State of Emergency: 1975
Indira was soon frustrated by the realization that she could not implement her more radical measures as the judiciary kept overturning the amendments. Moreover, Raj Narain, a member of parliament candidate who lost to Indira in 1971, lodged a case of election fraud for use of state machinery for campaigning against Indira. In June 1975, the Allahabad High Court found Indira guilty of using state property for her electoral campaign and declared

the 1971 election null and void and barred her from standing for election for six years. Jay Prakash Narayan, a well-respected Gandhian and public servant, and Desai garnered the general public unrest about the state of the economy and outrage against Indira to create public pressure through large rallies to get her to give up her prime minister seat.

Facing political dissent from both the far-right and far-left and increasingly losing popular support, Indira decided to announce a state of emergency in July 1975 to bypass the judiciary and implement the policies she believed would lead to radical social change. The state of emergency bestowed unlimited power to the president of India, Fakhruddin Ali Ahmed, who on behalf of Indira ordered the cessation of the democratic apparatus of the country, including the legislative and judicial institutions, placed curbs on the media, and arrested opposition leaders. Another bold set of measures called the 20-Point Program (All India Radio 1975) was announced following the Emergency, including land redistribution, a ceiling on land ownership, housing for the landless, liquidation of rural indebtedness, and piecemeal policies towards aggravated sections, such as subsidies to students, worker participation in industrial decisions, allocation of credit to small entrepreneurs, subsidies to informal service industries, projects for marginal farmers and agricultural laborers, and so on. Indira hoped that she could pass through her policies without legislative and judicial intervention and gain back the support of the masses. The Emergency is one of the strongest indications that Indira was a populist and hoped to get mass support in the face of criticism and antagonism from her political competition. Indira successfully passed a bill to allow the government to amend the Constitution without judicial intervention, allowing her to pass the Land Redistribution Bill.

The economy witnessed an economically prosperous period during the Emergency and the latter part of the 1970s, with increased growth and improvement in the trade balance. However, the INC failed to implement any of its more radical policies as it did not have the organizational strength to make ground-level changes. For example, while in principle land could be forcefully redistributed to marginal farmers, these farmers could not successfully cultivate the newly acquired land, since they had no new source of credit. So even if peasants could legally own redistributed land, they were still dependent on exploitative moneylenders and landlords for funds, and the rural status quo was maintained. The INC's failures demonstrated that radical social change was not possible within the framework of executive and judiciary checks and balances within which the economy was embedded. Since the Emergency, no major political party has promised socialist ideals. The Emergency was called

The Turn to Populism under Indira Gandhi

off in 1977, and a new election round was called by Indira. The first non-INC party, the Janta Dal, comprising opposition parties came to power.

Making Sense of the Indira's Political Regime: The Class Basis of Indira's Policies

Who benefited from Indira's mix of populist and socialist policies? Prem Shankar Jha (1980) has provided an illuminating account of the class basis of the Indira regime. Jha argues that the state created conditions benefitting commercial agriculture and peasant farmers. It did so by curtailing the growth of heavy private industries and the bargaining powers of organized labor. The complex set of policies – both successfully and unsuccessfully – created a regime of incentives and constraints that benefited the unorganized sector in general and the intermediate class in particular because they could avoid or work around the legal tangles created by the licensing era.

Jha's conceptualization of the intermediate class was derived from Kalecki's (1972) use of the term "intermediate regimes" to classify political regimes in which the lower middle class and rich peasants perform the role of the ruling class. He argues that in the early stages of development, big business allied with the remnants of the feudal system drives the process of capitalist accumulation. However, due to certain specific conditions, the capitalist accumulation process in underdeveloped countries is driven by intermediate classes. The conditions he identifies with this phenomenon were the numerical dominance of the intermediate classes, independence from dominant classes, and the existence of state-driven capitalism.

The key identifying criteria for these classes are those who earn their income partly through capital (land, money, property, social capital, skills) and partly through labor, a category that is referred to as mixed income of the self-employed in the National Income Accounts. One of the crucial analytical values of intermediate classes is that they do not have a homogenous class interest. The perpetuation of intermediate class domination requires a strong state which directs the process of capital accumulation.

Jha defined the politics of intermediary class in India as follows:

> The power of the intermediate class is based not only on its growing share of the national product but also on its sheer numerical dominance. While the total number of wage earners in industry [sic] does not exceed 13–14 million. Against this, the number of farmers cultivating 10 acres or more amounts to nearly 11 million. Add to this 5 mil [sic] shopkeepers, a mil [sic] or so bus, truck,

taxi and, scooter rickshaw operators, 4 [*sic*] mil self-employed and, their relatives in the unorganized sector, making the intermediate class the largest single class in the country. (Jha 1980, 103)

Jha has argued that intermediary classes comprising the unorganized and informal sector were the main beneficiaries of this regime, partially by design and partially by benefiting from the increasingly complicated set of regulations and licensing practices created under Indira's tenure. Price controls were placed on 84 major commodities produced by large business houses. However, over 100 industries were reserved exclusively, in this regime, for the small-scale sector – defined as an enterprise with less than 10 workers. Small-scale enterprises functioned in consumer industries that had no price controls and faced little regulation, allowing them to enter new markets and expand their production based on market conditions. They also benefited from the nationalization of banks which led to a re-allocation of credit to small-scale enterprises.

Large landlords had dominated the agricultural sector and benefited from colonial and Nehruvian policies. In this regime, the agricultural intermediate classes – rich peasants or small–medium landholders who were from backward communities and lacked social power, moneylenders, wholesalers, retailers, and so on – were invested with power through policies. Allocation of cheaper credit and publicly disbursed information allowed smaller farmers to benefit from Green Revolution technologies. Moreover, the few land redistribution acts allowed local politically dominant peasants to appropriate lands from absent landlords and tenant farmers. This class benefited tremendously from the crippling inflation which affected the economy for most of this period: the rich farmers from higher food prices, the traders because of the opportunities for black marketing, and the owner-entrepreneurs because they were able to slip through the government's price control and tax system. However, when prices were low due to a glut in the market, these classes benefited from artificially raised minimum support prices (MSPs) by the government through the FCI.

The rise of the intermediate classes in this regime was partly because it represented an important mass vote base for the Congress (I) which lost the traditional support base of the INC under Nehru. The intermediary classes represent a predatory form of capitalism, one where the surplus is appropriated by the middle classes and is not accumulated and directed towards long-term development goals. This was felt most profoundly by public sector enterprises that languished with a lack of resources and policies to support it. The rising importance of the informal sector will become more evident after the introduction of liberalization policies.

Crisis of 1979

In 1979, the economy experienced its worst crisis since independence as the GDP growth rate fell by 6 percent (RBI 2017, table 2). The crisis was symptomatic of multiple instabilities that had developed during this regime. The crisis had been catalyzed by a drought and a fall in agricultural production by 12 percent (RBI 2017, table 3). Industrial stagnation and a significant fall in investment, the driver of growth in the Nehruvian regime, were the main reasons for the crisis. Public investment was steadily reduced during this period as the government shifted its resources towards agricultural support and populist policies. Moreover, rigid controls were placed on heavy industry such as price freezes and complicated licensing procedures in this regime, which contributed to a fall in profitability of large investments and a steady decrease in private corporate investment (Figure 3.2).

The instabilities of this regime were felt not only in the industrial sector but also within the external sector and government expenditures. Devaluation in 1966 had led to a steady increase in the import bill. While the growth of exports had been significant in this period, the unstable international economy – two oil price shocks in 1973 and 1979 and the end of the Bretton Woods international monetary system in the 1970s – had led to an increase in the imports bill from INR 2,062 crore in 1967–68 to INR 7,806 crore in 1979 (RBI 2017, table 131). This was in sharp contrast to the increase in imports from INR 650 crore to INR 1368 crore in the Nehruvian regime. While under Nehru India had financed its import bills by foreign aid, external assistance was phased out in the second regime, and the government was forced to borrow at commercial rates to finance the growing import and petroleum bills. Indira's populist policy and an unstable global economy contributed to increasing fiscal profligacy as government revenue expenditures tripled from INR 3,130 crore in 1970 to INR 11,803 crore in 1979 (Figure 3.3). This was a consequence of higher defense expenditures (due to the Bangladesh War in 1971), increasing wage and salary bills in the public sector to compensate for high inflation, increasing subsidies (Green Revolution, redistributive policies), and increasing interest payment (increase in commercial borrowings in this regime).

This increase in revenue expenditures was unsustainable as government revenue could not keep up in a stagnating economy. The government financed its expenditures by taking commercial borrowings, which contributed to growing inflation and a vicious spiral of increasingly funding interest payments by taking further loans. The fiscal deficit as a proportion of the GDP increased

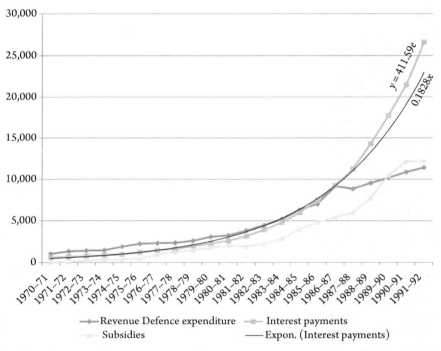

Figure 3.3 Trends in components of revenue expenditure from 1970 to 1992 (rupees, crores)

Source: Calculations by the author using data on GDP and fiscal deficit from RBI's *Handbook of Statistics on the Indian Economy*, table 93.

manifold from 1.69 percent in 1970 to 2.56 percent (Figure 3.4) in 1980. While the rise in fiscal deficit was not comparable to the one India would face at the beginning of the 1990s, it still represented a growing culture of financial profligacy by the state to gain political popularity. This change in fiscal policy contributed to the fall in public investment – an important foundation of policies introduced by Nehru – in this period (Figure 3.2). Lastly, the policies of the Indira regime had led to the alienation of classes that had benefited in the first regime: private industry, public sector employees, formal sector workers, and professionals. These alienated groups were mobilized by the JP (Jaya Prakash) movement and politicized by the Janata Party that pushed the Congress (I) out of power following the aftermath of the Emergency. The loss of hegemony of the Indira government led to the dilution of her policies and brought the second regime to an end. The crisis was initiated by a drought in the agricultural sector. However, the crisis was itself the culmination of multiple instabilities that had developed in the second regime.

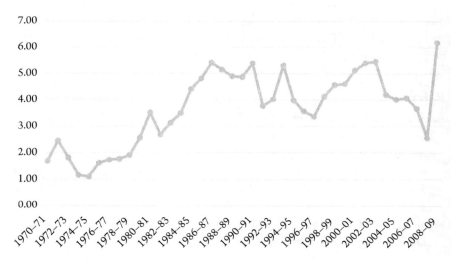

Figure 3.4 Trends in fiscal deficit as a proportion of GDP from 1970–71 to 2008–09

Source: Calculations by the author using data on GDP and fiscal deficit from RBI's *Handbook of Statistics on the Indian Economy*, table 90.

The food crisis of 1965–66 shaped the shift in economic policies in this period. The 1979 crisis marked the end of this period. The discovery of HYV of wheat which was conducive to Indian conditions was the contingent event that shaped the enthusiasm towards Green Revolution technologies and started a chain of events that overturned Nehruvian policies. Political contestation in the shape of infighting within the INC, diplomatic conflict with the USA regarding aid, and popular mobilization against Indira's policies shaped the economic policies introduced in this period.

If we analyze the period from 1950–80 through a macro political economy lens, then we can perceive certain broader trends. Primarily, the first moment of liberalization in India occurred in the mid-1960s and not in the 1980s. Secondly, the evolution of the economy to a corporate and market-driven form of capitalism was paved in the 1970s, especially with the realization that socialist policies were not possible in a democratic set-up. In some ways, Indira's imposition of the Emergency was done to initiate radical socialistic policies and bypass democratic mechanisms (legislature and judiciary). The failure of the Emergency influenced Indira to undertake liberalized reforms in the third regime. Thirdly, the economic upheavals faced during the crisis of 1965 influenced the state to embark on a radically different agricultural policy from that of the Nehruvian regime, and as a consequence diverted the direction and nature of capitalist development in the Indian economy. Lastly, some of the instabilities of the third and fourth regimes like exploding fiscal deficit and eroding BOP have their roots in the second regime.

References

All India Radio. 1969. "Bank Nationalization." Broadcast, July 19, 1969. As cited in *Indira Gandhi Speaks on Democracy, Socialism, and Third World Non-Alignment*. New York: Taplinger Publishing House.

———. 1975. "The 20-Point Programme." Broadcast, July 1, 1975. As cited in *Selected Speeches and Writings of Indira Gandhi*, vol. 3: *September 1972–March 1977*. Delhi: Publication Division: Ministry of Information and Broadcasting.

Frankel, F. 2006. *India's Political Economy 1947–2004: The Gradual Revolution*. Delhi: Oxford University Press.

———. 2015. *India's Green Revolution: Economic Gains and Political Costs*. Princeton, NJ: Princeton University Press.

Fourth Five-Year Plan: A Summary of the Draft Outlines. 1966. New Delhi: Publication Division, Ministry of Information and Broadcasting, Government of India, September 14.

Government of India. 1972. "Approach to Fifth Five-Year Plan." September. New Delhi: Publication Division, Ministry of Information and Broadcasting.

Indian National Congress. 1969. "Resolution on Economic Policy." 73rd Plenary Session. AICC Publication, December 28–19, 1–29.

———. 1972. *Statement on Economic Policy*. Minutes of Congress Working Committee Meeting. 73rd Plenary Session. Bombay, December 28–29, 1972.

Jha, P. S. 1980. *India: A Political Economy of Stagnation*. Bombay: Oxford University Press.

Kalecki, M. 1972. *Selected Essays on the Economic Growth of the Socialist and Mixed Economy*. Cambridge: Cambridge University Press.

Lakhanpal, P. L. 1970. *Two Historical Judgments*. Delhi: International Books.

Rao, M. J., and S. Storm. 2000. "Distribution and Growth in Indian Agriculture." In *The Indian Economy: Major Debates since Independence*, edited by T. J. Byres, 193–248. New York: Oxford University Press.

Reserve Bank of India (RBI). 2017. *Handbook of Statistics on the Indian Economy*. Mumbai.

The Hindu. 1966a. "Check on Inflation Plan Object." June 29, 1.

———. 1966b. "C. M. Attacks Critics of Devaluation." June 28, 8.

———. 1966c. "Delicensing of More Industries." June 23, 1.

The Turn to Populism under Indira Gandhi   95

———. 1966d. "Devaluation Linked to Aid - Govt Note." June 8, 8.

———. 1966e. "Impact of Devaluation on Plan: No Agreed Solution." June 21, 1.

———. 1966f. "Impact of Import Policy Only after 18 Months." June 24, 1.

———. 1966g. "Imports Liberalized: 59 Industries Will Benefit." June 22, 1.

———. 1966h. "Insidious Moves to Pressurise India." June 28, 6.

———. 1967a. "Banks Urged to Implement Social Control." November 15, 9.

———. 1967b. "Bell Mission Considers Fourth Plan Reasonable." March 8, 1.

———. 1967c. "Banks Takeover Will Help Credit Planning: Hazari." November 17, 8.

———. 1969a. "33 Gheraoes in Calcutta in 2 Months." May 3, 1.

———. 1969b. "Clash of Views of PM and Congress President at Party's Plenary Session." April 28, 1.

———. 1969c. "Desai Opposes Total State Control of Means of Production." April 29, 8.

———. 1969d. "Gap between Right and Left Group in Congress as Wide as Ever." April 29, 1.

———. 1969e. "Ideological Showdown Averted at Faridabad." April 28, 1.

———. 1970a. "Bill on Privy Purses in Current Session: PM Reaffirms Aim." March 11, 8.

———. 1970b. "Govt Not Averse to Taking over All Banks: Stabilisation first." March 25, 1.

———. 1970c. "Mrs. Gandhi's First Installment of Socialism." March 1, 1.

———. 1974. "Curbs on Dividends: Compulsory Deposits of Extra Wages and DA." July 1, 1.

Tomlinson, B. R. 1996. *The Economy of Modern India: From 1860 to the Twenty-First Century*. New York: Cambridge University Press.

4

The Early Liberalization Years
1980–2003

'Liberalization' is imagined as a magic bullet that makes economic processes and allocation of resources efficient, competitive, and meritocratic. However, liberal reforms are anything but one thing; implementation of liberal policies can be radically different in sequence and pace and quite tricky to evaluate without understanding the context. In this chapter, I will not attempt to evaluate whether liberal reforms were a success or failure in India, but will instead try to analyze the conditions – politics, social context, economic dynamics, and contingent events – which shaped the timing of the introduction and the pace and sequence of reform policies.

Liberalization is linked to 1991 for most informed Indians and is perceived as a watershed moment when the Indian economy emerged from the heavy state-centric "license Raj" regime and entered its modern high-growth phase. The National Council of Educational Research and Training's (NCERT) class 11 textbook explains liberalization in 1991 as follows: "India agreed to the conditionalities of World Bank and IMF and announced the new economic policy [NEP]. The NEP consisted of a wide range of economics reforms" (NCERT 2023 [2006], 39). However, I will contest the claim that liberalization was introduced in 1991 and instead argue that the economy had already been reoriented towards private enterprise and markets since the return of the Indira-led INC government in 1980; there were few liberal reforms introduced in 1991, and reforms introduced in the 1990s did not significantly impact growth, investment, or industrial growth. To explain these arguments, I will focus on two specific questions: what were the events that led to the introduction of reforms in India, and why is liberalization linked to 1991?

What Are Liberal Reforms?

Liberal reforms renew the beliefs of early modern and especially 19th-century "classical" liberalism that economic growth will be most rapid with the existence of unfettered markets unimpeded by government regulation.

The Early Liberalization Years

The free movement of the price mechanism will create conditions for the most efficient allocation of goods, services, and capital. The efficacy of "free markets" was based on a myth that the international economic system was free – in the sense of being self-regulating, with natural flows of money and capital – before WW1 which contributed to significant growth in the global economy. As I had argued in Chapter one, the global economy before WW1 was inequitable and supported the appropriation of resources and labor from the Third World to the First World. Liberal reforms refer to policies that promote market forces to determine production, consumption, and distributive decisions. The sequence and pace of reforms differ across countries as there are both economic and political costs involved.

Liberalization in 1980

Kohli's (2006) influential article on the politics of economic growth demarcates why 1980 should be considered the year of the introduction of reforms. I will summarize his article to highlight my argument.

India was going through its deepest crisis since independence in 1979 – the GDP had fallen by over 6 percent, key indicators such as BOP, fiscal deficit, industrial growth, and investment were on a downward trajectory, and the INC had lost its hold on the government and favor with the masses. Nehruvian policies had a clear direction: identify a growth driver (heavy industry), control scarce resources and direct them towards the growth driver, and have a separate set of policies to deal with the question of poverty and redistribution. The policies got convoluted under Indira, where it was not clear which policies were driving growth and which policies were complementary. Initially, it became about control under the garb of socialism. In rhetoric, there was talk of more equitable distribution of capital and assets, but it quickly turned towards giving concessions and benefits to supporters and punishing the antagonist. Somewhere, in the maelstrom, there was a loss of economic vision and an inability to cobble together political support. The year 1979 marked the end of the state-directed heavy industry-oriented growth plan. In hindsight, one can say that we never had the state capacity to withstand the inequities and democratic oversights that come along with accelerated growth models.

By 1980, it was clear that no major party could fill the political void left by the INC and there was no economic policy or ideology upon which multiple parties could agree – demonstrated by the failure of the Janata Party to forge a united opposition to the INC in 1977. This provided an opportunity for

Indira to come back under the INC umbrella but also pushed her to rethink her policies. Indira took the first step towards adopting liberal reforms early in her third tenure as prime minister. This was not publicly announced in her budget or manifesto, but if one looks closely at her rhetoric and policies, then the seeds of reforms can be traced to this period.

Liberal reforms under Indira had a three-pronged approach: prioritizing growth-oriented policies, supporting big private domestic industries, and driving growth through government spending. The key to Indira's policy change was to create the framework to bring in further reforms in industry and trade while not publicizing it, as it would not be possible to get mass support for it – the majority of India's voters were still dependent on the agricultural economy. Reforms under Indira focused on supporting private corporate business to drive industrialization. Indira diluted the bureaucratic hurdles and licensing loopholes that prevented businesses from making quick investment decisions based on profitability. Instead of creating conditions for markets to function and allowing competition to pick the winners, Indira bet on big private companies driving the process of industrial development.

She nominated three powerful committees headed by senior bureaucrats L. K. Jha, Abdul Hussain, and M. Narasimhan, well regarded by the Indian business committee, to overhaul economic administration, review trade policies, and introduce financial reforms. The government diluted some important constraints such as licensing and restrictions under the MRTP Act and encouraged big businesses to expand in core industries such as chemicals, drugs, ceramics, and power generation. They gave tax incentives for businesses to invest and eased restrictions on imports and foreign investment. Indira used different state- and police-centric measures to control labor strikes and union activities. Crucially, these changes were beneficial to certain large domestic enterprises which had the financial resources, industrial acumen, and political links with the government.

Rajiv Gandhi entered the political arena, after Indira's untimely death, in 1985 and became the face of growth-orientated, private enterprise-driven economic policies. His first step to getting the private industry on board with this vision was to bring in a group of young, Western-educated economic advisors without a political background to aid in this transformation: L. K. Jha, Montek Singh Ahluwalia, Manmohan Singh, and Abid Hussain. The state, under Rajiv, reduced direct taxes to agitate more consumer spending and encouraged businesses to invest in consumer durables – in stark contrast to the Nehruvian policy emphasis on heavy industries like infrastructure,

The Early Liberalization Years 99

coal, power, railways, and so on. He also encouraged investment in industries based on emergent technologies such as electronics, software, computers, and automobiles. He was personally invested in rethinking telecommunication as the heart of the new growth regime. He hired Sam Pitroda – an Indian-educated American electrical engineer – to undertake a restructuring of the telecommunication infrastructure in India; few have acknowledged Rajiv's contribution to the telecom revolution in India. He continued the process of internal reforms by eliminating licensing processes, reducing trade restrictions, and deregulating sectors previously reserved for the public sector. While there were no major changes in foreign direct investment (FDI) procedures, his government eased the process of gaining foreign investment for priority industries. If reforms under Indira were introduced by stealth, reforms were the plank under Rajiv's ministership.

Kohli (2006) argues that INC reforms in the 1980s were pro-business – directed towards benefiting certain big businesses – as opposed to pro-market. Pro-market reforms encourage more competition – including foreign competition within an industry. Rajiv's brand of reforms was oriented towards large domestic businesses – they were financially equipped to undertake production in a new industry since there were few channels of raising capital in India. The government further supported large domestic industries by getting economic bureaucrats to work alongside industrial federations such as Federation of Indian Chambers of Commerce and Industry (FICCI) and the Associated Chambers of Commerce and Industry of India (ASSOCHAM) to identify particular industries and ease the process of entering and accessing new markets, identifying investment opportunities, gaining foreign collaboration, and so on. The ability to raise capital and tap into well-entrenched bureaucratic networks essentially meant that large domestic industrialists like Tata and Birla and the new industrialists such as Reliance were the main beneficiaries of the reforms. From the government's perspective, having successful results from the first round of reforms were important, and a large domestic enterprise was the safest bet to achieve this.

Impact of Partial Reforms in the 1980s on the Economy

Partial reforms in the 1980s led to a transformation in the Indian economy – a transformation, as I will argue later in this chapter, that was not matched by the 1991 reforms. The GDP growth (Kohli 2006, 1254) rate went up between 1980 and 1991 and was higher than the growth achieved in any decade from 1950–80. The GDP growth rate was driven by government consumption and investment (Table 2.1). While government consumption had been driving growth in the previous regime, investment growth has significantly increased in this period. The pro-business reforms led to significant growth in the manufacturing and service sectors and an increase in imports and exports. There is sufficient evidence that partial reforms in the 1980s changed the structure of the Indian economy and coaxed it towards the path of private enterprise-driven industrialization.

For all the positive indicators in the Indian economy, there were a couple of destabilizing tendencies. Since the oil price hikes of the 1970s, the Indian government had been borrowing commercially to fund increasing expenses, especially in subsidizing the cost of food and oil for the masses. Moreover, the current account deficit continued to deteriorate due to an increase in imports caused by reforms in the trade regime and was funded in equal part by commercial borrowings and foreign aid. The increasing fiscal deficit and a deteriorating BOP were identified as important indicators of economic instability. However, the INC government, under Indira and Rajiv, was unable to manage it. The government had failed to generate revenue and had to borrow more to fund the increasing interest payments (Figure 3.3) from loans, leading to the ballooning of fiscal deficit as a percentage of GDP from 2 percent to 5.5 percent (Figure 3.4) by the mid-1980s. Further, the government was unable to reduce expenditures as they were the main driver of GDP growth in the 1970s and 1980s (Table 2.1). The government had provided tax cuts and decreased import duties in the 1980s, taking away a major source of revenue. Given the unequal distribution of benefits from reforms, the government could not cut public expenditures or subsidies; as a consequence, the fiscal deficit kept increasing, and the government was politically unwilling to make unpopular cuts in expenditure.

Liberalization in 1991

One would probably expect that the 1991 reforms would accelerate the developments made in the 1980s. However, the data does not corroborate this fact. Consider this: there was not a significant increase in GDP growth from the 1980s to the 1990s or a significant acceleration in India's growth rate since 1991 (Nagaraj 2017). Additionally, the secondary sector witnessed a modest statistically significant slowdown. The share of industry in the GDP hovered around 27.6 percent (Kohli 2006, 1254) which was the same as in the 1980s; the share of manufacturing did not change either. There was no statistically significant acceleration in growth rate in the tertiary sector or the

The Early Liberalization Years

primary sector. If one were to just look at the data, there is no indication that a significant change in economic policy took place in 1991.

Why 1991 Is Associated with Liberal Reforms

Economic policies, their impact on the economy, and the public discourse shaping it do not always move in a linear direction. In public discourse, 1991 is associated with crisis and liberalization. However, neither does the data reflect this nor were liberal reforms first introduced in 1991. To understand why this narrative is popularized, one needs to understand the conditions that led to liberalization in 1991. When Rajiv became prime minister in 1985, he paved the way for greater acceptance of reforms. Mass support of reforms was important but hard to achieve because reforms or opening up the economy to market forces – albeit partially – would have a detrimental impact on large parts of the economy. The initial benefit of reforms would be gained by modern sectors – companies and entrepreneurs who could produce for market requirements and consumers who drive demand for consumer goods. However, the majority of Indians, still living at or below subsistence level and dependent on the agricultural sector, would not benefit from reforms. While growth would translate into more employment, most of these jobs would go to skilled urban employees. There was no direct benefit for the rural masses and no straightforward way to sugarcoat it.

The Nehruvian brand of industrial growth – focused on long-term stable growth, infused by ideals of independence and autarky, buttressed by a benevolent neutral government that protected the economy from the drive for profit of private enterprise, intermixed with Gandhian ideals of equity, empowerment of the masses and respect for the traditional mode of production like peasant-based agriculture and small-scale industry – was far more palatable for politicians to sell to the voters. Even the right wing of the INC, represented by the Syndicate, had been careful not to overstep these tenets. Few political parties in India had flirted with rightist economic ideals of markets and private enterprise-driven economy. For the INC, to push for liberal reforms would engender losing their traditional voting base.

The Foreign Exchange Crisis of 1991

The INC had hoped that as Rajiv becomes the face of the modern Indian economy – fueled by technology, global competitiveness, and consumer growth – the growth generated by reforms could be used to justify these policies to the masses. However, the end of the 1980s led to a succession of internal and external events which would upend this cart. Rajiv got embroiled in the Bofors corruption scam and faced public backlash. His finance minister, V. P. Singh – known for his strong stance on corruption – resigned from the government and initiated a probe into the charges on Rajiv. The Rajiv-headed government tenure ended in 1989, and a new coalition government – the first of its kind – headed by V. P. Singh and backed by the newly upcoming BJP came to power (Bajoria 2018, 5). The RBI had been closely monitoring the deteriorating fiscal deficit and BOP situation. Funding the current account deficit had become increasingly complicated and had been a drain of India's foreign exchange reserve. The RBI artificially raised the exchange rate in India to stabilize the Indian rupee in the face of an unstable international exchange market. The RBI apprised the V. P. Singh government about this, but the government was unable to take any action – keep in mind that cutting expenditures or creating new taxes creates a public backlash.

Two destabilizing external events exacerbated the pace of the oncoming crisis: the dissolution of the USSR led to the USA becoming the dominant economy in the world – India had depended on USSR aid and assistance and geopolitical balance of power – and more urgently the Gulf War broke out in Kuwait. Oil prices started to rise with the unrest in the Middle East, and many Indians working in the Gulf region, whose remittances buttressed the deteriorating current account, were forced to leave the region. This double blow of increasing prices of oil imports and falling foreign remittances put the Indian economy on the brink of a foreign exchange crisis.

The V. P. Singh government stayed in office for a year after losing majority support in the legislature. They were followed by a Chandrashekhar-led minority government. However, that did not have the political stability to issue major changes in policies or tackle the growing fiscal crisis, BOP deficit, or fall in international reserves. In January 1991, the RBI had talks with the International Monetary Fund (IMF) for funds to eviscerate the foreign exchange crisis and sent a proposal to the government to use its gold holdings, impounded through crackdowns, to raise foreign exchange. As the political situation in the Middle East deteriorated, India's currency reserve was vastly depleting. To add fuel to this fire, the Chandrashekhar government collapsed in March 1991, even before the then finance minister, Yashwant Sinha, could present his budget. By April 1991, India had barely two weeks of foreign exchange to maintain its current import requirement, leading to the downgrade of its international credit rating. The RBI swiftly made the requisite arrangements to lease out 20 tons of gold in exchange for USD 200 million. However, this exchange could not be arranged until a new government was formed. In these challenging times, tragedy struck the Indian polity as Rajiv Gandhi was assassinated on

The Early Liberalization Years

the campaign trail. Amid political instability, the INC had lost its main prime minister candidate, and the situation threatened to desist into chaos.

The INC, unexpectedly, won the elections by a majority and chose to have P. V. Narasimha Rao as the prime minister. Rao was neither popular within the INC nor known for his ideology or economic vision. However, he was perceived as an agreeable candidate amongst seniors in the party. Rao, after consultation with trusted bureaucrats, decided to make Manmohan Singh the finance minister. This turned out to be a shrewd move, especially given that he had no political baggage, was a respected economist, and was perceived by the business community and international agencies as a reform-minded economist. On June 20, 1991 (Bajoria 2018, 8), the RBI provided an eight-page document to the prime minister, apprising him of the extent of the situation and suggesting a laundry list of reforms created in discussion with the IMF; IMF loans were attached to various conditionalities. Along with Manmohan Singh, the Finance Ministry was stocked with other reform-minded bureaucrats such as Montek Singh Ahluwalia, Bimal Jalan, Y. V. Reddy, and Rakesh Mohan. The INC was technically equipped to make reforms and politically stable to introduce them. However, making reforms palatable to all would be a different challenge altogether.

The Introduction of Reforms in 1991

The first step on the journey towards reforms was two sets of devaluations in early July which roughly led to a fall in the value of the rupee by a fifth – immediately making imports more expensive. However, another event happened on July 3 which captured the nation's imagination. In the early hours, trucks had been loaded with the RBI gold which was to be shipped to the BOE and the Bank of Japan for an emergency loan of USD 405 million. The operation was meant to be done in secrecy, but news of it got leaked and printed by the *Indian Express*, creating a national scandal. Financial independence had been an important foundation of economic policies and used to justify unpopular Nehruvian industrial policies. The news of the drain of gold and the fear of IMF dictating terms with the government brought back fears of colonial appropriation and discriminatory trade policy. This was not a good start to the reform process.

The Role of Private English Media

Unlike in the 1980s, the INC planned to introduce reforms to the larger public, and under Rao, they decided to make liberalization the focus of the new budget. Rhetoric plays an important role in explaining and justifying policies to the larger public, and certain policies can get conflated with specific meanings in the public imagination based on how they have been spoken about. For example, Nehru used to justify industrial policies by focusing on the need for economic independence and valorizing the sacrifice made by the people. Reference to Gandhian morals was also commonly used to justify policies that create hardship for the masses. The INC decided to rebrand its economic policies around the time when public support had been waning.

The private English media played a key role in introducing and making reforms palatable for urban educated classes – the primary beneficiaries of reforms (De 2017). The media interprets policies by framing them within certain terms of the debate. The frame provides the categories within which we understand an issue, establishes the limits of the discussion, and defines the range of problems that it can refer to. Tone, headline, quotations, and placement of an article within a paper have an important role in determining the framing of the article. I will demonstrate through examples how Manmohan Singh changed the rhetorical approach in his budget speech and how the private media framed reforms as a necessary change from economic policies in the past.

Days before the 1991 budget, the media started creating an exciting buzz around the prospect of the introduction of reforms by Singh. This can be gleaned from surveying newspaper headlines from this period. Within days of the new INC government being formed, the media was flush with a "call to open up the economy on all fronts" (*Times of India* 1991c), "to evolve a 'minimum' program acceptable to all to rejuvenate the economy of India" (*Times of India* 1991a). An increasing amount of space was given to speakers from institutions that were lobbying for liberal reforms, which included IMF chief Micheal Landessen (*Times of India* 1991b), chairman of Tata Steel, Russi Mody (*Times of India* 1991c), and president of the Confederation of Indian Industries, Dhruv Sawney (*Times of India* 1991a). Private media framed the narrative around the lack of liberalization as one in which vested-interest groups who have been profiting from the license regulation raj were resisting changes. The following is one amongst many articles which argues that the opposition towards reforms was due to "the political class by and large which is dominated by the Congress party would [*sic*] want to continue to have a say in an economy as well as to retain its capacity to favor one industrial house over another" (*The Hindu* 1991b).

There were intense discussions about the "loss of economic sovereignty" (*The Hindu* 1991a). However, this was recast as a debate based on economic

The Early Liberalization Years

merit and not loss of economic autarky. The article argues, "The resistance is understandable only when we view it from the perspective of political science. What the opponents of the loan resist is the loan of economic sovereignty that taking the IMF loans imply [*sic*]." Such articles argue that while economic sovereignty is a noble aim foisted by our colonial past, the truth of the matter is that we live in a world where all economies are dependent on each other, and we cannot ignore the benefits of this. Once again, liberalization was treated as an objective solution to problems brought about by an increasingly interlinked global economy. Interestingly, there was a serious dearth of articles talking about the possible harmful repercussions of loans. The only critical article that I came across was nestled in the middle pages of *The Hindu*, following the day after the budget, titled "Warning Note on the IMF Remedy" (*The Hindu* 1991c). The article is fairly abstract and ends with a counterfactual question. "Even without such changes [a reference to reforms] it may be difficult to say how the economy would have performed if the program had not been implemented."

This change in public discourse is highlighted by an article that came out in *The Hindu* on the same day as the second budget proposed by Manmohan Singh. The article refers to the breaking away from Nehruvian discourse and commends the finance minister for "taking the economy out of the woodland and the entrepreneur out of the bureaucracy of the 'License Raj' which replaced the British Raj." Moreover, the writer suggests that this budget will be appreciated by entrepreneurs as "this particular budget will be remembered because it is the first change-oriented, strategic, more economic and less political budget." He further refers to the death of Nehruvian rhetoric; he says, "Terms with political undertones such as 'the socialist, etc' have almost disappeared out of the budget document" (*The Hindu* 1992). These are arguments to break the consensus around the Nehruvian ideals and justify reforms. It is pitched that this change is based on objective economic judgment and the tendency to hold on to Nehruvian ideals of socialism and autarky is regressive, as it benefits a small political class that feeds on it. Liberalization is pitched as freedom from government intervention and freedom to connect with the rest of the economic world.

Manmohan Singh's Budget Speech

Unlike previous finance ministers who always qualified structural changes as being founded on Nehruvian ideals, Manmohan went in a completely different direction by urging the need for structural change. Parallel to the media-created fervor around reforms, Manmohan Singh took a very different rhetorical approach from the finance ministers in previous years: he introduced new buzzwords such as growth, dynamism, competitiveness, and stability which overthrew the older rhetoric of economic independence, socialism, equity, and justice.

It is worth taking a closer look at Manmohan's budget speech of 1991. He starts his speech by confirming that the economy is going through a deep crisis caused by political instability, fiscal deficiencies, the Gulf War, and a drop in international confidence. He then makes an interesting statement claiming that "the origins of the problem are directly traceable to large and persistent macro-economic imbalances and the low productivity of investment" (Singh 1991, 1). He goes on to clarify that this is a result of poor performance of public sector enterprises, low returns on public investment, indiscrete protection of industry weakening competition, and the sheer number of budgetary subsidies. These were important foundations of Nehruvian industrial policy.

The following is the key passage that indicates that reforms and liberalization are the way to tackle these issues:

> Macro-economic stabilisation and fiscal adjustment alone cannot suffice. They must be supported by essential reforms in economic policy and economic management, as an integral part of the adjustment process, reforms which would help to eliminate waste and inefficiency and impart a new element of dynamism to growth processes in our economy. The thrust of the reform process would be to increase the efficiency and international competitiveness of industrial production, to utilize for this purpose foreign investment and foreign technology to a much greater degree than we have done in the past, to increase the productivity of investment, to ensure that India's financial sector is rapidly modernised, and to improve the performance of the public sector, so that the key sectors of our economy are enabled to attain an adequate technological and competitive edge in a fast changing global economy. (Singh 1991, 3)

Manmohan identifies that piecemeal macro-stabilization and fiscal adjustments only impact the symptoms of the crisis; reforms are necessary to infuse dynamism in the industry, and the larger goal is to modernize the industry and make it globally competitive. However, to recommend reforms, he has to criticize the economic policies of previous INC governments without criticizing his party. This places him in a tricky position, and he has to undertake some rhetorical gymnastics. Following this paragraph, he thanks the contributions Nehru, Indira, and Rajiv made in shaping

The Early Liberalization Years

industrial policy. However, he mentions that the licensing procedures and barriers placed towards entry and exit into industries have contributed to the lack of dynamism in industry and its inability to translate into growth in the economy. This contradictory move of valorizing the policies of earlier ministers but criticizing its impact on the economy was necessary to not alienate long-term INC supporters and party members and anticipate that the opposition would use reforms to criticize the earlier government.

After clearly setting up the issues and origin of the problems, Singh proposes the following reforms:

1. adjusting the Indian rupee towards market-determined value and changing trade policies away from licensing and quota requirements;
2. Fifty-one percent foreign equity being allowed in high priority and exporting industries;
3. setting up a mechanism to privatize and disinvest loss-making public sector enterprises; and
4. setting up the Securities and Exchange Board of India to regulate the stock exchange.

After the budget, the government decided to formulate a new industrial policy and abolish industrial licensing in all except 18 industries. They also reduced and reframed the MRTP Act and the FERA, which regulated large companies. Further, they set up three high-powered committees to make recommendations regarding further reforms:

1. the committee headed by former RBI governor, M. Narsimhan, would review reforms in the financial system;
2. the committee headed by Raja Chelliah, a public finance expert, would look into tax reforms; and
3. the committee headed by the deputy governor of the RBI, C. Rangarajan, would look into BOP issues.

The Impact of Reforms on the Economy

Along with solving the BOP and exchange reserve issues, the government was under pressure to reduce the fiscal deficit, especially with the conditionalities attached to IMF loans. However, the fiscal deficit is politically challenging to cut down, as attempts to both increase taxes and reduce expenditures directly affect a part of the population. The government focused on cutting down expenditures. The biggest impact of this was seen in a cut in public investment, which fell from 43 percent of total investment in the economy to 30 percent by 1995–96 to 23 percent in 2003–04 (Figure 4.1). This represented a larger change in the industrial policy being choreographed in the economy: as liberal reforms opened up restricted industries to private enterprise, the government scaled back or intended to privatize public sector enterprises. Interest payments were the largest component of revenue expenditure followed by subsidies. There was no scope in reducing the first while the second would be politically risky to reduce. The government instead focused on cutting developmental expenditure, which became less than non-developmental expenditure by the mid-1990s. Developmental expenditure includes expenditure on education, public health, family welfare, housing development, employment, and scientific research. Public investment and developmental expenditure create positive externalities for society as they contribute to investment in public assets and human capital. It was politically easier to cut down expenditure in these categories rather than increase revenue or cut down on other forms of expenditure; these cuts contributed to the increasing inequality in the 1990s – more on this later in the chapter. These expenditure cuts helped India reduce its fiscal deficit as a percentage of the GDP from 5.4 in 1991 to 3.3 by 1996 (Figure 3.4). However, new governments were unwilling to make unpopular expenditure cuts, leading to the fiscal deficit returning to 5.4 percent of the GDP by 2003. This emphasizes the point that the fiscal

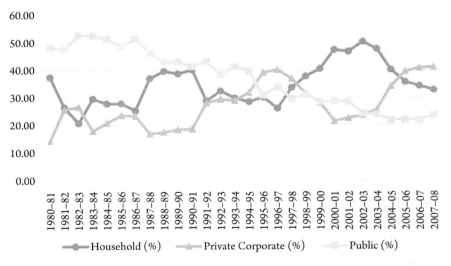

Figure 4.1 Trends in investment in proportion (percent) from 1980 to 2007

Source: Prepared by the author using data from RBI's *Handbook of Statistics on the Indian Economy*, table 13.

The Early Liberalization Years

crisis of 1991 was not equivalent to the 1965–66 food crisis or the 1979 industrial crisis.

The initial euphoria around reforms and the promise of more led to a surge in the GDP driven by industrial growth – 10.6 percent (Kohli 2006, 1255) and private investment (Figure 4.1). However, this surge stagnated over the latter half of the 1990s with both industrial growth and GDP growth becoming negligible – this has been argued with empirical evidence by Nagaraj (2017). While the reforms initially gave strong encouragement towards export orientation, it did not translate into a better BOP situation, and the economy was unable to improve its current account deficit (Figure 4.2). While FDI started increasing in the initial years after liberalization, Nagaraj (2003) shows that it was significantly less than that achieved by other emerging economies in Asia. Nagaraj suggests that foreign investors did not perceive optimal business conditions to compete with domestic rivals or stability of the reforms process to enter the Indian economy even though there were clear advantages of cheap labor to be found in India. The Indian government for various reasons failed to alleviate the two main symptoms of the 1991 crisis: fiscal mismanagement and an unsustainable dependency on commercial borrowings to finance the current account deficit.

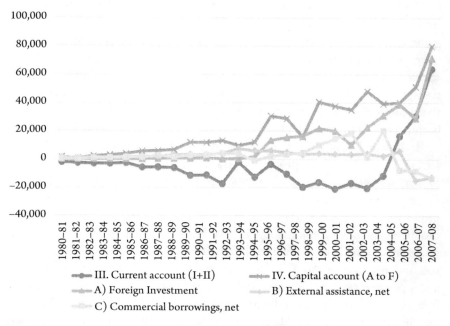

Figure 4.2 Trends in BOP from 1980 to 2003 (rupees, crores)

Source: Prepared by the author using data from RBI's *Handbook of Statistics on the Indian Economy*, table 133.

Why Reforms in 1991 Did Not Have the Desired Effect on Industry and Exports

The reason for the reduced pace of reforms after a couple of years of euphoria and lack of structural transformation initiated by reforms is not easily discernible – and there is no agreement about it amongst commentators on the Indian economy. There are no clear answers to this question, and it is worth analyzing multiple factors that may have led to the lackluster performance of the economy in the 1990s.

What conditions should exist for reforms to be successful? The fundamental idea is that opening up multiple parts of the economy to the market would lead to competitive behavior, dynamic and long-term decision-making, and efficient allocation of scarce resources. In a capital-and skilled labor-scarce economy like India, one would expect that capital and labor should flow towards the highest growing industries such as heavy industries, export-oriented industries, and high consumer-demand industries. This was the first part of the challenge for India – that it did not have well-developed export or consumer industries. Therefore, the primary surge would have to come from heavy industries which were controlled or dependent on public enterprises. The process of privatization is complicated: bad examples abound from Russia and China where oligarchs rigged the privatization process and gained control of public sector assets. India's proclivity had been towards opening up key industries to private enterprises rather than privatizing public sector enterprises such as banking and finance, telecommunications, and air transport. India – with good reason – was reluctant to completely deregulate the trade regime and tap into export possibilities and foreign investment – both necessary to grow at a fast rate like the South Korean model.

It is worth thinking about how an entrepreneur in India would take advantage of the reform process. With de-licensing, he or she will not have to negotiate the complex underbelly of the Indian bureaucratic complex to get permission to open a company. The first step would be to identify a product and get finance to initiate production – finance is the first barrier for producers in India. India did not have a well-developed banking system that was able to provide large credit to industries; India's public capital market was still underdeveloped and was a difficult route to raise capital from, especially if a company was not well known; and there were still many obstacles to attract foreign investment. Large industries had a competitive advantage in the post-reform economy as they had access to capital from their successful industries. This was the advantage that allowed sunrise industries like Reliance, GMR, and Wipro to leapfrog into the major product markets in India. Suppose a

The Early Liberalization Years

company manages to get funding. Then they have to solve the supply problem. Industries have to procure land and gain access to fundamental infrastructure like power, water, fuel, and transport connections to shipping and markets – all of which require well-functioning local governance institutions.

The political capacity and the changes in infrastructure and governance required to move to a market-based economy were underdeveloped and regionally heterogeneous. It is not a coincidence that large industrialists – Tata, for example – had developed complete townships around heavy industries to ensure that they have the supporting infrastructure required to run a large-scale operation. This normative reasoning was to provide the reader a sense of the perspective of business owners – especially because there is very little available data beyond anecdotal evidence on why businesses did not invest in the economy at the pace that was expected.

The domestic business community and foreign investors did not feel confident in the government's ability to sustain reforms and to make the heavy investments required to build industries. However, a look at the history of reforms in the Global South might bring some lessons for the challenges of introducing reforms. Most nations had to introduce reforms as a conditionality to get loans or debt written off by the IMF. These were forced onto economies going through major financial crises, making it easier to justify reforms. Further, all these economies like Mexico, Chile, Brazil, Egypt, Indonesia, and so on, had a dictatorial government that could force policy changes and used coercion to get different interest groups to accept reforms. Lastly, most of these economies had a presence of large multinational corporations which could immediately reap the benefits of reforms.

The Indian government in similar circumstances did not have to undertake fast reforms which have a severe cost to the economy to structurally adjust and lead to inequitable distribution of the gains. Neither did India want to lose its autonomy to foreign interests through multinational corporations or foreign capital, which is a way of fast-forwarding the impact of reforms. Moreover, the late 1990s were times of unstable governments that were unwilling to take the political risk of reforms, especially given the lack of benefit to the majority in the agricultural sector or being fiscally constrained to undertake a substantial redistributive program.

How Reforms Reshaped Federal Politics in India

Jenkins (2000) in his substantial analysis of the early period of reforms demonstrates how the complexity of the Indian polity shaped the reforms process. In some ways, India adopted a slow pace of reforms, so vested-interest groups could reconfigure their interests as they got used to changing market conditions since reforms created an environment where it was not clear which interest groups should collude or whose interests match. Politicians and bureaucrats who enjoyed rent-seeking opportunities in the licensing era discovered new sources of revenue – through land appropriation, colluding with industrial interest groups, or playing off different interest groups. Industrialists, speculators, financiers, and business owners also had to learn to negotiate the changing environment where it was not clear who the winners or the losers were, but there were ample opportunities to gain short windfalls. The process of reforms became a constant dialogue between politicians, the government, and business interest groups; a slow pace of reforms with constant negotiation became a necessity due to a situation of uncertainty and changing economic calculations. One of the primary outcomes was that reforms were displaced or taken up at the state level as state governments were in a better place to negotiate the different interest groups, and there was a clear push – especially by the more developed states – to gain independence from rigid central government policies.

This change in the balance of federal power began in the 1970s and provided an alternate pathway for implementing reforms. The INC government had been the dominant political force in India since independence; they had won majority seats in every Lok Sabha election, riding on being the face of the independence movement and taking up the mantle of unifying a very diverse population. The INC plank was based on centralized production of key industrial sectors to speed up the pace of industrialization in the economy. However, by the 1970s, amidst infighting within the INC, a stagnant industrial sector triggered worker strikes and protests and increasing inequality in the rural economy. And on the back of Indira's victory in 1972, which demonstrated the efficacy of wooing the masses through populist policies, political conditions were ripe for the rise of multiple regional parties taking over state governments. These included the left parties in Bengal and Kerela, the DMK in Tamil Nadu, the Telugu Desam Party (TDP) in Andhra Pradesh, the Akali Dal in Punjab, and the Janta Party in northern India – which would later fragment into the Janta Dal, the Lok Dal, the Samajwadi Party, and so on. Each of these parties was different in its ethnic composition, political ideology, and history of formation. However, there were certain commonalities between how these parties ascended to power – they contained personnel who had left the INC due to differences or grievances, each focused on prioritizing the region over the center, and each built its vote bank on linguistic, ethnic or caste-based identities – mobilizing people sharing an ethnic identity. Each focused on the

The Early Liberalization Years

rural economy which had been ignored by INC policies, and each used various populist political strategies to gain popularity.

By the 1980s, the INC had lost further seats in the Lok Sabha and major states such as Kerala, Tamil Nadu, Karnataka, Andhra Pradesh, Punjab, and Bengal. These were the most economically developed regions in India which in different ways were held back by the lack of allocation of funds by the center. Each of these state economies had the potential and conditions to grow and industrialize at a faster rate than the rest of the Indian economy. Each of these states represented powerful agricultural interest groups and industrialists who had not been able to access or benefit from central policymaking and licensing procedures as this was dominated by the north-centric government and relations. Each of these states had the political backing and conditions required to have state-level industrial policies.

The INC government had to come up with strategies to manage the increasing power of regional parties, especially since they would require their support to implement central policies. One of the ways the INC maintained relations with the state government was by increasing subsidies and allocating funds to state governments to spend on development and redistribution. Subsidies increased 20 times from INR 2,028 crore in 1980 to INR 44,323 crore in 2003 (Figure 4.3). The state government would

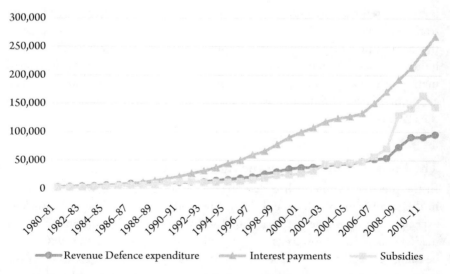

Figure 4.3 Trends in revenue expenditure from 1980 to 2011 (rupees, crores)

Source: Prepared by the author using data from RBI's *Handbook of Statistics on the Indian Economy*, table 93.

direct these developmental funds – subsidies, cheap loans, cheap housing, and re-distributive policies – towards its major voting planks who were usually from certain ethnic majorities – though in many cases socio-economically backward – and maintain its vote bank.

The 1991 fiscal deficit crisis forced the government to cut down its expenditures, and the allocation of funds to states became one of the first victims. Net transfers to state governments as a percentage of central government receipts fell from 31 percent in 1990–91 to 26 percent in 1994–95 (Jenkins 2000, 131). During the 1980s, central government transfers to the state government had grown at an annual rate of 17 percent. However, the annual growth rate grew by only 7 percent from 1990–95. As the amount of state government expenditure funded by central government transfers decreased, states had to look for new sources of funds, increasing revenue through their tax bases or commercial borrowings. The more developed states with stable governments – Andhra Pradesh, Tamil Nadu, Karnataka, Maharashtra, Gujarat, and so on – had an advantage on both counts. They generated more revenue and took charge of their industrial development projects by initiating reforms and raising money directly from international agencies. They could procure land, build infrastructure – roads, electrification, and water supply – and had well-developed and urbanized metros to attract private industry. State governments were in a better position to introduce piecemeal reforms and negotiate with interest groups who were not benefiting from reforms as they could mobilize voters on regional identities, control the distribution of government benefits and subsidies, and initiate regional industrial development around a historically urbanized and developed metropolitan city – Chennai, Hyderabad, Bangalore, Mumbai, and so on. The changing matrix of federal power explains both the slow pace of reforms and the regionally diverse impact it had on the economy.

The Impact of Reforms on the Agricultural Sector

In the previous chapter, I had described how liberal reforms were introduced in the production of wheat and rice in the mid-1960s and how policymakers expected that over time the agricultural sector will expand based on increasing market penetration. However, there was little evidence for this in the 1980s. I will be using Rao and Storms's (2000) analysis of the agricultural sector to study the impact of Green Revolution policies on the evolution of the agricultural sector.

The total growth of output of food grains increased in the period between 1981–82 and 1991–92 to 2.92 percent from 2.21 percent in the Indira regime.

The Early Liberalization Years

This was not a substantial increase in growth rate, especially given that the growth rate of food grain output was 2.93 percent in the Nehruvian regime. A closer look at individual food grains is equally telling. There was a substantial fall in the growth rate of wheat, the poster child of the Green Revolution, from 5.21 percent to 3.33 percent. This fall in the growth rate is indicative of the inability of producers to scale up from the initial success of Green Revolution policies. Rice production, however, showed an improvement in output growth from the Indira to the liberalization periods, from 2.16 percent to 3.87 percent. Another important change in dynamic was the substantial improvement in output growth in non-food grain production. Non-food grain production increased from 2.40 percent to 3.43 percent, indicating greater commercialization of agriculture. The results were mixed for other major food grains and there is no evidence that liberal reforms led to a structural transformation in the agricultural sector (Rao and Storm 2000, 204).

Mohan Rao concludes, based on this data, that the Green Revolution had been successful in generating agricultural growth by increasing the yield of the land. However, it has failed to tap into the existing potential provided by other sources of growth, such as increased land-use intensity and shift in cropping patterns. He analyzes two kinds of issues with agriculture in India which led to the failure to translate reforms into increased growth in the agricultural sector. The first had to do with the nature of growth of capitalism in agriculture, and the second was an outcome of a lack of public investment in agriculture.

The IADP, introduced in the 1960s, provided subsidies to increase the adoption of modern technologies in the production of wheat and rice. This created incentives for the development of a market for modern inputs such as seeds, fertilizers, and pesticides, and encouraged private investment in improving productivity. The expectations were that growth and increase in income of farmers who successfully integrate modern inputs will have dynamic effects on the agricultural sector. Commercial farmers will expand production by raising more capital, procuring or leasing more land, hiring more labor, and producing more output. This would lead to increased employment in rural areas, and the income would trickle down to poorer classes. However, the Green Revolution became restricted to certain regions in India as there were institutional barriers to growth in many regions.

The market for capital, land, and labor is not well developed in India. In many regions, land ownership is highly fragmented, making it near impossible to procure large chunks of land. Money or capital markets in rural India are dependent on informal lending institutions which charge exorbitant rates of interest; long-term loans needed for investment are tough to procure in informal markets. Lastly, due to barriers of caste and class, labor mobility in the regional economy was restricted. These peculiar institutional factors made the Indian agricultural sector non-responsive to changes in market prices – a fundamental condition for the success of liberal reforms. Rao and Storm (2000, 196–99) has cited multiple econometric studies which have shown that the supply response of agricultural output was low even in the long run. Typically, a 10 percent increase in prices would only lead to a 2–5 percent increase in real total output, and even these meager gains were wiped out by population growth. Only those agricultural capitalists who had a monopoly over land and capital and political clout to harness resources to take advantage of price rises could expand the scale of production. The gains of agricultural growth were reaped by a few and largely by those who shared an ethnic background with the regional party in power (Rao and Storm 2000, 197).

Rao further evaluates if the agricultural economy is structurally equipped to grow through patterns of investment and the use of modern inputs in agriculture. The first thing that stands out is that there has been a dearth of public investment in agriculture: private investment has increased three-fold from INR 1,188 crore in 1961 to INR 3,760 crore in 1991, and public investment has barely risen from INR 589 crore to INR 1,318 crore (Rao and Storm 2000, 210–11). Almost 50 percent of the total investment has been in machinery and implements; land improvements account for 15 percent of the investment while irrigation is about 25 percent. Additionally, the largest component of private investment has been in diesel and electrical pumps. There has been negligible investment in public infrastructure such as irrigation and canals, power supply, roads, and so on. While the net irrigated area has doubled in India since the Green Revolution, 50 percent of this has been through pumps and tube wells. The largest investment in India is in getting a private supply of water through pumps or tube wells. Moreover, the battle over groundwater has led to a steady drop in water levels, which has further exacerbated the difficulty of small farmers in gaining access to it. There has been a promising increase in the use of modern inputs such as HYV seeds, fertilizers, and so on – about a third of all cropped land use HYV seeds. Moreover, a third of all inputs used in agriculture are modern. However, access to institutional credit was still quite low in India as it increased from INR 281 crore in 1980–81 to INR 657 crore in 1990–91. The majority of this credit went to farmers with large landholding. Most farmers did not have access to formal credit channels due to a lack of information, bureaucratic hurdles, and lack of assets to use as collateral. Farmers had to depend on informal credit markets which charged high-interest fees or other modes of finance gained through ethnic networks.

The Early Liberalization Years

These reasons led to a very diversified development of agriculture in India focused on non-food grains and rice in particular and towards specific regions – fertile with large landowners. Institutional mechanisms and social norms restricted the ability of farmers to modernize and increase the scale of production and respond to changing market conditions. The incentives provided by the government were largely appropriated by a certain dominant class of agriculturists, while the lack of public investment in infrastructure prevented smaller farmers from benefiting from the increasing marketization of agricultural production. The agricultural sector stagnated through the reform period and grew at a 3.5 percent GDP growth rate, while the non-agricultural sectors grew at more than 6 percent (Table 2.2). The lack of growth in the agricultural sector was a structural impediment to successful industrial growth fueled by liberal reforms, especially since the majority of India's population was still dependent on the agricultural economy. This had severe implications for the distributive impact of liberal reforms on the masses.

Who Benefited from Reforms?

Growth generated through reforms is distributed unequally, and this is reflected in inequality and poverty data in India. Urban inequality remained constant and high throughout the reform period from 0.340 percent in 1983–84 to 0.344 percent in 1993–94 to 0.376 percent in 2003–04 (Table 2.3). Rural inequality interestingly came down in the first phase of reforms from 0.310 percent to 0.286 percent – growth was driven by high government expenditures which translated into benefits and subsidies for the majority of landless peasants and small farmers – but rose again to 0.305 percent in 2003–04. Nagaraj (2017) cites data which shows that the proportion of people living in poverty has been steadily decreasing from 55 percent in 1973–74 to 36 percent in 1993–94. Economists have analyzed that there is a direct link between growth and poverty – though there is no consensus on the precise mechanism. Nagaraj (2017) counters this claim by demonstrating that there is no statistically significant association between growth rates and poverty reduction. Moreover, he claims that the link between poverty and growth is a bit of a mirage as it is determined by poverty level: poverty can be reduced by not adjusting for price changes in the determination of poverty line. If one uses nutritional status, defined as the minimum calorie count required by different age groups to survive, as a measure of poverty, then it has not improved in rural India. As mentioned earlier, reforms in the agricultural sector in the form of the Green Revolution did not lead to improvements in the overall sector or gains received by the larger landless or small farmer masses.

Vakulabharanam (2010) has conceptualized an elaborate class analysis of changing inequality in the Indian economy to argue that reforms benefited and strengthened a sub-class of urban owners and managers, urban professionals, and certain categories of the rural elite – moneylenders, professionals, and large and medium farmers. Vakulabharanam uses the Yitzhaki method to decompose how much sub-classes (as listed in the National Sample Survey Organisation [NSSO]) contribute to inequality to empirically demonstrate which classes have become more unequal with the introduction of reforms. There is a clear three-pronged shift in class structure with the introduction of reforms. First, inequality between rural and urban areas has increased slightly, and the main increase in inequality has come from urban areas. Second, within urban areas the biggest winners are urban professionals – high income and educated class and skilled workers. Interestingly, owners and managers in the informal sector have done better than in the formal sector, while the primary classes to become more unequal are unskilled working classes. Third, inequality in rural areas has not changed much. Rural elites and farmers with any land ownership have done slightly better as have agricultural workers. But the class which has performed significantly worse are non-agricultural workers and the non-agricultural self-employed – the class which got dispossessed from land. With a lack of infrastructural development, public investment and growth mechanisms in agriculture, and the concurrent cutting down and politicization of subsidies, more and more small and marginal farmers have got dispossessed of their lands and have become dependent on middlemen and moneylenders for survival. Out of increasing desperation, these workers are migrating to urban areas for work and flocking to the growing informal service industries in urban areas. I will discuss this phenomenon in more detail about the role of footloose migrant labor in the urban informal sector in the next chapter.

The urban sector has driven growth in post-reform India, specifically the organized service sector which includes professional services, IT and software industry, business process outsourcing, finance and insurance, real estate, and hotels. Within these industries, the highly educated and skilled – especially the professional and managerial classes – have benefited the most. The urban informal sector – small businesses, vendors, and merchants – have provided the consumption needs of this class of population and benefited. While there is a lot of disparity within this class, there is a clear increase in income within certain parts of this class.

Overall, the growth in the 1990s has been driven by the export of services, luxury consumption, and non-agricultural investment. Vamsi Vakulabharanam (2010) has conceptualized this as enclave-led growth: a small percentage of urban classes are driving and benefiting from the growth generated by reforms. There is no clear evidence of this growth trickling down to the rural economy and other classes; what is fairly clear is that reform-led growth has increased inequality in India.

Reforms under the NDA Government

When the BJP came to power in 1998, it provided a perfect opportunity for them to bring in reforms – owing to their market-centric philosophy from the beginning – but they did not have the political stability to make radical changes or the longevity required to see it through. The BJP was unable to focus on reforms and instead got mired in the Kargil War, relations with Pakistan, and building up their political cache. The Indian economy did not perform well in this period from 1997 to 2003. According to figures from the Annual Survey of Industry (ASI), there was negative manufacturing growth, while the Index of Industrial Production (IIP) estimates were 5 percent, which was the lowest in any five years between 1980 and 2009. The growth rate of the GDP was also the lowest in any five years since 1980 at around 5.2 percent. Nagaraj (2017) argues that private investment went down during this period due to multiple shocks in the international markets, most importantly the Asian Financial Crisis. A closer look at patterns of capital formation provides empirical evidence for this claim as private corporate investment did indeed have a downward trajectory in this period. This can be taken as evidence of distrust amongst private enterprises about market conditions and failure to see a sustained benefit from reforms. In parallel, the agricultural sector continued to stagnate; one of the issues that highlighted the plight of small farmers was the steady increase in suicides, especially in certain commercial agriculture belts in India – Maharashtra, Andhra Pradesh, and so on. The GDP growth rate was at its lowest since 1980 in 2003 when the BJP finished its first successful tenure at the central government level. They decided to market their political campaign for elections in 2004 to be around the idea of 'India Shining', highlighting the growth achieved and modernization that occurred in India after the introduction of reforms. This campaign spectacularly failed, and a historically unique coalition between the INC and the left came to power in 2004. The failure of the BJP's India Shining campaign highlighted that liberal reforms could not be the economic philosophy to get popular support.

The masses did not perceive any benefit from reforms, and opposition parties mobilized voters based on their frustration against the exclusive nature of liberalization, modernization, and urbanization in India.

Conclusion

Unlike in 1965 or 1970, there was no growth crisis in 2003. However, there were multiple economic trends that indicated unsustainable growth dynamics from the reform process. The GDP growth rate was a robust 5.6 percent (Table 2.1). However, monsoon failure had led to significant negative growth in the agricultural sector, highlighting the lack of investment and increasing inequality in agriculture. This had translated into agrarian distress, increasing migration and urban inequality, and negative voters' perceptions of the BJP's India Shining campaign. Important variables which should have been stimulated by liberal reforms such as industrial growth, investment, FDI, and exports did not show a significant turnaround. The fiscal deficit as a proportion of the GDP had risen to the 1991 level of 5.5 percent (Figure 3.4). The 2004 election marked a turning point in the Indian economy and pushed it towards a new growth regime.

This period started on the back of a severe economic and political crisis, shaping the space for reforms to be introduced. This crisis marked the end of the INC's domination of the government and the efficacy of a centralized industrial policy. The changing political circumstances compelled Indira to start the process of liberal reforms in the early 1980s; reforms had to be introduced by stealth as it was challenging to get popular support for them. Liberal reforms were targeted towards large domestic industries in the 1980s. With changes in governance and licensing procedures to kickstart industrial growth, there was a dearth of big policy changes that strengthened the market. Two contingent events in the late 1980s created conditions for a potential foreign exchange and a BOP crisis in the Indian economy. These were the corruption charges raised against INC minister Rajiv Gandhi which led to a non-INC coalition government being formed at the center and the Gulf War in the Middle East affecting India's BOP situation. The 1991 crisis was exacerbated as India lacked the political stability to introduce policy changes to alleviate the conditions of the crisis. A new INC government came to power in 1991 and was compelled to address the problem, providing them the impetus to introduce liberal reforms in a public manner. Reforms were introduced with great fervor and support from the private media. However, they did not lead to a structural transformation or higher industrial growth through the 1990s.

The Early Liberalization Years

While reforms did translate into growth in certain industries, they contributed to an increase in inequality, and the government was unable to reduce the fiscal deficit or solve the BOP situation. There are multiple explanations for why reforms were slow and not successful in the 1990s.

In this chapter, I have highlighted three specific explanations: (*a*) reforms generated growth and prosperity in urban enclaves which did not trickle down to other sectors and regions; therefore, there was no multiplier effect on aggregate demand to agitate more growth; (*b*) the agricultural sector stagnated in the 1990s, leading to further increase in inequality and farmer distress; and (*c*) there was competition and contestation amongst state governments negotiating the pace and introduction of reforms. These issues culminated in a static economy in the late 1990s and the failure of a stable BJP central government to continue the process of reforms. The year 2003 marks the end of the first period of reforms; political and economic changes after this period carried India onto the path of high growth.

References

Bajoria, R. 2018. *The Story of the Reserve Bank of India.* New Delhi: Rupa Publications.

De, R. 2017. "India's Liberalisation and Newspapers." *Economic and Political Weekly* 52 (27): 7–8.

Jenkins, R. 2000. *Democratic Politics and Economic Reform in India*, vol. 5. New York: Cambridge University Press.

Kohli, A. 2006. "Politics of Economic Growth in India, 1980–2005." *Economic and Political Weekly* 41 (13): 1251–59.

Nagaraj, R. 2003. "Foreign Direct Investment in India in the 1990s." *Economic and Political Weekly* 38 (17): 1701–12.

———. 2017. "Economic Reforms and Manufacturing Sector Growth." *Economic and Political Weekly* 52 (2): 61–68.

NCERT. 2023 (2006). *Indian Economic Development.* https://ncert.nic.in/textbook.php?keec1=3-10. Accessed on September 20, 2022.

Rao, M. J., and S. Storm. 2000. "Distribution and Growth in Indian Agriculture." In *The Indian Economy: Major Debates since Independence,* edited by T. J. Byres, 193–248. New York: Oxford University Press.

Singh, Manmohan. 1991. *Budget Speeches: Union Budget.* July 24. https://www.indiabudget.gov.in/bspeech.php. Accessed on September 9, 2022.

The Hindu. 1991a. "Loss of Economic Sovereignty." Chennai, July 24, 8.

———. 1991b. "Politician vs Economist: Sabotage from Within Inevitable." Chennai, July 17, 6.

———. 1991c. "Warning Note on the IMF Remedy." Chennai, July 20, 8.

———. 1992. "A Structural Reforms Budget." Chennai, March 31, 9.

Times of India. 1991a. "An Agenda for Economic Revival." Delhi, July 4, 8.

———. 1991b. "Budget Speech." Delhi, July 23, 1.

———. 1991c. "Call to Open Up the Economy on All Fronts." Delhi, July 4, 8.

Vakulabharanam, V. 2010. "Does Class Matter? Class Structure and Worsening Inequality in India." *Economic and Political Weekly* 45 (29): 67–76.

5

Maturity of Reforms in the UPA Years
2004–13

How Was the UPA Different from Other Coalition Governments?

The UPA, which formed the central government after elections in 2004, was a unique coalition built on the back of secularist opposition to the BJP government. The INC won slightly more Lok Sabha seats than the BJP but gained powerful coalition partners to get a clear majority. The three largest coalition partners were the left with 43 seats, Uttar Pradesh-based Samajwadi Party with 36 seats, and the Bahujan Samaj Party with 19 seats. A few powerful regional parties also supported the coalition, such as the Telangana Rashtriya Samiti in Andhra Pradesh, the DMK from Tamil Nadu, and the National Congress Party from Maharashtra. Coalition governments had become the norm in the 1990s, but the UPA was different from the earlier coalitions in composition. First, the main opposition party, the BJP, had a significant number of seats which gave more impetus for the coalition members to stick together. Second, few of the coalition members had significant seats in the Lok Sabha, making them an important part of the coalition. Third, the coalition member had different political and ideological stances which meant that there was no straightforward economic plank which they could agree upon. These differences determined the mode of policymaking under the UPA government.

Ruparelia (2005) reviews theories about coalition politics and argues that there is a consensus regarding principles that lead to successful coalitions: parties that share policy goals are more likely to form a coalition, and diverse coalitions that fail to devise explicit pacts to accommodate their differences are vulnerable to sudden events which may trigger their demise. This knowledge may be common sense, but it foregrounds the fact that the UPA coalition was not a match of ideologies or political mandate but one of convenience – based on keeping the BJP out of government. But for the INC, to make the coalition work would require keeping members happy through cabinet berths, including partners in policy discussions and finding a plank on which everyone agrees.

124   A History of Economic Policy in India

The author adds that historical failures of coalition governments – of the Janta Dal in 1977, the V. P. Singh government in 1989, the NDA in 1996 – faced severe cleavages which could not be overcome. In 2009, the UPA came to power again. However, the INC had won a majority of seats in Lok Sabha and did not require the coalition partners in the same way as in 2004.

Common Minimum Program

The UPA followed two institutional mechanisms to make the coalition inclusive and effective: the Common Minimum Program (CMP) and the National Advisory Council (NAC). After winning the elections, the UPA government introduced a CMP to indicate the areas of priority for this government. The CMP was different from the INC election manifesto and was drafted after consulting all the coalition partners. The CMP provided a framework for deciding the direction of policies under the UPA government based on a broad consensus amongst coalition partners. It was primarily rhetoric rather than a policy document, meant to brand and differentiate UPA policies from previous governments, especially the NDA. But it is of analytical significance if one is to understand how the process of introduction of liberal reforms was different under the UPA than the previous INC governments.

The presidential speech in the Rajya Sabha on June 7, 2004, by A. P. J. Abdul Kalam introducing the UPA government and its policies stated, "This calls for speeding up economic reforms that ushered the country into rapid economic reforms." He further added that "the reforms will have a human face and will ensure that the benefits flowing from reforms reach the urban poor and rural areas, where the majority of people live." This quotation is in stark contrast to Manmohan Singh's budget speech which did not make any link between reforms and inequality or the BJP's India Shining campaign. Commentators have linked this position of the UPA government to the influence of left parties and other regional parties which had an agricultural backward caste voter base. The first phase of reforms had led to increased urban inequality, agrarian stagnation, and farmer distress. Therefore, it became important for the INC to qualify reforms by addressing their costs on marginalized classes. The CMP covers many themes but says little in terms of specific economic reforms, especially regarding industry, trade, and finance – three key themes in the 1991 budget. Instead, it is focused on policy changes in agriculture and identifying different marginalized groups that need to be assisted by government policy, such as backward castes, forest dwellers and tribals, women, the disabled, and workers in the unorganized sector.

It also lists basic needs that UPA policies would address, including health, education, employment, housing, sanitation, and access to loans. The most significant point was the inclusion of two innovative social policies, namely the National Rural Employment Guarantee Act (NREGA), 2005, and the Right to Information (RTI) Act, 2005. The CMP brands policies under the UPA focused on social distribution and poverty alleviation.

National Advisory Council

Another institution created by the UPA was the NAC, a government policy development forum created and headed by the INC president, Sonia Gandhi. It comprised academics, former bureaucrats and civil servants, and social activists. It was not surprising that the UPA did not choose Sonia as prime minister as it would not have been acceptable to its coalition partners and would have been heavily criticized by the opposition. The NAC provided an institutional mechanism through which Sonia could still influence the policymaking process and participate in negotiations with coalition members in the UPA. However, the NAC was equally important in bringing non-political actors in direct contact with the policymaking machinery. The NAC could only make recommendations and did not have any legislative powers to enforce them, but Sonia's presence meant that they wielded significant influence.

The NAC was to play a crucial role in the INC's attempt to give "reforms a human face": create a set of social policies as well as mechanisms that made the government accountable to complement the inequitable process of liberal reforms. The NAC provided a forum through which the UPA enlisted civil society organizations in the drafting of social policies. I will discuss some of the crucial social policies introduced and the role of civil society activists and organizations in drafting later in this chapter. It is worth mentioning that UPA I's success at introducing social policies has been connected to the success of the NAC in linking non-political actors to the policymaking process (Khera 2013). This impetus, however, ran out of steam as the INC became the majority party and did not have to accommodate the demands of coalition members in UPA II.

An additional step to ensure the successful working of the UPA coalition government was the appointment of Manmohan Singh as prime minister. While Manmohan was not presented as the prime minister candidate in the INC's election campaign, he emerged as the consensual candidate as he lacked a political base and was not considered a political threat by coalition leaders or to the political ambitions of younger power brokers in the INC. Manmohan had a good working relationship with Sonia, allowing her to influence central government strategies and policies without a ministerial post. Crucially, Manmohan had been the face of economic reforms in India and was well received by both domestic capital and industrialists as well as foreign economic institutions. His image fit with the idea of a progressive, reform-minded government committed to themes of social equity and distribution. These steps to make governance and policymaking more inclusive contributed to the success of the UPA government.

The Economy under the UPA

The Indian economy surged to a 7.94 percent growth rate in the last year of the NDA government and achieved the highest growth rate in any regime in this period at 7.52 percent (Table 2.1). This was comparable to the fastest-growing economies in global history. Even more impressive was the fact that this was achieved amidst the global financial crisis of 2008, which led to significant stagnation in world economy. This regime benefited from the introduction of reforms over the last two decades and grew at an average of 7.5 percent, higher than any year or period since the introduction of reforms in 1980. In the rest of the chapter, I will first discuss the macroeconomic dynamics that drove growth in this period and then discuss the policies that contributed to them.

This period was driven by 10.53 percent growth in investment and 13.8 percent growth in exports (Table 2.2), benefiting from greater embeddedness of the economy in global markets. The surge in investment came mainly through private corporate investment – registered companies. The increase in private corporate investment (Figure 4.1), which became the largest component of investment in 2006, was indicative of the optimism amongst large industries regarding the prospect of reforms under the UPA. This translated into an impressive manufacturing growth of 7.91 percent. Within manufacturing, the fastest growth was in the capital goods industry at 9.7 percent and consumer durables at 9.8 percent, in stark contrast to basic and heavy industries which drove growth in previous regimes (Nagaraj 2017, 64). However, this did not lead to any structural change in the economy: the share of industry in total GDP remained at 27 percent in 2013 (Nagaraj 2017, 62), and the industry employed less than 10 percent of the employed population.

Trade reforms led to a surge in exports and imports, leading to a steady deterioration of the BOP. The increase in exports was promising, especially as India had tapped into the global commercial services market and its share of global trade in commercial services increased from 1 percent to 3.5 percent from 2000 to 2014 (Nagaraj 2017, 62). However, the gains in exports did not drive the country's growth rate as had been the case with the East Asian tigers. China's contribution to manufacturing trade in the world doubled from 7 percent to 15 percent from 2000 to 2010, while India managed to increase its share from 1 percent to 2 percent in the same period. These measures are indicative that exports did not drive India's growth rate in the way it had done in other successful East Asian economies (Nagaraj 2017, 63).

Why Manufacturing Sector Growth Was Not Sustainable in This Period

Nagaraj (2017) has argued that the surge in exports and investment in this period was unsustainable. He attributed the increased growth dynamics in this regime to the Special Economic Zone Act (SEZA), 2005. I will discuss the SEZA in more detail later in this chapter, but fundamentally through the SEZA, the government was able to introduce a set of policies that concentrated growth in certain regions and industries and maximized growth potential while circumventing political obstacles. The introduction of reforms through the SEZA and a complementary set of mechanisms to ensure their efficacy led to a surge in private corporate investments, encouraged FDI, and growth in imports and exports. Bhaduri (2008) and Levien (2012) argue that the SEZA, which was meant to promote investment in industrial infrastructure and exports, instead became a mode of "predatory growth" where private developers were more interested in maximizing the value of real estate rather than leading to sustained industrial development. The SEZA and how it impacted the economy will be described in more detail later in this chapter.

One of the primary motivations for the SEZA was to attract FDI. However, Nagaraj (2017) argues that most of the FDI in this period was speculative and did not lead to a transfer of technology or improvements in productive capacities. FDI comes in multiple forms, and India attracted it largely in the form of investment funds such as venture capital, private equity, and hedge funds. The most important vehicle of FDI in India was private equities whose objective is to acquire underperforming and undervalued assets, restructure, and improve them over three to five years and then sell them for a higher valuation. The majority of FDI was coming to India in search of fast profits rather than long-term development. This stands in stark contrast to the East Asian tigers like South Korea where the government enticed and integrated FDI into the economy through incentives.

Nagaraj suggests that while growth in investment, FDI, and net exports were a vindication of liberal reform policy, there were four deeper structural issues in the economy that prevented this dynamic of growth from being sustainable. First, the agricultural sector continued to stagnate through this period, achieving average growth of 3.5 percent (Nagaraj 2017, 65), and could not provide a growing market for industrial goods or surplus to be invested as industrial capital. Reinvestment of surplus capital from agriculture and absorption of cheap excess labor provided the backbone of development in First World countries such as Britain and Russia. Second, since liberalization, public investment in infrastructure did not keep pace with industrial requirements, in stark contrast to Nehruvian policy. Fixed investment in infrastructure as a percentage of the GDP hovered around 6–8 percent from 1991 to 2014 (Nagaraj 2017, 65). Nagaraj has argued that after the global financial crisis, public investment in infrastructure was even more necessary as the private corporate sector was mired in debts and the banking sector was stuck with non-performing assets. Third, one of the big differences in the industrial environment in China and India is access to long-term capital necessary for expansion or improvement in productive capacity. After reforms in 1991, financial institutions such as IDBI and ICICI were turned into commercial banks, resulting in a shortening of loan maturities and drying up of funds for long-term investment. The domestic debt market was expected to fill this vacuum but had failed to do so. Lastly, there were no reforms to provide incentives for research and development. In 1996, both China and India spent 0.6 percent of their GDP on research and development (R&D). By 2011, China had tripled its R&D spending to 1.8 percent of its GDP, while India was still at 0.8 percent of the GDP (Nagaraj 2017, 67). One of the key reasons for this was that in pre-reform India, licenses to import technology and capital were conditional on setting up domestic R&D units. After reforms, firms did not have to make this effort while foreign firms had no incentive to set up R&D units in India. In summary, the SEZA provided the platform for growth in this regime, but this did not translate into industrialization or an increase in the share of global trade.

Government Spending Troubles and Fiscal Responsibility and Budget Management Act of 2003

Government final consumption expenditure (GFCE) (Table 2.2) was an important driver of growth in this regime. GFCE grew at 7.31 percent in this period, which is higher than any other period – it is worth looking at the composition of this increased expenditure to understand how it impacted the economy. GFCE includes revenue expenditures of the government, such as wages and salaries to government employees, revenue expenditures in defense, interest payment, subsidies, expenditures on social programs such as the NREGA, and so on. Since, the Great Depression, fiscal stimulus has been the policy of choice for driving growth, especially at a time when the economy is stagnating. However, since the 1970s government debt measured through fiscal deficit became an important variable in the economy: de-colonized nations took commercial loans to fund development. However, failure to repay debts threatened their hard-fought sovereignty. Many economies in the Global South had to accept IMF conditions to get assistance to repay loans.

In India, government spending became an increasingly important driver of growth over the 1970s and 1980s, culminating in the fiscal crisis in 1991. Gross fiscal deficit measures the degree of overspending by the government or indicates an excess of expenditure. In 1990–91, the gross fiscal deficit was 7.61 percent of the GDP (Lalvani 2009, 57) – the highest it has been since independence. After taking IMF loans in 1991–92, the government took various measures to cut spending, including disinvestment of public enterprises, reducing capital investment, and tax reforms to improve revenue collection. This saw a fall in fiscal deficit over the 1990s but it ballooned back to 5.28 percent of the GDP in the last year of NDA. It was in light of the rearing head of fiscal deficit that the government introduced the Fiscal Responsibility and Budget Management (FRBM) Act, 2003, which sought to make government expenditure sustainable and de-linked from political considerations.

Under the FRBM Act, the government was committed to keeping the gross fiscal deficit (GFD) to GDP ratio at 3 percent and reducing revenue deficit, defined as revenue income minus revenue expenditure, to zero in three years. Under the UPA regime, neither was the government able to maintain its commitment to meeting the FRBM Act targets nor was the pattern of spending an encouraging one from a developmental perspective. The government reduced the GFD-to-GDP ratio to below 3 percent by 2006–07 due to a significant increase in revenue collection, especially direct taxes on the back of faster growth. The government also steadily reduced expenditure by bringing down capital investment. Government capital expenditure as a percentage of the GDP reduced from 3.84 percent in 2002–03 to 1.8 percent in 2004–05 and averaged 1.92 percent over this period (Lalvani 2009, 57). Public investment has historically played an important role in complementing private investment by funding public infrastructure and basic industries. In a capital-scarce nation like India, a fall in public investment had multiple detrimental developmental outcomes.

The government was forced to inject fiscal stimulus into the economy in the aftermath of the global financial crisis of 2008, especially because it affected the exports and IT industries. The government was unable to reach its FRBM Act target, averaging a 5.24 percent GFD-to-GDP ratio under the UPA II government. Lalvani (2009) argues that the inability to hit the FRBM Act targets is indicative of fiscal irresponsibility in the government. The increased expenditure of the government stimulated aggregate demand and GDP growth but did not necessarily translate into better developmental outcomes. One of the biggest increases in expenditure came in the form of subsidies, which grew from 1 percent of the GDP in the 1990s to 1.4 percent under UPA I to averaging 2.3 under UPA II. Subsidies (Figure 4.3), especially agricultural, are used by politicians to compensate aggrieved farmers, especially after bad monsoons or to build vote banks. However, subsidies distort the market price and reduce the incentive to innovate, if the same amount spent on agricultural or infrastructural investment would create more sustainable growth and affect a larger group of farmers. Another component contributing to increasing expenditure was the hike in wages of government employees based on the recommendation of the Sixth Central Pay Commission. This measure has a negligible impact on developmental outcomes as the majority of the poor in India do not have access to government jobs.

By far, the clearest indication that increased government expenditure has not translated to developmental outcomes is that the expenditure on social services was 1.2 percent of the GDP. In 2008–09, education stood at a mere 0.44 percent of the GDP, while health's share was 0.11 percent. This is a far cry from other countries like China which invest more than 1 percent of the GDP in education alone (Lalvani 2009, 58). The share of expenditures on economic services has fallen since the 1990s. The share of expenditure on agriculture is a mere 1.5 percent of the GDP, which is meant to serve 70 percent of the population. The share of rural development which accounts for the majority of the population is 0.54 percent (Lalvani 2009, 58). This figure is particularly disappointing given the NREGA expenditures come under rural development and should show a spike in spending. Instead, the NREGA funds have come from reducing expenditure on other rural development schemes. Overall, while government spending has driven growth in the UPA regime, this spending is both fiscally unsustainable and irresponsible.

Informal Labor

Since the introduction of industrial reforms in 1980, the industrial sector has failed to absorb additional labor and provide employment to less than

Maturity of Reforms in the UPA Years

10 percent of the labor population, and most of India's population works in the agricultural or service sector, leading to the phenomenon of jobless growth. The Indian labor market has peculiar characteristics which make employment figures unreliable, such as disguised unemployment and the persistence of the self-employed, and there is little data about trends and patterns of employment, let alone about wage rates and working conditions. This makes studying labor issues in India a difficult and contested phenomenon. But the question of why the growing industrial sector does not absorb labor remains. The answer lies in understanding a distinctive feature in labor markets in developing countries – informality.

The UPA government listed informal labor as an important theme in its CMP and tasked the Sengupta Committee to provide a report on the nature and characteristics of informal employment in the country. In 2007, the report of the National Commission for Enterprise in the Unorganized Sector (NCEUS), headed by the Sengupta Committee, titled "Reports on Conditions of Work and Promotion of Livelihood in the Unorganised Sector," provided undeniable evidence that GDP growth in the Indian economy was not translating into better employment opportunities or higher pay. The report found that 92 percent of all workers in India are employed in the informal sector; the key contribution of this report was to define and identify what is referred to as the informal sector in India. Moreover, 75 percent of employment in industries and services is in the informal sector, and more than 95 percent of employment in agriculture is in the informal sector. There are many definitions of the informal sector; the Indian government had defined all enterprises in India which hire less than 10 workers as unorganized enterprises. However, the NCEUS defined informality as employment without labor rights, job security, or prospects of upward mobility. The largest component of the informal sector – accounting for more than 85 percent of all employment – are small businesses hiring less than five employees, also referred to as petty commodity production. The NCEUS report found that the majority of labor in India – 9 out of 10 workers and businesses – earn just enough to survive, have no protection against illness or accidents, and have no prospects for growth.

The growth and persistence of informal labor in industry is a consequence of industrial policies in India. Glancing backward at the historical development of industrial capitalism in the first world – the UK, France, Russia, and so on – one finds a consistent pattern of development described by renowned economist Arthur Lewis and referred to as the Lewisian transformation. All these countries were agriculture-dominant economies; initially, industries were a small part of the economy, and the agricultural sector in these economies grew by appropriating land from small farmers and tenants, and large landlords monopolized the profits made from commercially developing the agricultural sector and invested it in infant industries, tapping into the global colonial market. As the agricultural sector mechanized, more and more workers got displaced from the land and their traditional way of life and had to migrate to work in the industrial sector, leading to a new mode of living referred to as urbanization and city life. The initial process of industrialization was harsh and brutal for workers. However, as the industrial economies developed and established democracies, workers were able to politically organize and unionize and demand better pay, working conditions, and rights for workers. In all the developed economies, workers gained formal employment rights over the early 20th century and saw steady improvements in their standard of living. However, the process of industrialization and development did not translate into the Lewisian transformation in India.

The informal sector is defined as irregular or casual employment: low pay, lack of prospect of growth or promotion, no legal support, and lack of support for ill health or accidents. More than three quarters of informal labor in India are owners of their enterprise; National Sample Survey (NSS) and other government surveys label such arrangements as self-employed or small businesses, and their working conditions are not discussed as labor issues. However, the NCEUS highlighted how this form of informality is symptomatic of the nature of industrial development in India and comprises some of the poorest and marginalized classes of India. Informal labor in the form of petty business is an important analytical category to understand why industry was unable to absorb more labor.

The informal sector is heterogeneous in form. I will use the categorization of Basole and Basu (2011) and De (2020) to explain what is common in their mode of operation and how the current proliferation of informal business is an outcome of the nature of industrial development in the Indian economy. About a quarter of wage labor in India are casual laborers who are hired without contracts for short-term works; this includes landless laborers working in someone else's field, workers in the service sector (construction, domestic help, delivery boys, waiters, manual laborers, and so on), or daily wage workers in factories. The dominant form of informal labor is in the form of petty businesses or self-subsistence agriculture where there is no divide between owner and worker. These firms can range from self-subsistence agriculture, *kirana* shops, roadside vendors, small retail shops, and petty professionals like electricians and mobile repairers, or vertically linked with larger manufacturing

Maturity of Reforms in the UPA Years

units such as Chikan embroidery in Lucknow, leather shoes in Agra, and cotton textile in Tirrurpur.

Basole and Basu (2011, 62) have used NSS data from 1984 to 2008 to analyze the structure of informal enterprises. They find that the number of informal enterprises started increasing from 1990, indicating a correlation between informality and reforms. Ninety-five percent of rural enterprises and 75 percent of informal urban enterprises hire no external labor: they use family or community-based labor with shared caste or ethnic identity. In urban areas, these enterprises are either involved in sub-contracting or outsourced relations with industries or provide services to employees from these industries. A large part of informal enterprises is embedded within the enclave-led growth economies. Businesses' success depends on their ability to compete in the market; over time, loss-making businesses exit the market and successful businesses expand their scale of production and claim a larger share of the market. Basole and Basu (2011, 66–69) found evidence that the number of informal firms has increased since 1990, but the size of individual firms has remained stagnant. In 2008, a petty producer was generating an annual profit of INR 19,000, and firms with less than five workers were generating annual revenues of INR 120,000. Even if we assume that this sector dealt with black or unaccounted money, these incomes are below the per capita income of metropolitans in India. The incomes made by these firms are comparable to the salary of the lowest strata of the salaried class. This is referred to as the logic of reproduction as opposed to profit; the primary aim of these firms is to maintain their current standard of living.

Basole and Basu (2011, 67–68) found that informal enterprises were embedded in unequal relations with middlemen or contractors and moneylenders. In 2008, 50 percent of petty producers sold their products to other enterprises or middlemen or contractors rather than the final consumer. About 75 percent of enterprises hire equipment from middlemen, 90 percent of enterprises procure their raw materials and product designs from middlemen, and 25 percent of loans in these enterprises come from informal moneylenders. What this data highlights is that informal firms do not grow in size because they are interlocked in unequal contracts with contractors, agents, middlemen, and factories. The producer does not have access to the market, is unable to procure loans, rental equipment, raw material, and designs at a competitive price, and is unable to sell to consumers at a competitive price. Instead, the middlemen siphon off profit made by these firms through higher interest for finance, higher rents for space and equipment, higher prices for raw materials, and lower prices for final goods. There are different arrangements through which petty business gets embedded in unequal relations. However, unequal social relations through caste, gender, and religion play a pivotal role in reproducing these dynamics. There are no laws protecting or directly increasing the bargaining power of these businesses. Moreover, as they are largely migrants from marginalized communities, they are unable to unionize or gain political representation. Liberal reforms have not addressed the needs of informal enterprises. These petty businesses survive by using free family labor and cutting down household expenses to finance production.

Basole and Basu theorize that larger firms benefit by procuring goods and services from the informal sector at a cheaper rate than having to employ their labor. Moreover, petty businesses provide cheap consumer goods and services to employees of larger firms, thereby subsidizing their standard of living and wage requirements. The proliferation of petty businesses without any prospects for growth has contributed to the phenomenon of jobless growth in the manufacturing sector; large firms can outsource the labor-intensive parts of their production and not have to deal with providing competitive wages and provide legally mandated security and benefits.

This twin phenomenon of jobless industrial growth and an increase in the number of informal enterprises is only possible if there is a growing supply of unskilled labor available. This condition exists as a result of failed attempts at land redistribution and the unequalizing effects of the Green Revolution, leading to the steady dispossession or fragmentation of land owned by peasants and small farmers. Stagnation in the agricultural sector and a dearth of redistributive policies led to the immiseration of peasants across the major agricultural belts in India; as peasants got increasingly indebted, they were forced to migrate to the new urban and industrial growth centers in India. Surplus agricultural labor migrates under distress to high-growth enclaves for income to survive and is forced to accept work under adverse terms. Informalization is symptomatic of the nature of industrial growth in India and will remain this way until there are significant policy changes. The industrialization policies in India have encouraged heavy capital-intensive production which primarily employs skilled and managerial labor. Moreover, the social barrier of class and caste has prevented marginal classes from accessing good jobs. As a consequence, workers have been forced to enter the informal sector on adverse terms for survival.

In response to the NCEUS report, the government introduced a group of social security schemes under the Unorganised Workers' Social Security Act, 2008. Under this act, a group of targeted social security schemes was provided to any worker who registers under it. These include life and disability cover, health and maternity benefits, and old age protection covered by central government schemes. State governments were given the mandate to devise schemes for provident funds, employment injury and accident benefits, housing, skill-enhancing, and education schemes. Some of the policies under this act, especially centrally sponsored schemes, have been successful in providing benefits. However, none of these policies alleviate the structural modes through which these enterprises are trapped in unequal relationships with no recourse to upskilling or improving bargaining power. Despite the social policies, industrial policies introduced by the UPA exacerbated the informal labor crisis, especially the SEZA.

SEZA: Decentralizing the Process of Reforms

The most significant reform policy under UPA I was the SEZA introduced in 2005. The main objective of the SEZA was to attract investment in the development of export-oriented infrastructure. The belief was that growth in exports would lead to growth and employment opportunities in other interlinked industries in the economy. India's SEZ policy was based on a series of export enclaves established in Gujarat and Maharashtra in the 1960s, called Export Processing Zones. Under this scheme, private operators managed ports and industrial zones to increase the trading efficiency of certain key exportables, such as gems and jewelry, electronic components, and so on. These zones were exempted from the trade and customs regulations applicable to Indian industry in the 1960s with the hope that Indian traders would have a competitive advantage in the global market. The SEZA also borrowed from the experience of industrial townships such as Jamshedpur, Bhilai, Bokaro, and Rourkela, where a town was created around the needs of an industry. These towns contained all the requirements of the industry and its employees such as easy access to raw materials, infrastructural development, schools, hospitals, and residences. These townships necessitated the creation of specific exemptions from the creation of an elected local government. The experience of carving out geographical regions where different economic regulations were applicable contributed to the formation of the SEZA. Fundamentally, the SEZA follows an export-oriented industrial growth model – external demand drives growth in the economy – which introduces liberal reforms over a limited area, bypassing the political backlash and the various bureaucratic hurdles that affect industrial development. The SEZA allowed for zones to be developed by state governments and private promoters where different rules would be applicable.

The success of the SEZA depends on its instituting mechanisms: the central government eased the process of SEZ allocation by the formation of the Empowered Group of Ministers (EGOM), who coordinated decision-making between cabinet members, coalition partners, and different ministries. The EGOM of the INC consisted of Pranab Mukherjee (defense), P. Chidambaram (finance), Kamal Nath (commerce), Kapil Sibal (science and technology), Dayanidhi Maran (telecommunications), H. R. Bhardwaj (Law), and Montek Singh Ahluwalia (deputy chairman of the PC). While the EGOM could not make regulatory changes, they were equipped with the authority to streamline and create efficiencies in the SEZA process. At the state level, power is vested in the hands of a development committee that is responsible for the overall plans for the SEZ, providing common infrastructure, facilitating the transfer of land parcels, and maintaining civil services such as security, public health, education, and civic amenities. The development committee included representatives of state government and private developers, providing an institutional mechanism for public and private interests to administer the SEZ. The District Committee (DC) had to consult local government officials, but was able to exercise a combination of legislative, executive, and judicial powers. This kind of private control of administrative measures allowed a speed of decision-making that was impossible in the past.

These institutions were a culmination of the decentralization of the reforms process to state governments and the increased partnership between private industry and public agents which had been initiated in the 1980s. Under the SEZA, the process of reforms was democratized or made accessible to the regional industry. SEZs were built on piecemeal reforms introduced in the 1990s by bringing together independent reforms under one institution: deregulating the licensing process, providing tax and other incentives, modes of bypassing the multiple levels of bureaucracy that industries had to deal with, ability to attract foreign investment, and state-level management of reform and space to provide public–private collaboration. We will discuss some of these in more detail, but it is worth reiterating that SEZ allowed bypassing the political challenges of introducing a homogenous set of liberal reforms at the central level.

If industrial policy under Nehruvian and Indira's regime was driven by public enterprise, reforms in 1980 tipped the scale towards private enterprise. The SEZA introduced an arrangement for a partnership between central and state governments, private stakeholders, and industrialists. Historically, high-growth states such as Maharashtra, Tamil Nadu, Andhra Pradesh, Gujarat, Karnataka, and so on, were well placed to take advantage of the

Maturity of Reforms in the UPA Years

dilution of powers available under the SEZA. Regional parties, which had formed governments in this state, were equipped to negotiate the complicated politics of initiating liberal reforms. These states had landed capital and young industrialists who were unable to enter major industries due to large domestic capitalists dominating the central industrial plans. These capitalists were eager to partner with the state government: in many instances, they had been financially assisting the party's efforts. The state government was positioned to control the process of acquiring land, create partnership models with private investors, attract capital to develop infrastructure, borrow from multilateral agencies and private banks, control the bureaucratic regulatory machinery, and negotiate with the stakeholders who get dispossessed due to building SEZ. This was a far cry from the situation in the 1970s and 1980s when industries had to negotiate multiple bureaucratic hurdles through political patronage networks to enter major industries. This arrangement was beneficial for both the state government looking to kickstart regional growth and employment opportunities and develop metropolitans by attracting surplus capital from agriculture which was being invested in speculative ventures such as real estate, informal moneylending, distribution, and small-scale retail.

The Process and Politics that Shaped the SEZA

What does the process of making an SEZ look like? The SEZA instituted a legal framework to create a distinct regulatory zone called an SEZ. Let us take an example of an IT-based SEZ in the Hyderabad–Madhapur area called HITEC (Hyderabad Information Technology and Engineering Consultancy) City to understand the process of building SEZs. An SEZ was founded on the benefit of agglomerative economies: benefits from being in close proximity but also continuous competition leading to dynamic decision-making. Satyam Computers built an SEZ of over 50 acres for the IT industry. This allowed multiple Indian and foreign firms which had backward and forward linkages with IT to get offices in the SEZ. Offices based in the SEZ further benefited from sharing information and contracts with Satyam and having access to IT professionals from around the country migrating to this region for jobs. The Andhra (later Telangana) government attracted investment and built more than 20 SEZs in Rangareddy district, adjacent to Hyderabad, by developing world-class public infrastructure: roads, uninterrupted supply of electricity and power, well-functioning municipal services such as police and garbage disposal, a new airport which was linked by a toll road, and subsidized land to develop high-end housing facility, malls, schools, and other services to cater to the needs of high-income labor in the SEZs. These were meant to both attract skilled labor and create a multiplier growth effect through consumer spending from these high-income individuals. Within a decade of development, Rangareddy transformed from a primarily agricultural area into one of the most urbanized and industrialized regions in the country.

The most visible and politically contested aspect of the SEZA was the process of acquisition of land. The act empowered the government to acquire private agricultural land and redevelop it. While there were variations across states, SEZ developers and governments were economically vested in acquiring land for cheap and increasing the value of the real estate by developing it. SEZs were a real boon for real-estate developers to profit from speculation. However, the SEZA had a substantial socio-political cost; the management of classes that were adversely affected by the plans was important for the long-term viability of these projects. Let us take a hypothetical example to understand why this process was contested: the DC and approval committee identify a piece of land, and the government procures it at the current rate – most of the lands were agricultural lands whose values were determined by an underdeveloped agricultural market in India. Private developers would procure the land for cheap and develop the infrastructure and SEZ facilities and purchase additional land near the SEZ. Once the area was developed, the value of these lands would compound, and the developers would make large profits at the cost of the farmers who were not compensated for the full value of the land.

The land was acquired through the Land Acquisition Act, created in 1894, which justified colonial appropriation of land; its relevance was limited in India's current political set-up. Under this act, land could be acquired for the purposes of public use, and the state had to reimburse the affected party fairly. The state in cohort with local vested groups like *pyravikaar*s – Telegu word for influence peddlers in Andhra whose main function was to sow doubt and fear in property owners to sell the land without resistance – would convince the stakeholders to sell their land and prevent collective bargaining. There was a significant political backlash in multiple regions: Nandigram and POSCO SEZs in Orissa are two examples that captured the national imagination.

The political resistance in multiple states came through civil service organizations that took up the cause of the affected parties. The resistance was articulated on different grounds but had three common principles: First, how is acquiring lands for the benefit of the private corporate considered public interest? Second, what is the "fair" price for land – given that the land is valued on its current use as agricultural land, but its value balloons after it is

Maturity of Reforms in the UPA Years

developed as industrial or urban land? Third, there are many communities that do not own land but depend on this land for livelihood and identity. The lost value of these aggrieved parties should be accommodated in the evaluation of land. Protests against SEZs were scooped up by the national media and weaponized to critique the policies of the UPA.

The UPA responded to the widespread criticism by initially amending the Land Acquisition Act and introducing the Land Acquisition and Rehabilitation and Resettlement (LARR) Bill in 2011. This was one of multiple rights-based social redistribution bills introduced by the INC which will be discussed in more detail later in this chapter. There were three features of the bill which are significant, concerning the evolution of India's approach to land acquisition. The bill acknowledged that "public purpose" could not be used to justify the forceful acquisition of private land. The bill articulated that the public benefit of appropriated land had to be balanced against the social cost. The bill further redefined the conceptual underpinnings of compensation for the land: the cost of the land should not be the value of the loss of individual landowners but also include local stakeholders whose economic well-being is connected to the land – this includes tenants, sharecroppers, artisans, tribals, and traditional forest dwellers. The second key feature of the bill was the specification of livelihood rights and mechanisms to make the state accountable. Under this bill, citizen participation was invited at multiple points of the land acquisition and rehabilitation process. A land parcel can be identified for appropriation only after consultation with the Gram Sabha. Views of affected families were to be expressed through a social impact assessment report created by an expert group which should contain two non-official social scientists. The expert group was empowered to judge whether the project meets the needs of the larger public interest. Third, the bill created dedicated institutions to exercise accountability for the implementation of its provision. This bill made a substantial contribution to the changing discourse on economic rights. It also demonstrated the UPA government's commitment to engaging with stakeholders alienated from the reform process.

Reforms with a Human Face: Rights-Based Social Policy Introduced by the UPA

The UPA had promised reforms with a human face and, parallel to economic reforms, initiated a host of rights-based social distribution policies which were meant to compensate the masses who were not benefiting from reforms. This was the largest scale of the introduction of social policies in India, since the introduction of poverty alleviation schemes under Indira's prime ministership in the 1970–80s. Over its two tenures, the UPA introduced many rights-based policies, such as the RTI Act of 2005, the NREGA of 2005, the Forest Rights Act 2006, the Right to Education Act of 2009, and the National Food Security Act (NFSA) of 2011. Before describing and evaluating these policies, it is important to understand the common principles upon which they were founded. These policies are rights-based: they entitle people to receive certain social benefits, and it is incumbent upon the government to deliver them.

This is in stark contrast to the delivery-based social policies of earlier times: social policy since independence, and especially since Indira's government in 1972, has identified marginalized groups and provided targeted benefits. This was an outcome of limited resources available for social distribution – especially in the early stages of heavy industrialization. Those identified were the poorest income groups – referred to as Antyodhya ration card holders – and received subsidized rations and essentials through the PDS. Further, certain groups within the poorer classes such as women, especially lactating mothers, the elderly, the disabled, and forest dwellers were provided with further benefits such as highly subsidized healthcare, access to loans to build houses, and access to additional nutrition, care, and social security. While in principle these policies made sense, their execution was poor due to the complexity and inefficiencies of India's bureaucratic process. State and local governments were responsible for identifying the poorest and marginal sections of the population but would often allocate social resources to people with shared ethnic links for vote garnering. As a consequence, marginalized groups such as migrants, forest dwellers, SCs, single-women households and the disabled were ignored – they had no political voice. Moreover, due to multiple opportunities for corruption and pilferage, the targeted population rarely received their due. I will talk about this in more nuance when discussing the changes made to the PDS in the next chapter, but generations of activists and political groups have raised concerns about the failure of the government to identify and deliver social goods.

It is in this context that rights-based social policies were recommended by social activists, as they empower the masses to demand their rights and make the government accountable. Manor and Jenkins (2016, 16), two of the leading commentators on the politics of reforms in liberalized India, have referred to such rights-based policies introduced by the UPA as governance rights which confer "the right to participate in purpose-built governance institutions the delivery of particular benefits essential to the fulfillment of basic social and economic rights." These confer on the citizen the right to engage in making officials accountable for delivering state guarantees. These rights are different

Maturity of Reforms in the UPA Years

from civil and political rights in India, which circumscribe political action as choosing representatives, forming associations, or engaging in political speech. This new articulation of rights-based policies assigns a key role to civic associations.

The Infrastructure for Rights-Based Social Policy
Unique Identification Authority of India (UIDAI) and Identification

Three key institutions formed the infrastructural backbone to scaffold rights-based social policies in India. The first step was identifying who was entitled to these rights and empowering them in the spirit of the law. This was achieved by the establishment of the UIDAI in 2009, a statutory authority that provided a unique ID to each citizen of the country, popularly known as the Aadhaar card. Further, the UIDAI digitized their data, creating the foundation for digitally identifying and delivering subsidies and benefits to the citizens of India. After much debate, the Supreme Court made Aadhaar voluntary and not a requirement to gain government benefits. However, Aadhaar allowed a huge section of the marginalized, illiterate population to get official recognition as residents of the country – especially given the challenges of getting identification cards within an inefficient and corrupt bureaucratic machinery. There have been multiple challenges to the legality of Aadhaar by the civil rights movement with legitimate concerns about privacy rights. These discussions are still ongoing in the court of law.

The Role of Civil Society and Non-Governmental Organizations (NGOs)

The second key institution was the inclusion of activists in the policymaking process. The UPA-formed NAC included activists who have been deeply involved in contesting key social issues in India, such as Jean Drèze, Aruna Roy, Harsh Mander, Deep Joshi, and so on. The inclusion of activists in a politically influential group brought creditability to the UPA government's promise of "reforms with a human face." It also provided the UPA a mechanism to pressurize other parts of the policymaking machinery through NGOs and the private media. Since independence, a parallel set of non-politicized organizations have played an important role in demanding government accountability to social redistributive policies. The nature of these organizations has evolved from religious and charitable organizations, extensions of political parties such as Gandhians who worked for the most marginalized, people organized around occupation or caste protesting for rights, or even more militant institutions seeking radical structural changes at the grassroots. There was a clear need for civil society organizations to bring accountability to the government and especially the bureaucratic apparatus which delivers social goods because the Indian bureaucratic system was complex, opaque, controlled by elite classes and castes, and had no mechanism of accountability. This had allowed the vast political and bureaucratic apparatus in India to work the delivery machinery of redistributive policies for personal benefit.

The liberalization and privatization of the Indian economy were meant to break the monopoly nexus of politicians and bureaucrats in controlling scarce social resources. However, liberalization did not produce any alternate mechanism to achieve this. Instead, the 1980s and 1990s saw the rise of a new variant of NGOs which were organized like corporate firms – with daily staff, offices, budgets, management structure, and clearly defined area of work. Increasingly, a cadre of the educated middle class – including bureaucrats unhappy with the official machinery, academics, activists, and a slowly growing class of professionals – were part of modernizing NGOs. It was important for NGOs to avoid funding from political actors due to conflict of interest. Therefore, they were able to tap into the increasing amount of developmental aid channeled through multilateral institutions such as the World Bank, the UK government's Department for International Development (DFID), and the Ford Foundation. These agencies had been transferring funds and resources to achieve better developmental outcomes and delivery of basic goods. This transfer of resources was meant to compensate for the socio-economic collateral of colonization.

Private media had emerged in the early 1990s with the growth of televisions and deregulation of the telecommunication sector. However, most of the news media was interested in national or urban news which would be of interest to its clientele. NGOs increasingly found ways to make a public display of protest to get visibility from private news media. The traditional instruments of public protest such as *dharna*s, rallies, and strikes were transformed into more interactive modes of protest, such as public hearings christened by the Mazdoor Kisan Shakti Sangathan (MKSS) as Jan Sunwai (more on that later). Such political events created interest in important social issues amongst a wider audience and provided more opportunities for academics and educated activists to write in newspapers and frame the issue. Moreover, NGOs increasingly had legal and economic counsel to provide documentary evidence for their claims. They were able to anticipate attempts by political leaders to dilute the criticism against the government. The rise of modern NGOs, professional social workers, and the growing power of the private media to frame policy discussion created

Maturity of Reforms in the UPA Years

the conditions for the UPA to include activists and civil society in social policymaking decisions.

Right to Information Act, 2005

If Aadhaar provided a solution to the politics of identification in India, the RTI Act, 2005, provided the legal foundation to bring accountability to governing institutions and was the third important institution in the creation of a new ecosystem of rights. Fundamentally, the RTI Act allows any citizen of India to request information from a public authority – both central and state – and get a response in 30 days. This right is extended not only to official documents but also to records, notes, data, and documents regarding the provision of government services. The RTI Act is meant to promote transparency and accountability in the working of the government and provides a mechanism to tackle corruption deeply embedded in the Indian polity.

The interpretation of RTI in India is different from the Western liberal discourse around it. Jenkins and Goetz (1999, 608) point out that amongst advocates of human rights in the West, RTI is not considered an important right. Rights advocates are first and foremost concerned with first-generation rights such as the right to live, the right to expression, voting rights, and the right to a fair trial. After the establishment of basic rights, the focus is on the second generation of rights, such as the right to food, the right to education, the right to fair livelihood, and so on. The RTI is considered a third generation of rights required by society after the establishment of first- and second-generation rights. Moreover, RTI advocates in the West believe that it has low practical relevance for countries where the masses are illiterate and do not have the means to actualize this right into social change. Other criticisms of RTI were that it had limited efficacy to fight corruption, and citizens were not politically mature to use this right prudently; it will instead lead to wastage of time in the bureaucratic machinery or that it is just an accounting practice and cannot be used to engage in questions about the path of development or larger philosophy shaping policy.

Ideas of rights possess a degree of flexibility and do not have to be defined in the way they had been in the first world. The content of RTI and the role it was meant to play were re-engineered to suit the requirements of the Indian polity. Jenkins wisely notes that "the nature and utility of rights are linked to the process through which they are obtained." The Supreme Court granted that RTI was a fundamental right in 1982. However, the content of this right and how it was to be actualized was not decided. The MKSS, a grassroots-level organization based in Rajasthan, had been at the forefront of shaping the campaign demanding RTI. The MKSS worked around issues faced by the poor and the marginalized, and in the late 1980s they focused their activism on the failure of state governments to enforce minimum wage regulation in drought-relief work and the availability of subsidized foods through the PDS. As they investigated the reasons for poor delivery of government services, they discovered that corruption and malpractices existed at multiple levels: inflated estimates for public work projects, use of low-standard material and over-billing by contractors, fake names or missing names in the labor list, pilfering of stocks by PDS shop owners to be sold on the open market, and so on.

It was impossible to calculate who was to blame and to what extent for this malfeasance without having access to official documentation: about how much funds have been allocated, how much provision is provided for labor payment, the quantity of subsidized goods allocated under the PDS scheme, and so on. The MKSS was unable to break the veil of secrecy between local politicians, officials, and contractors. Instead, they pivoted their campaign towards a legislative claim for official documents which can be used to place blame for malfeasance and demand specific action from government officials. The MKSS used an innovative method for putting pressure on government officials through collective action. They procured some of the official documents through sympathetic bureaucrats. They organized a public hearing – called Jan Sunwai – where they shared details of public records and official expenditure accounts and invited local people to testify to highlight the discrepancy between public accounts and their own experiences of working on public works projects. These proceedings were overseen by respected individuals from within and outside the area – instead of it being overseen by elected representatives or Gram Sabha members who could pressurize locals not to participate. The *sunwai* was highly successful as it both exposed the scale of malfeasance and the multiple actors involved in it. The public display of this hearing is a way of putting pressure on politicians to take action, and the support of private media ensured that officials were hesitant to disrupt the event. However, it was difficult to reproduce this format across regions and issues as it was very hard to procure copies of government documents.

The MKSS pivoted its campaign to introduce legislative reforms in Rajasthan to allow locals to procure government documents. This campaign captured the imagination of other grassroots organizations who started supporting this demand. The increasing mobilization of organizations in this movement led to the formation of the National Campaign for People's Right to Information (NCPRI) in August 1996, which included activists, journalists, lawyers, retired civil servants, and academics who would focus

Maturity of Reforms in the UPA Years

on getting an appropriate law enacted to cover the whole country. The basic premise of RTI was accepted by the Rajasthan government, and a few other state governments followed. However, there was consistent resistance and backlash from the central government at various levels. The NCPRI was at the forefront along with NGOs in different regions to create awareness and get public support, educate the masses, and eventually be involved in the drafting of the bill. The bill took many different forms. However, it was the ability of the NAC under Sonia Gandhi's leadership that managed to channel the energies of activists to legislate an acceptable draft of RTI which covers both central and state governments. RTI in India was perceived as a participatory social audit that could be used as an aggressive tool to achieve accountability from local governments. The interpretation of RTI as a social participatory audit allows activists to highlight the multifaceted day-to-day exercise of corruption and forged a tool through which they could be tackled structurally rather than focusing on individual acts of corruption. RTI's primary purpose was to make the government accountable for the delivery of basic services. Therefore, it was catalytic of the social rights policies that arose under the UPA government.

The National Rural Employment Guarantee Act, 2005

Along with RTI, the most impactful social policy introduced under the UPA government was the NREGA. The NREGA Bill, passed on September 5, 2005, guarantees 100 days of paid unskilled manual work to any member who volunteers from a rural household. The worker is paid minimum wages, and if a state is unable to provide a job within 15 days, the applicant is entitled to daily unemployment insurance. A right to work or employment guarantee act is not a novel policy in India, and a whole host of them have been introduced by various central and state governments: the Jawahar Rozgar Yojna in 1989, the Employment Assurance Scheme in 1993, and the Jawahar Gram Samridhi Yojana in 1999. The most successful right-to-work program was the Maharashtra Employment Guarantee Scheme introduced in 1977, which provided the foundational principles of the NREGA.

The history of the formation of the NREGA has similarities to RTI, and I will not go into great detail. The roots of the activist movement can be traced back to the MKSS who were trying to ensure payment of minimum wages in drought-relief work provided to aggrieved parties in Rajasthan. In its original form, the demand for employment guarantee legislation in Rajasthan fought by about 50 grassroots organizations – called the Akal Sangharsh Samiti – was focused on the right to employment for drought-affected people.

The Samiti's *dharna* held in June–July 2001 in Jaipur demanding an extension of the drought-relief employment program captured the imagination of other activist groups fighting for food availability for the poor. A coalition of activists filed a public interest litigation (PIL) in the Supreme Court in 2001 that states were denying people the right to live by not implementing adequate nutrition and food programs. In response to the PIL, the Supreme Court gave an interim order that across the country the benefits distributed through government nutrition schemes should be treated as legally entitled schemes which would be supervised by a court-appointed commissioner. Buoyed by their success in gaining a legislative guarantee based on the right to food, the Samiti, the MKSS, and other activist groups began pressurizing parties to include employment guarantees in the election manifesto. There is some evidence that Sonia was herself lobbying for such a scheme, and with key INC members like Manmohan Singh coming on board, it was included as part of the party's national election manifesto.

A crucial role was played by the NAC in drafting the bill and pushing it through the parliamentary mechanism. The focus of the draft was to operationalize the right to work in such a way that it could combat the well-established shortcomings of the public service delivery mechanism, such as lack of transparency, lack of mechanisms to combat corruption, and political actors diverting funds from this program. The NREGA Bill built on the success of RTI to conceive of a mechanism through which poor people along with activist allies could be legislatively empowered to demand entitlements from the government. This principle led to the creation of one of the NREGA's most distinguishing features: a specialized implementation and oversight apparatus which was headed by the Central Employment Guarantee Council (CEGC) which included representatives of central and state government and civil society representatives – including non-elected officials and NGO workers. The CEGC was empowered to undertake an evaluation of various schemes under the NREGA by collecting statistics from the rural economy. An infrastructure of official posts was created to build supervision and accountability of the program at various levels, such as a state employment council, an officer in charge of implementing the program at the district level, and the creation of a national employment guarantee fund to ensure the availability of funds for the program. The NREGA made two significant contributions to the Indian economy. By guaranteeing minimum wages for 100 days, it ensured a minimum social safety net and boosted the bargaining power of the poorest in determining wages and working arrangements. Second, the NREGA work was focused on building assets in rural areas which served the needs of the community.

Maturity of Reforms in the UPA Years

This allowed stakeholders, including traditionally marginalized classes at the village level, to be involved in economic decision-making.

Social Rights Policies Introduced by the UPA

RTI and the NREGA were both parts of the CMP and provided a structure for introducing other rights-based social entitlement programs. For diverse reasons, each of these policies faced different kinds of successes and failures. The Right to Education Act, 2009, made education a fundamental right for every child aged 6 to 14. Under this act, the government is mandated to provide free and compulsory education to every child of that age group. This brought a gamut of education policies under one rubric. An annual citizen- and volunteer-led survey of primary schools called the Annual Status of Education Report (ASER) was set up in 2005 by NGOs in civil society to monitor the government's endeavors to fulfill the mandate of the right to education. As the government successfully achieved universal primary education, NGOs and the ASER have been constantly working with local governments to improve the delivery of education, nutrition, and awareness to the children of India. While there is significant diversity within outcomes in regions, educational outcomes have improved throughout the country since the inception of the right to education.

Another landmark policy introduced by the government was the Forest Rights Act (FRA), 2006. This act, which was part of the CMP, recognizes and vests forest rights to Scheduled Tribes (STs) and other traditional forest dwellers. This along with the LARR was a move to give land rights to people who have been traditionally dependent on land but due to historic injustices did not gain a legal right to the land. This population has faced significant costs of displacement and alienation due to large government projects, mining, and deforestation. The FRA provided provisions for social and participatory audits, and recognizing the legitimacy of claim on the land by local dwellers was a necessary first step to finding a sustainable solution to the cost of development projects on the environment and dwellers dependent on forest resources. For multiple reasons, including lack of emphasis from the UPA government, the FRA did not achieve the same success as the NREGA and the RTI Act.

The UPA government managed to pass the landmark National Food Security Act (NFSA), 2013. The NFSA was an attempt to consolidate several programs which entitled people to food across the country, including the mammoth PDS, nutrition for children and lactating mothers under the Integrated Child Development Scheme (ICDS), and mid-day meals in government schools. The NFSA legally entitles around 75 percent of the

148 A History of Economic Policy in India

population of India to subsidized grains under the PDS and provides provisions to ensure that state governments and local officials are accountable for this. In the past, the success of the PDS had been dependent on state government and local authorities. However, the NFSA brought it under the rubric of rights rather than welfare schemes. A broader discussion of the shortcomings of the PDS, the changes brought by the NFSA, and its impact on health outcomes and the agricultural economy will be provided in the next chapter.

Conclusion

The Indian economy had successfully transitioned from a public enterprise-driven economy to an economy embedded in the market and driven by private enterprise. However, the state continued to play an important role in supporting private capital. Both heavy industrialization and liberalization came at the cost of agrarian stagnation, increasing consumption inequality, and regional differences in growth. The UPA government continued the process of liberalization but changed the mechanisms through which liberalization occurs. It was able to build mechanisms to avoid the shortcomings of the reforms process in the 1980s and 1990s through rebranding reforms as "liberalization with a human face" and decentralizing the process of reforms at the state level. The UPA initiated reforms primarily through the SEZA – which allowed regional concentration of reforms and created an enclave that attracts investment, FDI, and skilled labor. Moreover, the process of reforms was divested to state governments and private developers who were better equipped to negotiate the political contestation of the SEZA – through political cache, subsidies, influence peddlers, and redistributive policies. Moreover, the governments finally deregulated the licensing procedure by creating committees to expedite necessary permissions and regulations. This translated into the economy becoming one of the fastest growing economies in the world, driven by growth in investment, exports, and government expenditure. Successful growth, however, masked persistent issues in the economy: agrarian stagnation, increasing fragmentation of land and indebtedness of small farmers leading to mass migration and informalization, unequal regional development leading to high growth metropolitans and low growth in the rest of the countryside, lack of development of capital and financial markets leading to industrial growth fueled by speculative finance, and government expenditure focused on populist policies rather than developmental outcome.

The UPA government introduced a host of social distribution policies in anticipation of the political backlash of enclave-led growth and agrarian stagnation. The social policies were based around governance rights which included mechanisms to make governments accountable for the delivery of redistributive policies. One of the innovations of the UPA government was to include civil society members and activists in the process of drafting the policies and institutional mechanisms to make the government accountable. This decentralization of the implementation process indicates a changed strategy of policymaking – especially on the back of ineffective reforms in the previous period. Two contingent events – the failure of the INC to get majority seats in the 2004 elections and the global financial crisis of 2008 – influenced the trajectory of policymaking.

The UPA government failed to win the elections in 2014. Unlike previous periods which were marked by an economic or political crisis, the UPA regime came to an end due to a lack of political support. The final regime under the NDA government marks a shift in economic policymaking due to the different political concerns that shaped their tenure.

References

Basole, A., and D. Basu. 2011. "Relations of Production and Modes of Surplus Extraction in India: Part II – 'Informal' Industry." *Economic and Political Weekly* 46 (15): 63–79.

Bhaduri, A. 2008. "Predatory Growth." *Economic and Political Weekly* 43 (16): 7–8.

De, R. 2020. "Mechanisms of Surplus Appropriation in the Informal Sector: A Case Study of Tribal Migrants in Ahmedabad's Construction Industry." CSE Working Paper Series, Centre for Sustainable Employment, Azim Premji University, Bengaluru. https://cse.azimpremjiuniversity.edu.in/publications/mechanisms-of-surplus-appropriation-in-the-informal-sector-a-case-study-of-tribal-migrants-in-ahmedabads-construction-industry. Accessed July 9, 2022.

Jenkins, R., and A. M. Goetz. 1999. "Accounts and Accountability: Theoretical Implications of the Right-to-Information Movement in India." *Third World Quarterly* 20 (3): 603–22.

Kalam, A. 2007. 'Presidential Address to Parliament' (Speech). April 6. https://eparlib.nic.in/bitstream/123456789/4011/1/kalam_07_06_2004.pdf. Accessed September 21, 2022.

Khera, R. 2013. "Democratic Politics and Legal Rights: Employment Guarantee and Food Security in India." IEG Working Paper No. 327, Institute of Economic Growth, New Delhi. https://econpapers.repec.org/paper/awewpaper/327.htm. Accessed September 21, 2022.

Lalvani, M. 2009. "Persistence of Fiscal Irresponsibility: Looking Deeper into Provisions of the FRBM Act." *Economic and Political Weekly* 44 (37): 57–63.

Levien, M. 2012. "The Land Question: Special Economic Zones and the Political Economy of Dispossession in India." *Journal of Peasant Studies* 39 (3–4): 933–69. https://doi.org/10.1080/03066150.2012.656268.

Manor, J., and R. Jenkins. 2016. *Politics and the Right to Work*. Hyderabad: Orient Blackswan.

Nagaraj, R. 2017. "Economic Reforms and Manufacturing Sector Growth." *Economic and Political Weekly* 52 (2): 61–68.

National Commission for Enterprise in the Unorganized Sector (NCEUS). 2007. *Report on Conditions of Work and Promotion of Livelihoods in the Unorganized Sector*. New Delhi: Dolphin Printo Graphics.

Ruparelia, S. 2005. "Managing the United Progressive Alliance: The Challenges Ahead." SSRN Scholarly Paper No. 2807204. https://papers.ssrn.com/abstract=2807204. Accessed September 21, 2022.

6

Reforms under the NDA Government
2014–19

In 2014, a resurgent NDA government under the prime ministership of Narendra Modi came to power. Neither was India going through an economic, political, or international crisis nor was there a substantial change in economic policy marked by this period. However, the period was significant due to the historic domination of the BJP. This final chapter is different from the previous chapters: the logic of periodization in previous chapters of crisis and change does not explain this one. The reason for including the NDA in a separate chapter was because its politics were in stark contrast to the INC, and I wanted to explore whether they had a different philosophy or ideology for economic reforms and welfare policies than the INC. At the time of writing this chapter, the BJP has entered its second tenure as the central government on the back of a successful election campaign. I have decided not to write about the second NDA government, as it is difficult to analyze contemporary events with objectivity, especially in the aftermath of the COVID-19 lockdown crisis.

How did the BJP come to power when there was no historical precedence of a non-INC party getting majority votes (the NDA government of 1998 was a coalition government)? Political analysts credited the BJP's victory based on their political ideologies referred to as Hindutva politics (Sharma 2003; Madhav 2021; Ananthamurthy 2016). While Hindu nationalism or Hindutva politics is perceived as the main identity of the BJP's voters, this does not completely explain how they dominated elections in 2013–14. I take recourse to Nalin Mehta's (2022) comprehensive analysis of electoral data to explain the BJP's electoral success, which, as Mehta has argued, cannot be simplified as Hindutva politics. His counterfactual for this was that much of the BJP's Hindutva politics based around the Ayodhya movement and L. K. Advani's Rath Yatra were in the 1990s. However, even at the peak of Hindutva popularity, the BJP lost the 2003–04 elections. What explains their return in 2014? Mehta empirically demonstrates that a key part of the BJP's

152 A History of Economic Policy in India

victory was based on its ability to capture electoral seats in Uttar Pradesh – the biggest constituency in India. It did so by changing the caste composition of its party and leveraging the use of digital technology in its campaign.

Electoral Strategy

In the last two decades, Uttar Pradesh's Lok Sabha seats were dominated by the Samajwadi Party (Other Backward Caste [OBC]-based party) and the Bahujan Samaj Party (SC-based party). The BJP gave an unprecedented number of seats to OBC candidates – 26 out of 79 Lok Sabha seats and 44 out of 79 seats to OBCs and Scheduled Castes (SCs), respectively – in the run-up to the 2014 elections to be able to compete with these parties. This data is based on the Mehta–Singh Social Index (Mehta 2022, 36). The BJP's social engineering of candidates was driven to maximize the competition with opposition parties, but they strategically gave seats to under-represented backward castes and SCs. While the Samajwadi Party's OBC Lok Sabha candidates were largely from the Yadav community, the BJP gave seats to non-Yadav OBCs, splitting the OBC votes. The Bahujan Samaj Party's SC Lok Sabha candidates were from the Jadhav caste, so the BJP gave seats to non-Jadhav SCs. Importantly, the BJP did not just give Lok Sabha seats to under-represented minorities but increased OBC representation at every level of its political organization in Uttar Pradesh, including district-level presidents to state unit leaders. This kind of transformation across the party increased the BJP's credibility as a backward castes' party and reaped benefits in the 2014 elections.

The second important electoral strategy was to maximize the use of newly emerging social media technology clubbed with increasing penetration of the internet in India. While digital media was a fairly new medium for Indian politics in 2012–14, with cheaper access to smartphones and faster internet connections, an increasing proportion of the nation was accessing digital media, especially the younger population – India has the largest proportion of youth, or new voters, in any democracy in the world. The politics and economics that shape digital media are very different from the traditional big media: newspapers, television, radio, and so on. A traditional media house like Star or Zee TV has a monopoly over its distribution channel and content. Moreover, there are barriers to entry in big media because of the scale of investment required to set up the infrastructure. Big media are an oligopolistic industry with a few large companies coexisting with each other. In new or digital media, anybody with a smartphone and editing software can create

Reforms under the NDA Government

and distribute content for free. The low cost of manufacturing and the lack of barriers to distributing content allow both a variety of mediums to reach out to voters as well as the ability to reach voters without mediation from a media house. For a party that generates such polarized opinions, having direct access to voters was one of the few advantages it had over the INC.

Since Mehta's analysis is based on data from the 2019 election, this analysis will give a sense of the BJP's ability to adapt to new technologies rather than the extent to which digital media contributed to their 2014 election campaign. However, this analysis has value to understand the differentiating electoral strategies of the 2014 NDA government. The BJP's placement of Modi as a digitally savvy leader began in 2012 when Modi took part in a Google Hangout session moderated by Bollywood actor Ajay Devgan. The use of social media to make Modi more accessible to the public was a deliberate strategy in opposition to Manmohan Singh who was perceived as a reticent prime minister figure – staying out of the limelight and being inaccessible even to INC members. In 2012, Modi had eight million Twitter users, which rose to 61.5 million by September 2020, and six million followers on Facebook (Mehta 2022, 132). He was already ahead of all Indian leaders – barring Sashi Tharoor – in having a digital presence. Modi had deployed 3D holograms in rallies for the Gujarat assembly election in 2012. After becoming prime minister, he had further entered the psyche of Indians through his radio show *Mann ki Baat*. This use of digital media to make Modi accessible to the public and seem digitally savant was particularly appealing to younger voters.

A large part of the BJP's digital strategy was hinged on its ability to have digital media experts on board before any other major party did so. There was a clear understanding in the party about how different platforms require different messaging to access different voter banks. Even though data on social media advertising is fairly recent, tech giants such as Google and Facebook have recently divulged advertising data under their ad transparency campaign. The BJP was way ahead of any other party in terms of digital presence. In the run-up to the 2019 Lok Sabha election, the BJP accounted for 41.4 percent of advertising on Google as opposed to the INC with 10 percent, and on Facebook, it accounted for 14.7 percent of advertising as opposed to the INC with 6.1 percent. Digital political advertising can be difficult to analyze because private individuals can also advertise for parties: seven of the top spenders on Facebook in March 2019 were sympathetic to the BJP (Mehta 2022, 139–40). The BJP's ability to use digital media as a campaign tool was empowered after 2016 as the price of mobile data per GB fell from INR 226 to INR 78 to INR 19.35 with the introduction of Reliance Jio networks, and data usage drastically increased per user per month from 0.4 percent in 2015 to 4.13 percent in 2017 (Mehta 2022, 137).

Aside from the digital spending, the party trained its cadre to use social media technology; in a telling quote, Amit Malviya, the BJP's national head for IT, said that its workers were taught how to create local WhatsApp groups and given guidelines on what kind of content to share and how to present it (Mehta 2022, 152). The confidence to use new media technology and support digital technologies marked out the BJP as a party for 21st-century India, and while the use of digital media does not solely explain the 2014 victory, it can be seen as an element that distinguished the NDA from the UPA. This is of particular importance in understanding how the NDA's economic policies were different from the UPA's.

The NDA's Economic Philosophy

How were economic policies, especially reforms and welfare policies, different under the NDA than under the UPA? More specifically, was there any difference in ideas around economic policy between the two?

Unlike the INC, which can trace its history from driving India's anti-colonial struggle in the early 20th century, it is tougher to trace the history of the BJP, especially because different organisations came together to form it. Different sources trace the roots of the BJP to the late 19th- or early 20th-century Hindu nationalist thinkers. However, the birth of the Akhil Bhartiya Jan Sangh on October 21, 1951, is largely agreed upon as its origin. The party set up by Syama Prasad Mukherjee was meant to be the cultural and political alternative to the secular INC. The INC and the Jan Sangh sharply differed on questions of politics and culture, and much of their debates revolved around issues that would become central to the BJP's political brand: the question of Muslims in India and Hindus in Pakistan, uniform civil code, no special status for Kashmir, and the Ram Janmabhoomi movement. From the eyes of an outsider, it is hard to glean if there was a coherent economic vision within the Jan Sangh and its later merger with the Swatantra Party. Elements of the Sangh were Gandhian in philosophy, believing in the importance of *swadeshi* development and placing agriculture at the center of the development model. There were leftist elements that criticized the Nehruvian partnership of state and heavy industry and even rightist elements that advocated minimizing government's role and introducing liberal reforms. While the INC had cemented itself as a reform-minded party since 1991, the BJP had never managed to position itself as having a different stance on reforms. Therefore, in the build-up to the 2014 elections, there was a lot of interest in how the BJP's policies of reform and social welfare would be different from the UPA's. One indication was that Modi would apply the Gujarat development model across India, but this was wishful thinking because Gujarat had been a historically highly developed region and much more amenable to the growth path that it took under Modi.

The BJP's Election Manifesto, 2014

One particular way to make sense of the BJP's economic vision would be to analyze its manifesto, budgets, and economic survey. The BJP's 2014 election manifesto suggests a leftward direction, with space and significance given to welfarism and a commitment to helping the poor and marginalized. In some sense, this is not a surprise, as the UPA, both in 2004 and 2009, focused more on social welfare programs in their manifesto, even though it made substantial reforms in the background. A focus on social welfare in the election manifesto is expected as it becomes a target for both voters and the opposition. Some of the new terms that stand out from the BJP's manifesto of 2014 were a program for "rural rejuvenation" which proposed a host of farmer-friendly policies which included issues around housing, irrigation, education, and health. There was no indication of how these programs would be different from those introduced by the UPA in the past decade. Another interesting term was the idea of "industry family", or the idea of setting up safety nets for labor by strengthening pension and health insurance. There was no specific mention of focus on growth or investment in new infrastructure or trade and foreign investment policies. The growth plan proposed was to harness the "5Ts – tradition, talent, tourism, trade and technology." There was no clear economic agenda or strategy, no reference to reforms, no mention of the Gujarat model. In some sense, the manifesto was very different from the infamous India Shining report and probably an indication that the BJP deliberately stayed away from discussion on reforms.

Economic Survey, 2013–14

After winning elections, the Modi government became associated with a group of economists who were market reform-minded: Ila Patnaik, who would become the chief economic advisor of the Finance Ministry, and senior economics such as Bibek Debroy, Arvind Panagriya – later to become head of the NITI Aayog – and Jagdish Bhagwati. In July 2014, the BJP finance minister, Arun Jaitley, tabled the Economic Survey of 2013–14, proposing a new economic alternative vastly different from the election manifesto. Economic surveys by their nature can be a fickle document, as there is no constitutional accountability. However, this survey was different enough from all other economic documents by the BJP and thus worth taking a closer look. The survey discusses the need to transition to a market economy and explicates the role the state should have in this transition. It distinguishes a market economy from the "regulatory framework of a command and control economy" (Government of India 2014, 155), referring to the Nehruvian state – a similar strategy had been used by Manmohan when introducing reforms in 1991. It defines a market economy as "the economy thrives because the state interferes only when there is 'market failure'." The document went on to discuss a different set of reforms that were necessary to move to such a market economy where the state's role is limited to providing public goods and addressing market failures. Such an account of the market economy is fairly standard in the Western, developed world, but was unusual in the Indian milieu – largely because the majority of the Indian population was immersed in the agricultural and informal economy which was only indirectly affected by markets. Moreover, most of India's population was dependent on government provision for their daily survival.

There is widespread skepticism amongst Indian voters about the intent of private industry driven by profit, born of centuries of appropriation by the colonial machinery. Even though the BJP had failed in its India Shining campaign, this seemed like pushing for bolder reforms, something akin to Manmohan's 1991 budget. However, it became clear pretty soon that the BJP's economic vision documents were more rhetorical than actually planned changes. Its economic policies have been more piecemeal or independent of one another, rather than a logical succession of policies as was introduced by the UPA in its first tenure. In the next section, I will discuss some of the important policy and institutional changes that were made by the NDA under Modi's PM tenure and I will highlight how even though they may not seem like a coherent plan, there are certain consistencies in the manner of conception and execution of these policies.

NITI Aayog

One of the first institutional changes that the BJP made, replacing the PC with the NITI Aayog, provides a revealing insight into its economic vision or ideology. Modi had been critical of the PC under the UPA government. According to journalist Puja Mehra (2019, 160), this was based on his experience as chief minister of Gujarat, having to approach the PC for funding. Of particular note was the PC's criticism of the Gujarat development model for its record on the Human Development Index. Maybe it is not necessary to see the replacement of the PC with the NITI Aayog as a personal slight but as symptomatic of the kind of institutional changes that the NDA wanted.

We must, however, keep in mind that the PC under the UPA or even previous governments was nothing like its role under Nehru. In Chapter two, we noted how the PC in its original incarnation was demolished after Nehru's death; in its place it became a committee that allocates funds to states and plays an ancillary role of advice on policies and monitoring and evaluation of schemes. The efficacy of the PC was always dependent on the ability of its cabinet members to be able to have links with the prime minister and the central government. In some sense, the PC was primed for importance under the UPA government as chairman Montek Singh Ahluwalia had professional links with Manmohan. However, the NAC ended up being a more important policy-influencing institution than the PC, largely due to Sonia Gandhi's role in directing its trajectory. Within this larger context, there is nothing transformational in Modi's decision about ending the tenure of the PC. However, it would be of interest to evaluate how the NITI Aayog was different from the PC and how successful it was in achieving its stated objectives.

Mehra (2019, 167) provides a detailed account of how the restructuring of the NITI Aayog was envisaged, bringing together an eminent group of senior officials which included Bimal Jalan, Yashwant Sinha, and Vijay Kelkar. A substantial amount of time and energy was spent on naming and branding the NITI Aayog, but, like other NDA documents, the role of the body was kept vague. In principle, the NITI Aayog was conceptualized as a think tank, which would make recommendations to the national economic agenda, including technical advice, creation of delivery mechanisms, and evaluation tools. The PC's responsibilities towards devolution of funds to states would be transferred to the Finance Ministry. However, the the NITI Aayog vision document launched by the BJP in April 2017 was vague and amorphous. It included quotes from across the ideological spectrum, ranging from Gandhi and Vivekanand to Ambedkar while advocating a "Bhartiya" model of development. It defined the NITI Aayog as an enabler rather than a provider whose main role is to diminish the role of the state as a player. However, from the beginning it was plagued by a lack of direction or vision: its acting head, Arvind Panagriya, had little to no link with the Prime Minister's Office, and it did not have a constitutional status, which meant it was not accountable to the parliament and had no mechanisms to ensure that its advice was taken. Over time, the

NITI Aayog was publicly perceived as a public relations institution for Modi's policies rather than having any involvement in influencing important policies such as the Goods and Services Tax (GST), demonetization, and so on. This can be seen most starkly in the controversy around its attempt to compute a set of GDP estimates, which was widely criticized and lowered the credibility of Indian statistics generated under the NDA regime (Mehra 2019, 177).

The Indian Economy under the NDA

There are certain challenges to discussing the impact of the NDA's performance on the economy. This is largely because the GDP data series released by the NDA in 2015 used a slightly different methodology to calculate the GDP and a different base year than earlier GDP data series, which means that we can study trends but cannot make a direct comparison with GDP data from earlier series. The new methodology changed the way in which data was collected from the manufacturing sector. However, what would have been fairly cosmetic changes led to substantial political firefighting. The growth rates of the GDP and important macroeconomic variables like government consumption, investment, and exports did not show any improvement from the UPA's tenure, which led to allegations that the NDA had not introduced any new reforms (Table 2.1). Moreover, the lower rates were impacted by demonetization in 2016 – more on this later – which affected growth rates over a short time horizon, decreasing the efficacy of the statistical aggregative study. This became a common point of debate among economists supporting and criticizing NDA policies, and without comparable GDP data made it impossible to objectively resolve. However, there is reason to believe that there may have been political reasons for the change in methodology as the NITI Aayog had blocked the release of data in 2015 based on the earlier method of computation of the GDP, which showed faster growth in the UPA years. It is important to remember that the use of statistics is always a political act as one can choose which statistics to present based on one's agenda. However, while GDP data is not directly comparable based on different methodologies, it does provide an intuition about trends and directions of policy which need to be substantiated through case studies or deeper analysis of policies.

NDA I's Economic Policies
Welfare Policy under the NDA

The economic policies that defined the NDA were its implementation of welfare programs under the direct beneficiary transfers (DBTs). DBTs were a certain philosophy of welfare which are very different from the welfare schemes under Indira's government or the rights-based schemes of the UPA. DBTs mean transferring benefits in cash directly to the beneficiary. In the context of India where it has been established that the governance system systematically and individually engages in leakages, frauds, and corruption, DBTs were proposed as a mechanism of bypassing systemic corruption – one of NDA's main critiques of the UPA government. It is worth noting that DBTs were not an invention of the NDA and has existed in multiple forms in the past. In fact, the DBT program was launched by Manmohan Singh's UPA II in January 2013 as a pilot scheme. However, DBTs became the face of policies under the NDA government and part of NDA's rhetoric differentiating it from UPA's welfare schemes. It is worth noting that both the BJP manifesto and Modi's speeches were oriented towards making pro-poor policies, and DBTs were given high visibility within their political discourse.

Given the benefits of DBTs, why did earlier governments not provide them universally? There are two aspects to this question. First, there are legitimate concerns about whether DBTs lead to increased welfare. Second, DBTs require a mechanism of delivery that did not exist in India before. Other modes of welfare policies in India were subsidized goods like fuel, rations – rice, wheat, pulses, agricultural inputs, and so on – or free or subsidized public goods such as education through government schools, health support through public hospitals, and so on. One of the criticisms of DBTs is that there is no guarantee that the beneficiary will spend the cash on goods and services which increase their welfare. For example, a poor household might spend their money on food lacking in nutrition or other needs that are not primary instead of spending it on health, education, improving homes or land, and so on. Second, there was no infrastructure to directly transfer cash; if the central government had to depend on the bureaucracy to distribute cash transfers, then the same issues of corruption and leakages would rear their head. The biggest DBT under the UPA government, the NREGA, had created an institutional mechanism that allowed the public and members of civil society to make the government accountable for the promised transfers.

DBT, however, was the most significant tool in driving Modi's popularity amongst the masses and one of the foremost reasons for the party's victory in the UP state election in 2017 and central elections in 2019. It is no surprise to find that the number of beneficiaries of DBTs increased from 10.8 crore in UPA II's final year of 2013–14 to 31.2 crore in 2015–16 to 76.3 crore in 2018–19. The amount of cash transferred increased at a similar pace from INR 7,367.7 crore in 2013–14 to INR 61,942.4 crore in 2015–16 to INR 214,092 crore in 2018–19 (Mehta 2022, 65). Most of the NDA's DBT schemes were UPA schemes that had been renamed. However, the way the NDA handled and presented it was different. For starters, the large cadre of NDA personnel at the village and block levels were recruited to ensure that the transfers were reaching the beneficiary, and journalists covering election campaigns have reported how BJP leaders would go to villages and ensure that the public knew that they were receiving the benefits from the party or would publicly make officials accountable if they were not. For poor masses, especially in the densely populated belt of north India, receiving cash in hand was immediately identified with the NDA, even though welfare policies have been the mainstay of multiple INC governments in the past. Attaching welfare policies to the party head's persona is not a new political strategy either and had been successfully done by the DMK in many election cycles. More recently, the head of the Samajwadi Party, Akhilesh Yadav, publicly gave free laptops to students in Uttar Pradesh. This is where the NDA's digital outreach was really powerful as it associated DBTs with the NDA and Modi in the voter's mind.

Digital Delivery Mechanism

The creation of a digital delivery mechanism is what differentiates the NDA from earlier governments' DBT delivery policy. Even if cash is directed towards beneficiaries, there is no guarantee that it will reach them as it is mediated through the bureaucratic system at multiple levels. The NDA focused on digitally delivering benefits directly to people. In this, they were favored by a few circumstances: the universal identification system created by the UPA 2 government called the UIDAI became the base infrastructure on which DBTs were based. Through the Aadhaar Act of 2016, the NDA created a statutory act to ensure the universal adoption of Aadhaar. Aadhaar solved the problem of identification by linking each Indian citizen to a unique identification number which could be used to provide multiple targetted government benefits. The second important policy which created the infrastructure was the Pradhan Mantri Jan Dhan Yojana, which provided accident insurance cover to 1.5 crore Indians but, more importantly, created bank accounts for them. Therefore, between an Aadhaar card, bank account, and mobile phone, the government could identify a beneficiary, directly put money in their bank account, disseminate information, and track details through the mobile phone. This addressed one of the toughest challenges in delivering benefits:

identifying who deserves it, especially, as it has been frequently reported across the country that the list of beneficiaries is politically manipulated. Two other factors benefitted the NDA: increased penetration of affordable phones in India and affordable data plans provided by the launch of Jio phones in 2015. The culmination of all these circumstances provided the NDA an opportunity to successfully start the largest DBT policy in the world and present it as one of its foremost economic innovations based on the idea of minimal digital governance.

Demonetization

On November 8, 2016, Modi made an unscheduled television address and announced that all INR 500 and INR 1,000 notes would stop being legal tender from midnight. He argued that this was a necessary step to fight corruption, capture black money and fake notes, and shut off an important mode of financing terrorist activity. Demonetization was one of the most publicly covered economic policies in recent times, and it is understandable because it affected every citizen but also paradoxical because it would have very little impact on the economy in the larger scheme of things. Even though it had little significance over the long run, it does provide us a window into understanding economic policymaking under the NDA government.

It is worth keeping in mind that there was a press blitzkrieg after the exercise of demonetization, leading to much misinformation about what it is meant to be theoretically and what its impact was on the economy. Demonetization is an exercise in absorbing cash from the public; there can be different economic reasons for doing so. Demonetization has been historically used to reduce purchasing power from people to reduce aggregate demand in the economy. Such a move would immediately lead to a fall in the GDP and could threaten the stability of a currency. However, this could be justified if the economy is going through a period of hyperinflation: an increase in prices of goods at unsustainable rates and/or a currency becoming unstable. There are many examples in the 20th century where demonetization was done successfully. These were largely countries that had gone through a major political crisis or war, and the local currency had become unstable. An exercise of demonetization had been done in India in 1978, which did not have any significant impact on the economy. The Indian economy was not going through any kind of economic or political crisis, and the Indian rupee is one of the most stable currencies in the world, so why would the government do this exercise which would immediately harm the economy?

The government argued that this exercise was to weed out black money, as people hoarding black money would have to either reveal it or lose its value. Black money had been a source of discontentment amongst the government for a long time, especially in earlier times when resources were scarce and the government was directing the economy. Black money exists in the cultural imagination as stolen or immoral money, and the NDA used this powerful idea to be connected to the exercise of demonetization. 'Black money' is an umbrella term that refers to illegal or unaccounted money, income on which tax has not been paid and has not been reported to the government. There is not any good estimate of how big the black-money economy is in India or how much of this economy is illegal or corruption-based money. There are fairly good theoretical reasons for believing that a substantial amount of black money is not generated through corruption. More than 90 percent of enterprises – including agriculture in India – are in the informal economy and do not pay taxes. Similarly, more than 90 percent of India's population has an income less than the minimum taxable income. Therefore, most of the money in the Indian economy can be considered black money, in the sense that it is not accountable and is largely in the form of cash. However, a part of the black economy is illegal money gained through corruption or the sale of illegal products which may have been used to finance terrorist activity. The government argued that this money would not be returned and would be weeded out of the system.

The NDA within the 50 days of initiating demonetization never clearly announced how much black money they planned to weed out through this process. The attorney general submitted to the Supreme Court that he expected INR 4–5 lakh crore not to be returned to the banking system. At some point, the RBI stopped publicly announcing the amount of cash returned because it was clear that it would be well below the target. At the final count, the unreturned notes were around INR 10,720 crore, which was 1 percent of the expected target. Demonetization as an exercise in weeding out corruption was a failure; the government had underestimated how much black money was already converted into assets such as land, gold, and other valuables and how much was placed in offshore accounts. The exercise immediately hurt the informal economy which was largely dependent on cash payments. Millions of workers and petty businesses who had no savings were forced to survive without access to sufficient cash and consumer demand plummeted, and it led to a significant reduction in the GDP – the gross value added reduced from close to 8 percent growth to 6 percent from 2016 to 2017. It continued to be around 6 percent even in 2018, indicating that the economy was unable to revive from the fall in demand caused by demonetization. There was a high cost to the banking system as the RBI reported that the cost of printing new notes was much higher and affected its balance sheet. The NDA, while never publicly admitting that the policy was a failure, did try to argue that demonetization was to push Indians to adopt digital modes of payments at a time when, conveniently, internet rates were at an all-time low and digital payment platforms like Paytm emerged in the landscape.

Mehra (2019) provides an interesting hypothesis to explain the strange exercise of demonetization by the NDA government. After coming to power, Modi had primarily projected himself as a global business-oriented prime minister with the Make in India campaign, liberalization of FDI norms, and building of relationships with world leaders. This seems to have affected his traditional voter base, which had perceived him as a pro-poor minister. The NDA had been hit by successive waves of electoral failures in 2015 with losses in Tamil Nadu, Kerela, and West Bengal, followed by embarrassing defeats in Delhi and Bihar. Mehra argues that demonetization was part of a campaign to rebuild its pro-poor image around the rhetoric of curbing black money from the corrupt rich in India. While demonetization was an economic failure, the BJP successfully raised political cache out of it by winning the Uttar Pradesh state elections in 2017 and the Manipur elections 2017. The exercise of demonetization highlights the contradictions of making sense of economic policy as its financial impact can be different for different sectors, classes, and regions, and can be used politically to celebrate or criticize the government depending on the composition of the voter base.

Goods and Services Tax

In July 2017, the NDA government introduced one of its most important reform policies, the GST. GST was initially recommended by the Kelkar Commission in 2004, tasked by the Atal Bihari Vajpayee-led BJP government. GST formed part of a larger policy push by the NDA government to improve governance by reducing the limitations of the governing system. Paradoxically, the UPA had tried to initiate GST but was met with obdurate objections by the opposition parties, especially the BJP. The indirect taxation structure in India was complicated with different rates and exemptions in different states. It was well established in the economic literature that tax compliance is directly correlated to the complication of the taxation system.

GST is an indirect value-added tax charged on all goods and services produced for domestic consumption. The tax is paid by the final consumer, instead of taxation at every point of the production process. For example, in the production of rice, instead of tax being collected from the farmer, the wholesaler, the transporting agency, and the final retailer, the full tax is collected directly from the consumer – through the retail price. The government does not need to collect taxes at multiple stages, leading to lower costs of tax collection and ensuring tax compliance. It should be kept in mind that just because consumers pay the whole tax does not mean that they bear the burden of it; this would be determined by the concept of tax incidence, which essentially means that who pays how much tax depends on the demand and supply elasticity of the good. In simple terms, it means producers pay a higher share of tax for highly competitive goods, while producers pay a lower share of tax for monopolistic or oligopolistic goods.

The principle of GST was one tax rate for the whole nation. However, in practice, there would be three rates depending on which category the good was listed in. The idea of GST fits in with the larger philosophy of the NDA government referred to by NITI Aayog as "cooperative federalism." The idea was to build stronger synergies and economic cooperation amongst states; it was implied that the central government will have to play a larger role in facilitating this. This was particularly relevant as more regional parties came to power in the state, and there was increased competition for capital, revenue, and business amongst states.

The primary complication in implementing GST was that state governments in India have historically had the right to decide what tax rate they want to charge, and GST would force a common tax rate for all goods, including special goods such as fuel, alcohol, land, all of which fund the largest part of the revenue bill. Moreover, taking away power from states to charge indirect tax and making GST collection at the point of consumption created certain complications, the most significant of which was that states would collect tax for goods that were not produced in there. Manufacturing-dominant states such as Tamil Nadu, Haryana, Maharashtra, and Gujarat would lose revenue to high-consumption states such as Bihar, West Bengal, and Assam. This would reduce the incentive for the state government to develop heavy industries as it will not receive the income from the infrastructure created. For example, creating an SEZ has a high cost, which is expected to be compensated by higher revenue in the future. This was the primary reason for resistance from states to implement GST. The NDA government alleviated this issue by promising to compensate for revenue lost by states for five years.

The second major issue with GST was the lack of rationality for how goods were placed in different tax brackets. Theoretically, goods should be placed in different brackets based on their demand and supply characteristics. In its simplest form, it would mean that essential goods would be placed in lower tax brackets and consumer goods placed in high tax brackets. However, in its final form, the rates of taxes were determined by political lobbying and would lead to irrational outcomes such as the same rate of GST charged for environment-friendly hybrid vehicles and petrol-guzzling SUVs or a lower tax rate for soaps and a higher rate for detergents. The GST for different products was dependent on the ability of the industry to lobby the government.

State resistance and business lobbies made GST a politically contentious process and led to the creation of an empowered decision-making constitutional body called the GST Council, chaired by the union finance minister with both the center and states getting a weightage of votes. The INC had demanded an independent dispute resolution authority with non-political actors with judicial authority, which would be empowered to adjudicate thorny differences of opinion, especially between states. But eventually it had to accept the GST Bill in the form rolled out by the NDA. The effectiveness of the GST is dependent on its proper adoption and also on the government's ability to modify and amend the act as different issues rear their head. It is still too early to evaluate the efficacy of GST as opposed to other tax systems in India, but institutional adaptation is the key to the successful nationwide implementation of GST.

Pradhan Mantri Jan Arogya Yojana

The NDA's focus on direct cash transfers and delivering welfare through better governance machinery and digital infrastructure was impressive. However, it did not have any welfare schemes that were different from the ones introduced by past governments, especially the UPA. Therefore, it is difficult to isolate what the NDA's social welfare philosophy was. In 2018, the NDA rolled out a large-scale scheme to push for universal healthcare called the Pradhan Mantri Jan Arogya Yojana (PM-JAY). This was not the first public insurance scheme in India. However, it was substantially larger in coverage than any previous insurance scheme. The PM-JAY is designed to cover 10 crore poor and vulnerable families (about 50 crore individuals) to provide INR 5 lakh per family per year, for secondary and tertiary care hospitalization. This would make it the biggest social insurance policy in the world. Moreover, if successful, it would provide a significant contribution to reducing poverty by providing a safety net to families across India, especially those who would be pushed into pauperism if the health of its earning members deteriorated.

166   A History of Economic Policy in India

Let me provide some context on what was different about the NDA's policy for public health and why this would be an important indicator of the future direction of social policies. India has invested close to 6 percent of its GDP in public health – an impressive number by the standards of a developing country. Over multiple decades, governments have set up a universal primary healthcare infrastructure with care workers accessible for all citizens; further, both the central and state governments have established public hospitals to provide secondary and tertiary care subsidized or free of cost to Indian citizens. Different governments in their tenure have made policies targeting vulnerable populations, such as lactating mothers, children under the age of five, the old and disabled, and so on. Social insurance is a different mechanism of delivering healthcare than rights-based healthcare and can transcend some of the issues that plague India's healthcare system: lack of infrastructure, illiteracy, caste and gender barriers, and big hospitals predominant in the cities. Health insurance provides an incentive to caregivers and hospitals to approach the ill and the diseased, by passing one of the primary barriers to healthcare in India – literacy and awareness. Aside from the size of coverage, this policy was different from other public health insurances introduced because it was designed to counteract the problems with previous policies – such as low quality of public hospitals and profiteering tendencies of private hospitals. Under this scheme, the insurance would be funded by the government and regulated by private management firms. Moreover, the government provided incentives to counteract issues faced by previous health insurance schemes. Since this policy was introduced towards the end of the NDA's first tenure, I will focus on the challenges posed by introducing this scheme and how the government counteracted these issues.

Two key ideas underpin the success of this policy – the first is a sustainable financing policy and the second is the execution of the public–private partnership model (PPP) model. The cost of providing insurance to about 40 percent of India's population is significant, especially given that the government invests funds into other aspects of health policy as well. The extent of insurance coverage determines the "notional premium" amount the government has to pay. The NDA government decided that the expense will be shared 60–40 between the center and the state, except for the northeastern states. Second, the extent of coverage would determine both the premium and the types of ailments that are covered. For example, if the insurance cover is low, then people would not be able to get care for high-cost illnesses, injuries, and accidents. However, if the cover is increased, then the premium required for the insurance would go up too. Gupta et al. (2020)

have provided a detailed analysis of the total cost to the government based on different amounts of premium. However, from the national economic perspective, the biggest challenge is that the central government allocation of funds for the insurance premium would lead to a decrease in funds allocated for other aspects of healthcare. In this regard, the government allocation has not been encouraging. In the 2018 budget, the government committed just 1.4 percent of the GDP to health as opposed to the promised 2.5 percent (Hooda 2020, 109).

The second issue is even more perplexing. The public healthcare system in India is severely underfunded and unable to handle the increase in patients from this scheme. As a recourse, the NITI Aayog proposed a PPP model where the government would both procure private facilities and convert them to public hospitals, and some private hospitals would be part of the approved network of hospitals. The hesitancy to include private hospitals under the scheme was understandable as private hospitals are not well regulated, and prior experience has shown that they have an incentive to charge higher or charge for unnecessary healthcare. This is particularly exacerbated because the population covered by the insurance is largely illiterate and unaware of their right.

Let us summarize some of the major issues in implementing the PM-JAY at this current juncture. This has been covered by the *EPW Engage*'s special issue (2020). First, if the government is unable to allocate separate funds for the insurance premium, it may move to a full insurance model where the healthcare is completely provided by private parties. This would lead to private lobbying for the government's budget allocation for health. Second, there are both inequities of access and corruption in its implementation. While public hospitals lack hospital beds and infrastructure, most of the private hospitals are in urban areas in southern states, making it difficult for common people to access. Those able to access healthcare face treatment-based discrimination – the tendency for hospitals, both public and private, to allocate limited beds to higher-costing treatments and invest in equipment for these kinds of treatment. There is already growing evidence of patients shunned from the hospital as the treatment is not covered in the medical package. Third, the insurance coverage does not provide support for post-hospitalization charges, and there have been reports of multiple out-of-pocket charges which are unaffordable for the poor. As a consequence, full treatment is not provided, or people are wary of accessing the facilities. Lastly, there are many accounts of corruption through overcharging, low-quality equipment, and excessive or unnecessary treatment, which limits the efficacy of the policy. The COVID-19

168   A History of Economic Policy in India

pandemic tested the limits of India's public healthcare system, and an objective assessment of the NDA's insurance policy is hard to do. However, currently, the issues of implementation and sustenance far outweigh the benefits that would come from a well-functioning public insurance system. Is this scheme fiscally sustainable? Only time will tell.

Agrarian Distress and Farm Bill

When Modi became the NDA's prime minister, he was perceived as pro-poor and pro-farmer in orientation. However, as his focus shifted to manufacturing growth and welfare policies, agriculture increasingly was put on the back burner. The NDA had to manage the agricultural economy on the back of two successive droughts in 2014 and 2015. However, it is difficult to make sense of what their policy stance was in managing increasing agrarian distress. It has been demonstrated throughout this book that inequality in landholding, control of agricultural output by large landlords and middlemen, and collusion with the government in raising MSP have effectively prevented the agricultural economy from developing. But it was specifically in the 1990s that the agricultural sector went into a downward spiral with its contribution to the GDP steadily decreasing from over 50 percent to less than 25 percent by the time Modi comes to power. It is a difficult exercise to demarcate the impact of NDA policies on agriculture, given the long-running neglect of structural issues in the sector. The data, however, suggests that agricultural trends worsened under the NDA (Himanshu 2015, 26). Based on the old GDP series growth rate of value added in agriculture, it had improved from 1.76 percent in 1998–2003 (the first BJP government) to 3.84 percent from 2004-05 to 2012–13 (UPA I and II). Using the new GDP series, the last two years of the UPA (2011–12 to 2013–14) achieved a 3.5 percent agricultural growth rate, which fell to 1.86 percent from 2014 to 2017–18. It is clear that the drought affected the growth rate, but it is equally surprising to find that the NDA did not address this through any direct intervention.

In the 2014 general elections, Modi had promised higher procurement prices for crops. By 2017, there were reports of large-scale farmer protests across the country, as there was little to show for this promise. This culminated in a 40,000-strong farmers' march in March 2018, demanding a rethinking of the implementation of the FRA of 2006, which was perceived to have been diluted by the NDA. This was followed by farmer strikes in 2018 regarding the price of tomatoes. This kind of public protests highlighted the growing nationwide dissatisfaction of the farming community with the NDA government.

Whether this an error of judgment or a deliberate strategy is hard to guess; lack of agricultural growth and agrarian stagnation had been a constant theme since the introduction of reforms.

The UPA managed the politicization of agricultural distress through different social policies. The NDA's approach to agriculture was very different and indicative of another philosophy. The most crucial component of agricultural policy is the MSP. Since the construction of the PDS, the government has played an important role in ensuring access to the market for small and marginal farmers in India. This was an important social policy as the majority of the Indian population's fortunes are either directly or indirectly linked to agricultural prices. The MSP has played a crucial role in delinking the fortunes of farmers from the vagaries of monsoon and made them less dependent on the powerful hold of moneylenders, hoarders, and wholesalers.

The agricultural sector was in a bad state by 2018 – highlighted by farmer unrest – due to several factors: agricultural stagnation, the economy-wide shock faced by demonetization, the high price of diesel, and so on. In the 2018 budget, the government promised to make MSP at 150 percent of production cost. However, controlling the MSP is not just a matter of procurement price but also maintaining buffer stocks to control market price and import–export strategy. For example, bumper monsoons in 2017 led to a glut of stocks in the agricultural market. This resulted in a decrease in prices of many crops. So the government raised prices but allowed a record volume of imports, leading to a surplus in the domestic markets which send prices crashing.

It is in light of the lack of intervention in the agrarian economy under NDA I that I will analyze the Farm Bill introduced by NDA II in 2019. While this period is outside the purview of this book, the Farm Bill provides a window into the BJP's agricultural policies, and at the time of writing in 2022, it has been repealed, providing closure to this version of the bill. In September 2020, the government introduced three bills, which were together referred to as the Farm Bill. The three bills were meant to liberalize and deregulate the agricultural sector. They were intended to provide a framework for contract farming, facilitate barrier-free trade of farmers' produce outside markets that are notified under the Agricultural Produce Marketing Committee (APMC) laws, and regulate the supply of certain food items. For our analysis, however, we will focus on how the Farm Bill wanted to dismantle the PDS infrastructure and create opportunities for competitive procurement of agricultural goods. More than half of India's population, even today, is dependent on agriculture as the primary source of income. The PDS, the MSP, and the APMC were crucial institutions through which the government intervened in the agricultural economy, regulating markets from the vagaries of monsoons and control from middlemen, moneylenders, wholesalers, and retailers.

The primary philosophy of the Farm Bill – and by extension governance under Modi – was that excessive state intervention had made these institutions inefficient, and farmers would benefit from private competition alongside the government infrastructure. Let us ignore the politics shaping MSP for now and understand the institutional intent behind the Farm Bill: MSP provides a price floor, ensuring that farmers do not have to sell their products below that rate. This is particularly useful in glut years when agricultural prices may plummet or to protect against cheap imports. The APMC is essentially a marketing board established by state governments in India to ensure farmers are safeguarded from exploitation by large retailers or by intermediaries who compel them to sell their produce at the farm gate for extremely low prices. All food products brought to the market yard (*mandi*) are sold through auctions, ensuring farmers face competitive prices. The Farm Bill intended to deregulate this infrastructure on the grounds of inefficiency and stifling competitive behavior. The Farm Bill would dilute the power of the APMC and allow private parties – primarily large corporates – to directly negotiate with farmers for prices. This competition would give more options to farmers and force the APMC and the MSP to be more competitive.

In theory, this seems like a win-win situation. However, the nationwide backlash, especially from agricultural competitive states like Punjab, indicated apprehension about corporates having an inherent incentive to undercut or pay lower prices to misinformed farmers, while the APMC – even given its failing – was more reliable and, most importantly, under state intervention. The extent of protest led to the repealing of the Farm Bill laws in 2022, with no way of knowing if the fears of farmer groups were real or not. However, this is one of the clearest indications of different reforms introduced by the NDA government and hints at the possibility of more to come.

Conclusion

In this chapter, I have chosen to analyze only NDA I's tenure because this book was written in NDA II's tenure, and it was not possible to provide a balanced analysis of contemporary times. Moreover, the COVID-19 lockdown crisis had affected economic and political variables in the short run, making it next to impossible to predict the repercussions of the crisis on the economy. This means that, unlike other chapters, a fair and balanced account of the NDA's tenure is not possible. Instead, this chapter highlights how the BJP came to power by using different electoral tactics and some of the important policies introduced in their tenure. The chapter poses the following questions: Were the NDA's development policies distinct from the UPA's? Did they have a different philosophy underpinning reforms and welfare policies? Was there a logic to the succession of policies introduced by the BJP?

In the analysis of economic policies under the NDA, I argued how there was no coherent economic philosophy, as the policies implemented were different from what the economic survey or the NITI Aayog indicated. Moreover, in the first two years of his tenure Modi focused on business and manufacturing but over the course of his tenure had to reposition himself to counter the BJP's losses in state elections and increasing agricultural distress. As a consequence, it is not discernible whether the lack of connection between policies was bad planning or an inexperienced government reacting to changing circumstances. However, there are a few common ideas that can be found across the NDA's political discourse, the policies introduced by them, and how they responded to public criticism which could be indicative of the future direction of policies. First, the NDA was focused on minimizing the role of the government in production and distribution; this was part of a larger criticism of corruption in the system. Attempts to minimize the role of the government can be found in many of their policies, such as introducing digital governance technology, DBTs, and encouraging more PPPs in public health and the Farm Bill. Another idea whose seeds were planted through GST was having more cooperation between states through the mediation of the center. This appears to be different from how the UPA pushed for more competition between states.

While it is tempting to say that the BJP does not have a clear economic philosophy beyond opportunism mixed with populism, it would be unfair to predict the future direction of the NDA based on its first tenure. As a counterfactual, the analysis after economic reforms introduced by Indira in the early 1980s, or UPA I, would be very different from the analysis done, accounting for Rajiv Gandhi's tenure in the late 1980s, or the policies introduced under UPA II. Instead, I would expect a longer-term perspective and learnings from past failures of the NDA government based on its first tenure. With the NDA taking the Indian economy on the path of digitalization, it is not difficult to imagine that the Indian economy will become more and more enmeshed in the global economy, requiring increased government intervention. However, reducing income inequality and creating stronger social security nets are crucial to any hope of a prosperous Indian economy in the future.

References

Ananthamurthy, U. R. 2016. *Hindutva or Hind Swaraj*. Noida: HarperCollins India.

EPW Engage. 2020. "Ayushman Bharat and the False Promise of Universal Healthcare." 8 July.

Bharatiya Janata Party (BJP). 2014. *BJP Election Manifesto 2014*. http://library.bjp.org/jspui/handle/123456789/252. Accessed September 22, 2022.

Government of India. 2014. *Economic Survey 2013–14*. New Delhi: Minsistry of Finance, Government of India. https://www.indiabudget.gov.in/budget2014-2015/survey.asp. Accessed September 22, 2022.

Gupta, I., S. Chowdhary, A. Roy, and Ramandeep. "Ayushman Bharat: Costs and Finances of the Prime Minister Jan Arogya Yojana." *Economic and Political Weekly* 55 (36): 56–64.

Himanshi. 2015. "Too Little, Too Late." *Economic and Political Weekly* 53 (9): 25–30.

Hooda, S. 2020. "Decoding Ayushman Bharat: A Political Economy Perspective." *Economic and Political Weekly* 55 (25): 107–15.

Madhav, R. 2021. *The Hindutva Paradigm: Integral Humanism and Quest for a Non-Western Worldview*. Chennai: Westland.

Mehra, P. 2019. *The Lost Decade 2008–18: How India's Growth Story Devolved into Growth without a Story*. New Delhi: Penguin eBury Press.

Mehta, N. 2022. *The New BJP: Modi and the Making of the World's Largest Political Party*. Chennai: Westland.

Sharma, J. 2003. *Hindutva: Exploring the Idea of Hindu Nationalism*. New Delhi: Penguin Books.

Index

20-Point Program, 88

Aadhaar Act of 2016, 160
Aadhaar card, 141, 143, 160
agrarian stagnation, 124, 148, 169
agricultural credit, 62
agricultural development, strategy for, 37
agricultural economy, 41, 98, 116–17, 148, 168, 170
agricultural intermediate classes, 90
Agricultural Land Ceiling Act (1972–75), 62
agricultural policy, in India, 54–56
  external policy, 56–57
  food pricing policy, 75
  food rationing program, 75
  Green Revolution, 54
  of increasing the productivity of agriculture, 75
  new agricultural strategy, 73–74
  subsidies and price incentives, 75
  See also minimum support prices (MSPs); New Agricultural Strategy (NAS); public distribution system (PDS)
Agricultural Price Commission (APC), 75
Agricultural Produce Marketing Committee (APMC), 169
agricultural productivity, 4, 16, 32, 55, 59, 62, 65, 69, 73–74, 76–77, 91, 117
  policy of increasing, 75
agricultural sector, in India

  American technical and financial assistance in, 55
  appropriation of forests and common lands from tribals, 54
  capitalist development in, 53
  commercialization of, 37, 53
  community ownership of, 55
  feudal heads and landlords, role of, 55
  growth of capitalism in, 115
  impact of
    Great Depression, 28–31
    Green Revolution policies, 114
    liberal reforms, 114–17
  liberalization in, 73
  public investment in, 55, 115
  regional and class inequity, 55
  resource allocation to industrial sector, 52
  social structure resistant to change, 54
  stagnation in, 134
  tenure system, 54
agricultural technology, 78
  capital-intensive, 62
Ahluwalia, Montek Singh, 98, 103, 136, 157
Ahmed, Fakhruddin Ali, 88
Aid India Consortium, 53
Akali Dal, 80, 112
Akal Sangharsh Samiti, 145
Akhil Bhartiya Jan Sangh, 154
All-India Congress Committee (AICC)
  Faridabad session of, 83
  Gandhinagar session of, 86
All India Kisan Sabha, 36, 49

174   Index

All India Trade Union Congress, 36
allocation of funds
  by the center to the states, 113–14
  for the insurance premium, 167
American Revolution, 13, 56
Annual Status of Education Report
  (ASER), 147
Annual Survey of Industry (ASI), 119
anti-colonial movements, in South
  America, 36, 86. *See also* Latin
  America
Antyodhya ration card, 140
Asian economy, 13, 15, 42, 127
Asian Financial Crisis, 119
Associated Chambers of Commerce
  and Industry of India
  (ASSOCHAM), 99

backward castes, 11, 22, 124, 152
Bahujan Samaj Party (BSP), 123, 152
balance of payment (BOP), 10, 94,
  97, 102
  crisis of 1964–66, 66, 69
  policies determining, 56
*bandh*s, 36
Bangladesh War (1971), 91
Bank of England (BOE), 23, 103
Bank of Japan, 103
banks and insurances
  nationalization of, 81–82, 84
  socialist control of, 82
Basole, A., 132–34
Basu, D., 132–34
Bengal famine (1943), 35, 46
Bhagwati, Jagdish, 155
Bharatiya Janata Party (BJP), 6, 49, 102
  "5Ts – tradition, talent, tourism,
    trade and technology" growth
    plan, 155
  Ayodhya movement, 151
  credibility as a backward castes'
    party, 152
  economic survey of 2013–14,
    155–56

economic vision documents, 156
election manifesto of 2014, 155
electoral strategy, 152–54
Hindutva politics, 151
"India Shining" campaign, 119–20,
  124, 156
L. K. Advani's Rath Yatra, 151
NITI Aayog, 156–58
placement of Modi as a digitally
  savvy leader, 153
political ideologies of, 151
program for "rural rejuvenation", 155
social engineering of candidates, 152
social welfare programs, 155
use of digital technology in election
  campaign, 152 (*see also*
  Facebook; Twitter)
See also National Democratic
  Alliance (NDA); Ram
  Janmabhoomi movement
Bhardwaj, H. R., 78, 136
"Bhartiya" model of development, 157
black-money economy, in India, 162
Bombay Plan, 36, 48, 51, 61
Bretton Woods international monetary
  system, 91
British administration, 15, 31, 33, 38
British economy, impact of Depression
  on, 34
British Empire, 23, 31
  decline of, 31
British industries, transfer of Indian
  revenue to support, 22
British landlords, 14, 53
British-made goods, 19
British parliament, 31, 34, 53
budgets, 8, 30, 47, 52–53, 55, 69, 73,
  98, 102, 104–05, 124, 142,
  155–56, 167, 169

capital, 13–28, 36, 40, 57, 78, 148, 164
  ability to raise, 99
  account, 57
  accumulation, process of, 46, 89

Index   175

British, 37
to develop infrastructure, 137
distribution of, 82, 97
domestic, 37, 44, 61, 126
foreign, 44, 111
formation, patterns of, 119
goods industry, 59
human, 108
industrial, 128
private, 52–53, 148
public, 110
reinvestment of, 128
capitalism, 8, 13, 24, 45, 69, 71, 82–83,
      89, 115, 131
development of, 23
market-driven, 93
state-driven, 89
capitalist
accumulation process, 89
agricultural, 116
classes, 16, 33
economies, 17, 46
capital-scarce economy, 16, 82
caste inequities, 11
Central Employment Guarantee
      Council (CEGC), 146
centrally sponsored schemes, 135
Chavan, Yashwantrao, 87
cheaper credit, allocation of, 29, 48, 90
cheap labor, 19–20, 41–42, 54, 109
availability of, 14
Chidambaram, P., 136
Chinese economy, 15
civil society organizations, 9, 125, 138,
      141–43
class conflicts, effects of, 55
"classical" liberalism, 96
coalition governments, 102, 120,
      123–25, 151
Cold War, 71–72
colonial bureaucracy, 41
colonial economy, in India
      (1776–1947), 5, 12–39
discrimination policies, 28

divergence with other economies of
      the world, 12–15
free trade policies, 20 (*see also* free
      international trade regime)
impact of economic policy on, 8
domestic industries, 25–26
Indian agriculture, 15
Indian industries, 18–21
importance of India to Britain,
      15–16
preferential treatment to British
      traders, 30
protectionist trade policies and
      monopoly trading, 20
resistance by Indian political actors,
      12 (*see also* home charges,
      critique of)
role in globalization of the Indian
      economy, 21
tariff policies, 20
textile industries, 20
theft of resources from India by
      Britain, 22
trade balance for India, 16
colonial government, 21–22, 25, 35,
      37–38, 42, 44, 46, 54
colonialism
discriminating protection, policy of,
      26
discriminatory tariff policy, 21
employment, in industrial centers, 24
colonial resistance, roots of, 21–22
Common Minimum Program (CMP),
      124–25
Communist Party of India (CPI), 80
Communist Party of India–Marxist
      (CPI–M), 80
community program, 55
Confederation of Indian Industries,
      104
Congress (I), 90, 92
Congress Working Committee
      (CWC), 8, 81
cooperative federalism, 164

cooperatives, creation of, 24, 55, 62, 73, 164
cotton plantations, in North America, 16
cotton textile industry, 24
COVID-19 lockdown crisis, 7, 151
  impact of lockdown on the Indian economy, 7
crisis
  of 1964–66, 66, 69
  of 1979, 91–94
  agricultural, 71
  foreign exchange crisis of 1991, 101–03
  See also food crisis of 1965–66
currency conversion, 23
  sterling–rupee exchange rate, 29
currency reserve of India, depletion of, 102
current account, 57, 66, 109
current account deficit, commercial borrowing for funding, 57

Debroy, Bibek, 155
debt servicing, 38
deficit financing, 53
deforestation, 16, 147
delicensing of industries, 72, 110
demonetization scheme, 161–63
Department for International Development (DFID), UK, 142
Desai, Morarji, 65, 70, 80
  dismissal as the finance minister, 84
devaluation of the currency, 32, 71–72, 73, 79–80, 91
*dharna*s, 142, 146
digital media, 152, 154
  contribution to 2014 election campaign, 153
  See also Facebook; Twitter
digital modes of payments, 163
digital political advertising, 153
direct beneficiary transfers (DBTs), 158–61, 171

District Committee (DC), 136
domestic industry, in India
  impact of colonial policies on, 25–26
  protection of, 36
  state support for the development of, 26
Dravida Munnetra Kazhagam (DMK), 80, 112, 123
Drèze, Jean, 141
drought-relief work, 144–45
  employment program, 146
dual economy, 17
Dutt, R. C., 22

East Africa, 48
East Asian tigers, 127
East India Company (EIC), 15, 19
  creation of Indian economy, 16–18
economic development
  goals of the Indian economy, 40
  models of, 42–43
economic growth, politics of, 14, 22, 40, 96–97
economic independence, 43, 104, 106
economic policies, in India, 3, 12
  Bombay Plan, 36, 48, 51, 61
  colonialism and, 12–39
  of Nehruvian government, 5
  populist policies under Indira Gandhi, 5–7
economic policymaking, 71, 149, 161
economic reforms, 6, 124, 126, 139, 151, 171
economic sovereignty, 105
  loss of, 104
Economic Survey of 2013–14, 155–56
economic theory and development discourse, 10
economies of scale, 52
Emergency of 1975, 6, 87–89, 93
Employment Assurance Scheme (1993), 145

Index 177

employment, in industrial centers, 24
Empowered Group of Ministers (EGOM), 136
enclave-led growth, 119, 133, 148
ethnic identity, 112, 133
European economies, 8, 21, 27
 during wartime, 46
exchange rate, 53, 102
 overvalued, 80
 policies determining, 56
 See also overvalued exchange rate
export
 orientation, 109
 of services, 119
Export Processing Zones, 135
external trade policy, 56–57

Facebook, 153
factory production, in India, 20, 41
"fair" price for land, 138
fair price shops, 75
Farm Bill Act (2018), 7, 9
 agrarian distress, 168–70
federal power, balance of, 112, 114
Federation of Indian Chambers of Commerce and Industry (FICCI), 99
feudal lords, of India, 23
financial capital, 17
First World countries, 97, 128, 131
fiscal deficit, 91–94, 97, 100, 102, 107
 crisis of 1991, 114
 gross, 129
 rise in, 92
Fiscal Responsibility and Budget Management (FRBM) Act (2003), 128–30
fiscal sustainability, 10
Five-Year Plan (FYP), 47, 73
 fifth, 86
 fourth, 76, 79
Food Commission of India (FCI), 90
 formation of, 74–76
 role in changing PDS, 75

food crisis of 1965–66, 5, 79–80, 93
 and end of the Nehruvian policy regime, 65–67
Food Grain Inquiry Committee of 1957, 75
food grain shortage, 51
Food Grain Trading Corporation. *See* Food Commission of India (FCI)
food imports, 80
food pricing policy, 75
food production, 54, 62
 impact of New Agricultural Strategy (NAS) on, 76–78
food rationing, 75
food security, 75, 140
food self-sufficiency, 76
food shortage, due to monsoon failures, 75
food stocks, 41, 65, 67, 75
 self-reliance in, 78
Ford Foundation, 55, 71, 74, 142
foreign aid, 53, 57, 60, 65, 69, 71–72, 91, 100
foreign capital, 44, 52, 57, 111
foreign direct investment (FDI), 65, 99, 127
Foreign Exchange Regulation Act (FERA) of 1973, 85, 107
foreign firms
 collaborations with Indian firms, 52
 as source of foreign exchange and technology, 52
foreign goods, boycotting of, 35
foreign policy, of India, 45
foreign reserves. *See* currency reserve of India, depletion of
foreign trade, imbalance in, 60
Forest Rights Act (FRA, 2006), 140, 147
free international trade regime, 23

Gadgil, D. R., 71
Gandhi, Indira, 70
 attack on heavy industry, 86–87

case of election fraud for use of state machinery, 87
class basis of policies of, 89–90
curb on the bargaining powers of organized labor, 87
defense of public enterprises, 83
election campaign of 1971, 85
Garibi Hatao campaign, 85–86
grab of power by, 84
liberal reforms under, 98
political dissent against, 88
populist policies under, 5–6, 84–86, 91
as prime ministerial candidate in the 1967 elections, 80
redistributive policies, 85
socialist policies, 10
state- and police-centric measures to control labor strikes and union activities, 98
state of Emergency in 1975, 87–89
victory in general election of 1972, 85
Gandhi, Mahatma
Dandi Salt March, 30
demands in his Satyagraha movement, 49
economic philosophy, 49
economic vision, 50
idea of non-violence, 50
influence on Nehruvian policy, 51
launching of Satyagraha movement, 29
method of politics and critique of colonialism, 49
notion of economic change, 50
vision of idealizing village life, 50
See also Gandhian philosophy
Gandhi, Rajiv, 98, 120
assassination of, 102
Bofors corruption scam, 102
contribution to the telecom revolution in India, 99
as prime minister of India, 101

Gandhi, Sonia, 125–26
Gandhian philosophy, 50, 55
Gandhi–Irwin Pact, 31
German economy, recovery of, 34
Gini coefficient, 60
Giri, V. V., 84
global economy, 13–14, 48, 56
shrinking of, 31
global financial crisis of 2008, 126, 128, 130
Global South
history of reforms in, 111
IMF conditions to get assistance to repay loans, 129
threat of nationalization in, 57
gold monetary standard, 23
end of, 24
gold reserves
for determination of country's exchange rate, 23
loss of, 29
stability of, 24
Goods and Services Tax (GST), 7, 158, 163–65. *See also* GST Council
government bureaucracies, 47, 64, 74
government debt, 129
Government of India Act of 1935, 33
Gram Sabha, 139, 144
Great Britain, 16
trade relations with
China, 32
India, 30
Great Depression of 1929, 5, 24, 49, 129
economic crisis caused due to, 27
impact on
British economy, 34
European economies, 27
Indian economy, 28–31
Satyagraha movement, 26–28
USA, 27
and national independence movement, 31
See also Smooth Hawley Act of 1930

Index 179

Great Divergence, phenomenon of, 12–15
Green Revolution, 54, 73, 76, 134
  beneficiaries of, 79
  impact on evolution of the agricultural sector, 114
  land-use intensity, 115
  rice production, 115
  scale-neutrality of, 79
  technologies, 90, 93
  See also high-yielding variety (HYV) seeds; Intensive Agricultural Area Program (IAAP); Intensive Agricultural Development Program (IADP); New Agricultural Strategy (NAS)
gross domestic product (GDP), 4, 31, 42, 129, 158
gross fiscal deficit (GFD), 129
growth-oriented economy, 39
GST Council, 165
Gulf War (1992), 102, 106, 120

handicraft industry, in India, 19, 41
  de-industrializing of, 44
  forms of, 19
handicraft production, 19
handlooms, in India, 20
heavy private industries, growth of, 89
hedge funds, 127
high-yielding variety (HYV) seeds, 74, 77
  discovery of, 93
Hindu nationalism, 151, 154
Hindustan Steel, 64
Hitler, Adolf, 34
home charges, critique of, 22–23
home industries in Britain, protection of, 20
Human Development Index, 157
Husain, Zakir, 84
Hussain, Abdul, 98

Hyderabad Information Technology and Engineering Consultancy (HITEC), 137
hyperinflation, 161

ICICI Bank, 128
IDBI Bank, 128
import
  licenses, removal of, 72
  substitution policies, 4–5, 26, 32, 60
    devaluation and the dilution of, 71–72
  tariff, rate of, 26
  See also food imports
Inclosure Act of 1773, 53
income, redistribution of, 86
independence movement, in India, 11–12, 17, 21–22, 29, 36, 71, 112
Index of Industrial Production (IIP), 119
Indian economy
  capitalist development in, 72
  colonialism and, 12–39
  dependence on American aid, 80
  in the early twentieth century, 31–32
  economic development goals, 40
  on the eve of independence, 37–39
  impact of
    COVID-19 lockdown, 7
    East India Company (EIC), 16–18
    Great Depression of 1929, 28–31
    liberal reforms, 107–109
    Nehruvian policies, 58–60
    New Agricultural Strategy (NAS), 76–78
    partial reforms in the 1980s, 99–100
  inheriting the colonial economy, 40–41
  liberalization and privatization of, 142
  market reforms, 72
  under the NDA, 158

180 Index

orientation towards foreign trade, 15
orientation towards exports of
    primary goods, 31
political economy framework, 9
rate of growth of, 58
role of monetary policy on, 10
Indian National Congress (INC), 6
10-point program for rebuilding of,
    81
abolishing of *zamindari* system, 55
creation of, 22
demolishing of PC, 71
destabilization of government and
    split in, 80–81
diplomatic conflict with the USA
    regarding aid, 93
Empowered Group of Ministers
    (EGOM), 136
as face of the independence
    movement, 32–33
failure in uniting Indian society, 29
freedom movement led by, 35
industrialization-led development
    model, 44
infighting within, 81–83
internal struggles in, 70–71
launching of Satyagraha movement
    under Gandhi's direction, 33
mobilization of votes in rural areas, 55
"Note on Economic Policy," 83
pro-business reforms in the 1980s,
    99
Quit India movement (1942), 36
rightist elements in, 80
rise of, 32–33
social redistribution bills, 139
split in 1969, 83–84
victory in the first election in 1935,
    31, 33
Working Committee reports, 8
See also Congress Working
    Committee (CWC);
    Syndicate; United Progressive
    Alliance (UPA)

Indian Ocean, 13
Indian peasantry, 28, 38, 49
Indian polity, complexity of, 111
Indian Tariff Board of 1932, 30
India–Pakistan War (1965), 65
"India Shining" campaign, 119
Indira government, ideology of, 86
industrial capital class, in India, 20
industrial development, 40, 132
    Bombay Plan, 36, 48
    goal of, 45
    government share of investment
        in, 58
    of India under Nehru's direction,
        43–44
        political responses to, 48–51
        protective policies, 48
    influence of multinational
        corporations in, 48
    market-directed, 45
    planning for, 45–48
    role of public and private enterprise
        in, 45
    in Russia, 43
Industrial Dispute Act of 1947, 61
industrialization
    Gandhian critique of, 45
    under Nehru's Leadership, 5
    planning-based, 56
    private enterprise-driven, 100
    rightist critiques of, 45
industrialization policy, of India,
    51–53
    of 1948, 52
    for capital goods industry, 59
    on deficit financing and aid from
        Western countries, 53
    public sector-led, 58
    Schedule C, 52
industrial know-how, 20
Industrial Policy Resolution of 1956,
    51
industrial production, 4, 17, 52, 59,
    106

Index

Industrial Revolution, 13
  in Britain, 14
  technological innovations used in, 19
industrial stagnation of 1979, 6, 91
industrial townships, 135
industries
  cottage industries, 52
  demand for, 52
  drive to Industrialize under Nehru's
    Leadership, 40–67
  growth trajectory of, 38
  heavy industrialization, stages of, 51,
    58, 140, 148
  heavy industries, in India, 20
    protection from foreign
      competition, 25
  impact of
    colonial policies, 18–21
    World War 1, 23–25
  industrial capital, 128
  industrial support for state control
    of, 37
  industrialized economy, 19
  industry family, idea of, 155
  licensing process, 64
  private enterprises, 64
  strikes and *bandh*s, 36
inequality
  agricultural, 80
  economic, 10, 21 (*See also* Gini
    coefficient)
  reform-led growth, impact on
    inequality in India, 119
  regional, 2, 25, 79
  See also urban inequality; rural
    inequality
infant industry, protection of, 56, 132
inflation of 1965–66, 71, 87, 90–91
informal
  business, proliferation of, 132
  employment, characteristics of, 131
  enterprises, structure of, 133
informal labor, 130–135
informal sector, definition of, 132

informal urban enterprises, 133
informality, 131–133. *See also* urban
    informal sector
information sharing, 137
institutional credit, 82
Integrated Child Development
    Scheme (ICDS), 147
Intensive Agricultural Area Program
    (IAAP), 74
Intensive Agricultural Development
    Program (IADP), 54, 74, 115
inter-class inequalities, 79
intermediate class
  concept of, 89
  politics of, 89
  rise of, 90
International Monetary Fund (IMF),
    96, 102–03, 111, 129
international monetary system, 28, 91
intra-rural spatial inequalities, 78

Jaitley, Arun, 155
Jalan, Bimal, 103, 157
Janata Party, 92, 97, 112
Jan Sangh, 80, 154
Jan Sunwai, 142, 144
Janta Dal, 89, 112, 124
Japan, 48
  export of cotton textiles to India,
    30
  export-oriented development, 42
Jawahar Gram Samridhi Yojana
    (1999), 145
Jawahar Rozgar Yojna (1989), 145
Jha, L. K., 71, 98
Jha, Prem Shankar, 89
jobless growth, phenomenon of, 131,
    134
job security, 49, 131
Johnson, Lyndon, 71
Joshi, Deep, 141
JP (Jaya Prakash) movement, 92. *See
    also* Narayan, Jay Prakash
jute industries, in India, 20

Kalam, A. P. J. Abdul, 124
Kamraj, Kumaraswami, 65, 70
Kargil War (1999), 119
Kelkar Commission (2004), 163
Kelkar, Vijay, 157

labor
  cheap labor, 19–20, 41–42, 54, 109
    availability of, 14
  high-income, 138
  protection of property from
    agitations, 87
labor market
  characteristics of, 131
  in developing countries, 131
  in India, 131
Lancashire cotton and yarn, 19
land
  collectivization of, 73
  common property lands,
    appropriation of, 53
  degradation of, 17
  fair price for, 138
  ownership of, 22
  for personal cultivation, 63
  productivity of, 41, 54
  redistribution of, 61–63, 73, 78, 88
Land Acquisition Act (1894), 138–39
Land Acquisition and Rehabilitation
    and Resettlement (LARR) Bill
    (2011), 139
Land Acquisition Bill, 84
land and indebtedness, fragmentation
    of, 148
land ceiling, 85–86
Land Ceiling Act, 63
land market, creation of, 16
land owned by peasants and small
    farmers, fragmentation of, 134
land ownership, 62
  ceiling on, 88
land productivity, 73, 77
Land Redistribution Bill, 88
land redistribution, failure of, 61–63

land reforms, 81
  failure in India, 63
  policies in the fourth FYP, 79
  Soviet-inspired, 36
land revenue, 22, 29–30, 62
land-augmenting technology, 77
landlords, 33, 41, 83
Latin America, 15, 41, 48, 86
left parties, 112
Lewis, Arthur, 131
Lewisian transformation, 131–132
liberal reforms, 96, 128, 134
  in 1991, 103
  association of the year 1991 with, 101
  beneficiaries of, 117–19
  distributive impact of, 117
  failure of reforms of the year 1991,
    110–11
  impact on the agricultural sector,
    114–17
  under Indira Gandhi, 98
  lobbying for, 104
  meaning of, 96–97
  under NDA Government, 119–20
  primary beneficiaries of, 104
  reshaping of federal politics in India,
    111–14
  role of private English media in,
    103–05
liberalization policies, in India, 73, 96
  in 1980, 97–99
  in 1991, 100–01
  first moment of, 79–80
  and Green Revolution, 76
  second moment of, 80
  third moment of, 80
"license Raj" regime, 96, 104–05
Lok Dal, 112
Lok Sabha, 62, 80, 112–13, 123, 152
luxury consumption, 19, 119

Mahalanobis, P. C., 51
Maharashtra Employment Guarantee
    Scheme (1977), 145

Index

Mahatma Gandhi National Rural Employment Guarantee Act (MGNREGA), 6, 10
Malviya, Amit, 154
Mander, Harsh, 141
Mann ki Baat, 153
Maran, Dayanidhi, 136
market
  economy, 6, 111, 156
  reforms, 72
  development, 45
  capitalist production driven by, 79
Mazdoor Kisan Shakti Sangathan (MKSS), 142, 144. *See also* Jan Sunwai
media, 120, 139, 141–42, 144
Mehra, Puja, 156
Mehta, Nalin, 151
Mehta–Singh Social Index, 152
merchant classes, 13, 17, 21–22
Middle East, 13, 102, 120
Middle Path, 44–45
minimum support prices (MSPs), 90, 168–70
mining industry, 24
mixed economy, 5, 44–45
  adoption of, 47
  political responses to Nehruvian industrialization development model, 48–51
modern economics, tenets of, 49
Modi, Narendra, 151, 156–57, 163
  popularity amongst the masses, 159
Mohan, Rakesh, 103
Monet plan, to restore the economy (France and Germany), 46
moneylenders, 17, 54, 90, 118
Monopolistic and Restrictive Trade Practices (MRTP) Act of 1969, 85, 107
  licensing and restrictions under, 98
Mughal kingdom, 13
Mukherjee, Pranab, 136
Mukherjee, Syama Prasad, 154

Nandigram, Orissa, 138
Narain, Raj, 87
Narasimhan, M., 98
Narayan, Jay Prakash, 88
Naroji, Dadabhai, 22
Nath, Kamal, 136
National Advisory Council (NAC), 124–26, 145
National Agricultural Party, 33
National Campaign for People's Right to Information (NCPRI), 144
National Commission for Enterprise in the Unorganized Sector (NCEUS), 131
National Congress Party, 123
National Council of Educational Research and Training (NCERT), 96
National Democratic Alliance (NDA)
  Agrarian Distress and Farm Bill, 168–70
  COVID-19 lockdown crisis, 151
  demonetization scheme, 7, 10, 161–63
  digital delivery mechanism, 160–61
  economic philosophy, 154–55
  economic reforms under, 7–11, 119–20
  failures of, 124
  Farm Bill Act (2018), 9
  Goods and Services Tax (GST), 163–65
  Gujarat development model, 157
  Indian economy under, 158
  "India Shining" campaign, 119–20
  Make in India campaign, 163
  Pradhan Mantri Jan Arogya Yojana (PM-JAY), 165–68
  Pradhan Mantri Jan Dhan Yojana, 160
  under prime ministership of Narendra Modi, 151
  social welfare philosophy, 165

welfare policy under, 158–60
See also direct beneficiary transfers (DBTs); Economic Survey of 2013–14; Modi, Narendra
national economy, functioning of, 18
National Food Security Act (NFSA), 140, 147
National Income Accounts, 89
nationalization of banks and insurances, 81–82, 84
National Rural Employment Guarantee Act (NREGA, 2005), 125, 129–30, 140, 145–47, 159
National Sample Survey (NSS), 132
National Sample Survey Organisation (NSSO), 118
Nehru, Jawaharlal, 4
  on achieving self-sufficiency in food production, 54
  death of, 67, 69
  dilution of public investment in agriculture under, 9
  direction for industrial development, 43–44
  drive to industrialize, 40–67
  food crisis and the end of the policy regime of, 65–67
  industrialization-focused development model, 44
  industrial policies, 104, 106
  mixed economy industrialization development model, 44–45, 47
    impact on Indian economy, 58–60
    political responses to, 48–51
  Planning Commission under, 7
  speeches on economic issues and policy, 8
  third tenure as prime minister, 65
  See also socialism, Nehruvian ideals of
Nehruvian policy regime
  agricultural and balance of payment crisis of 1965 and 1966, 67, 69–70

beneficiaries of, 84
dilution of, 70–71
on industrial development and self-reliance, 69
Nehru–Mahalanobis plan, 66
political economy of, 61
problem with the planning mechanism, 63–65
shortcomings of
  failure of land redistribution, 61–63
  structural, 67, 80
New Agricultural Strategy (NAS), 73–74
  criticism of, 78–79
  impact on
    food grain production, 76
    Indian economy, 76–78
new economic policy (NEP), 96
Nijalingappa, Siddavanahalli, 83
NITI Aayog, 156–58, 164
non-alignment movement, 72
non-governmental organizations (NGOs), 141–43
non-INC coalition government, 120

oil price shocks, in 1973 and 1979, 91, 100
Organization of the Petroleum Exporting Countries (OPEC)
  oil price crisis, 6
organized labor, bargaining powers of, 89
Other Backward Caste (OBC), 152
overvalued exchange rate, 53, 56–57, 60, 80

Panagriya, Arvind, 155, 157
Park, Chung-hee, 65
parliamentary democratic system, 53
partial reforms in the 1980s, impact of, 99–100
partition, of British India, 37
Patel, Vallabhai, 36, 83

Index

Patnaik, Ila, 155
patron–client networks, of large
    landlords, 73
peasant rebellion, 36
peasant-based agriculture, 101
peasants and farmer suicides, 2, 119
petty businesses, proliferation of, 134
Pitroda, Sam, 99
PL 480 agreement, between India and
    USA, 66, 69, 75
planning-based economy, 6
Planning Commission (PC), 44
  balance of power with the ministries,
    71
  dilution of the powers of, 71
  formation of, 33
  Modi's decision about ending the
    tenure of, 157
  report of 1938, 51
  weakening of, 70–71
political economy, 8–10, 93
political lobbying, 165
political unrest, due to food shortage
    crisis, 80
populist policies, under Indira Gandhi,
    5–6, 84–86, 91
POSCO SEZ, Orissa, 138. *See also*
    Special Economic Zone Act
    (SEZA, 2005)
poverty
  alleviation, 37, 63, 86, 125, 140
  impact on economy, 42
  traps, 29
Pradhan Mantri Jan Arogya Yojana
    (PM-JAY), 165–68
Pradhan Mantri Jan Dhan Yojana, 160
price mechanism, free movement of,
    97
private corporate investment, 91, 119,
    126–27
private equity, 127
private news media, 142
problem solving, 7
pro-market reforms of 1980s, 99

public distribution system (PDS), 75,
    140
public enterprise, 47, 51, 65, 74, 79, 83,
    85–86, 110, 136, 148
public health insurances, 166
public healthcare system, 167–68
public interest litigation (PIL), 146
public investment, 9, 51–52, 55, 58–59,
    66–67, 69, 73, 76–77, 80, 86,
    91–92, 107–08, 115–18, 128–29
Public Law 480 ("Food for Peace"), 66
public sector enterprises, 83, 106
  importance of, 83
public sector, job creation in, 60
public service delivery, 146
public–private collaboration, 136
public–private partnership model
    (PPP) model, 166
*pyravikaar*s, 138

Quit India movement (1942), 36
quota tariff, 53

radical land reforms, 49
Rajya Sabha, 124
Ram Janmabhoomi movement, 154
Rao, Mohan, 77, 115
Rao, P. V. Narasimha, 103
real estate, value of, 127
reallocation of credit, 85
Reddy, Y. V., 103
re-distributive policies, 114
Reliance Industries, 99
remittances, 16, 22, 24, 38, 102
Report of the Indian Fiscal Commission
    (1922), 26
Report of the Indian Industrial
    Commission 1916–18, 25
research and development (R&D), 128
Reserve Bank of India (RBI), 10, 102
  shipment of gold for emergency
    loan, 103
resource allocation, from agricultural
    sector to industrial sector, 52

revenue for Britain, sources of
income tax, 30
land revenue, 30
salt taxes, 30
through export and import, 29–30
rice production, 115
rights-based social policy,
infrastructure for, 141
Right to Education Act (2009), 140,
147
Right to Information (RTI) Act
(2005), 125, 140, 143–45
Right to Education, 6
Right to Information (RTI), 6
right-to-work program, 145
Roy, Aruna, 141
Roy, Rajaramohan, 22
rural consumption inequality, 79
rural debt, liquidation of, 85
rural economy, 16, 49, 112–13, 119, 146
rural inequality, 60, 69, 117
rural infrastructure, public investment
in, 76
rural land redistribution, 85
Russia
Bolshevik government, 43
industrial development in, 43
nationalization of all industries, 48
Russian Revolution, 36

salt taxes, 30
Samajwadi Party, 112, 123, 152, 160
OBC Lok Sabha candidates, 152
Satyagraha movement
demand to
abolish the salt tax, 30
impose customs duties on foreign
cloth, 31
reduce the rate of land revenue, 30
Gandhi–Irwin Pact and suspension
of, 31
Gandhi's demands in, 49
impact of Great Depression of 1929
on, 26–28

impact on sterling–rupee exchange
rate, 29–30
launching of, 29, 33
Scheduled Castes (SCs), 140, 152
Scheduled Tribes (STs), 147
Securities and Exchange Board of
India, 107
self-subsistence agriculture, 132
Sengupta Committee, 131
Reports on Conditions of Work and
Promotion of Livelihood in
the Unorganised Sector, 131
Shastri, Lal Bahadur, 70–71
Sibal, Kapil, 136
Singh, Manmohan, 98, 103, 146, 159
budget proposed by, 105
budget speech of 1991, 104–07,
124
introduction of reforms by, 104
as prime minister of India, 125
working relationship with Sonia
Gandhi, 126
Singh, V. P., 102, 124
Sinha, Yashwant, 102, 157
Sino-India War (1962), 65
Sixth Central Pay Commission, 130
slave trade, with Africa, 16
small-scale industries (SSI), 82, 87,
101
re-allocation of credit to, 90
Smooth Hawley Act of 1930, 28
social distribution policies, 139
social hierarchies, 78
in rural India, 50
social insurance, 29, 32, 165–66
social media, use of, 153. *See also*
digital political advertising;
Google; WhatsApp
social policies
delivery-based, 140
rights-based, 140
social redistribution bills, 139
social welfare policy, 75, 155
socialism, Nehruvian ideals of, 105

Index

socialist control of banks, 82
socialist policies, 81
  definition of, 83
socialist revolution, 36, 62
socially redistributive policies, rights-based, 6
South Africa, 48
South Korea, 48, 65, 127
  planning mechanism, 71
Special Economic Zone Act (SEZA, 2005), 127
  decentralizing the process of reforms, 135–37
  objective of, 135
  political contestation of, 148
  process and politics that shaped, 137–39
  success of, 136
  See also District Committee (DC); Empowered Group of Ministers (EGOM); Export Processing Zones
stakeholders of capitalism, 83
standard of living, 23, 35, 132–34
state-directed heavy industry-oriented growth plan, 97
state economies, 113
steel production, in India, 64
Subramaniam, C., 71, 74
subsidies, politicization of, 118
Suez Canal, 18
swadeshi development, 154
Swatantra Party, 48, 80, 154
Syndicate, 80, 82–85, 101

tariff barriers, 20–21, 56
tariff war, 20, 28
Tata Steel plant, 24–25
tax incidence, concept of, 164
technical know-how, 19, 74
tehsils, 18
Telangana Rashtriya Samiti, 123
telecom revolution, in India, 99
Telugu Desam Party (TDP), 112

tenancy rights, 17
tenant farmers, 90
textile industries
  growth in India, 20, 46
  Indian textiles, 19, 24, 30
  in Japan, 42
  See also cotton textile industry
textile mills
  British, 14, 56
  Indian, 20
  steam-powered, 20
Third Reich, 46
Third World, 97
trade policy, of India, 56
trade quotas, 57
trade union, in India, 36, 49
trusteeship, idea of, 50–51
Twitter, 153

unemployment insurance, 145
Union of Soviet Socialist Republics (USSR), 42
  aid and assistance to India, 102
  dissolution of, 102
  state-controlled capitalism, 45
Unique Identification Authority of India (UIDAI), 141, 160
United Progressive Alliance (UPA)
  Common Minimum Program (CMP), 124–25
  difference with other coalition governments, 123–24
  economic liberalization under, 6
  economy under, 126–27
  manufacturing sector growth under, 127–28
  mode of policymaking under, 123
  National Advisory Council (NAC), 125–26
  politicization of agricultural distress, 169
  rights-based schemes of, 159
  rights-based social policy introduced by, 139–41

social rights policies introduced by, 147–48
social rights policy under, 9
trade reforms under, 126
work on social distribution and poverty alleviation, 125
See also Common Minimum Program (CMP); National Advisory Council (NAC)
United States of America (USA)
decision to withdraw aid to India, 71
as dominant economy in the world, 102
free enterprise-based capitalism, 45
global leadership of, 42
PL 480 agreement with India, 66, 69
Unorganised Workers' Social Security Act (2008), 134
unorganized enterprises, 131
urban educated classes, 104
urban inequality, 60, 117. *See also* rural inequality
urban informal sector, 118
urban land ceiling laws, 85
urban–rural inequality, 60

Vajpayee, Atal Bihari, 163
Vakulabharanam, Vamsi, 118–19
value-added tax, 163

venture capital, 127
vernacular regional parties, rise of, 11
Versailles, Treaty of, 46
vote banks, 49, 112, 114, 130

wage labor, in India, 132
wartime repatriations, payment of, 46
welfare policy, under the NDA, 158–59
WhatsApp, 154
working classes, 118
World Bank, 53, 71, 96, 142
World War 1 (WW1), 97
collapse of the international trade due to, 23
economic damage caused due to, 24
expenditure faced by the British government in, 26
impact on Indian industries, 23–25
World War 2 (WW2)
India's involvement in, 33, 34–37

Yadav, Akhilesh, 160

zamindari system
abolition of, 36, 55
Zamindari Abolition Act, 63
*zamindar*s, 54